INTERNATIONAL DISCORD ON
POPULATION AND DEVELOPMENT

INTERNATIONAL DISCORD ON POPULATION AND DEVELOPMENT

JOHN F. KANTNER
AND
ANDREW KANTNER

palgrave
macmillan

INTERNATIONAL DISCORD ON POPULATION AND DEVELOPMENT
Copyright © John F. Kantner and Andrew Kantner, 2006.

All rights reserved.

First published in hardcover in 2006 as THE STRUGGLE FOR
INTERNATIONAL CONSENSUS ON POPULATION AND DEVELOPMENT by
PALGRAVE MACMILLAN®
in the United States—a division of St. Martin's Press LLC,
175 Fifth Avenue, New York, NY 10010.

Where this book is distributed in the UK, Europe and the rest of the world,
this is by Palgrave Macmillan, a division of Macmillan Publishers Limited,
registered in England, company number 785998, of Houndmills,
Basingstoke, Hampshire RG21 6XS.

Palgrave Macmillan is the global academic imprint of the above companies
and has companies and representatives throughout the world.

Palgrave® and Macmillan® are registered trademarks in the United States,
the United Kingdom, Europe and other countries.

ISBN: 978–0–230–62113–8

Library of Congress Cataloging-in-Publication Data is available from the
Library of Congress.

A catalogue record of the book is available from the British Library.

Design by Newgen Imaging Systems (P) Ltd., Chennai, India.

First PALGRAVE MACMILLAN paperback edition: January 2010

10 9 8 7 6 5 4 3 2 1

Printed in the United States of America.

Transferred to Digital Printing in 2009.

CONTENTS

LIST OF TABLES

PREFACE

To designate our area of interest as lying somewhere in the wide domain of "population and development" is something of an enlargement of what we are about. Our defense for this elastic usage of both terms is that the issues we confront are often packaged that way. This is particularly true of the very influential conferences that have been held every ten years by the United Nations. Since much of what we have to say is in reaction to these conferences, we decided to follow their usage and fence our subject in the same way.

But to do so is to be false to both terms. In both there are many mansions. "Population" is a term that covers a vast range of topics having something to do with aggregates called populations—their properties, their dynamics, their interrelationships with determining factors and their consequences. It deals with what the famous demographer Alfred Lotka, called necessary relations inherent in the properties of a particular population aggregate all the way to the analysis of the external causal relations that give shape to a particular population and set bounds for its possible effects. Our purchase on this extensive subject is as a canoe paddle to the giant screw of an ocean liner. While to round out our discussion, we do recognize certain large implications of current population trends, our main concern throughout is with the policies and practices that began with the attempt to control population growth, primarily through technological innovation, behavioral modification, and organizational response, which have more recently morphed into a tangle of assorted welfarist proposals and ideological derivatives.

We, perhaps, do even less justice to the term "development." It is extensive in its reach. There is an entire subdiscipline in social science concerned with social, economic, cultural change and development, not to mention the field of human development, which has its roots in social context. Various aspects of population have long been considered as factors in and limiting conditions to the course of development. These interconnections have been grasped, with a greater or lesser degree of precision, over the length of human history—from Confucius, Ibn Khaldun, Malthus, Marx, the Club of Rome, to pick some of the low hanging fruit. They are still an active frontier of scientific investigation.

But here we are concerned with issues of lesser scope. So why till such a restricted field? Is there a crop worth harvesting there? Metaphor aside, the answer is simple: because this is where argument over policy has taken us. Sides are lined up, trenches dug, and this is where the action is. Consensus about what actions to take are proclaimed and challenged, strategies for action are proposed, but there is little agreement on the ends in view. Were the issues involved not serious ones one might be tempted to leave all this as an ideologically inspired, politically motivated cat fight. But it is not so readily disposed of. At issue here are questions of human welfare, of the efficient allocation of scarce resources, and even the proper role of the institutions and agencies of government and what today is popularly called civil society.

And what is the squabbling all about? It is about population policy and what that should mean. What human goals are properly the ends to be achieved? And by what means? Whose agendas are being pursued? Toward what ultimate ends? What factors stand in the way of success or promise achievement? Our aim is to recount the struggle for consensus on these issues, to review, with cautionary intent, the mantras and shibboleths of competing factions, and to look ahead to the possible resolution of differences between them. Finally, as a matter of providing some perspective, we give brief consideration to the larger context in which population and development policy will play out in the future.

ACKNOWLEDGMENTS

There are many generous souls who have helped us in this effort to recount the story of population assistance over the past 50 or so years and to size up the situation in its present unstable state. Understandably, some of our best informants might prefer a degree of anonymity in these contentious times of the struggle for consensus regarding the framing of issues and related questions of policy and strategy. Rather than risk "outing" some informants and possibly slighting others, we let the matter pass. Suffice it to say we could not have prepared this account without their help, both in granting interviews and comments on early drafts. If you recognize yourself in any of the points we make and we got you right, we are pleased. If we didn't, we take full credit for these errors of interpretation.

We are happy to acknowledge the assistance of some who need have no fear of the winds of contention. First we must thank the William and Flora Hewlett Foundation for the grant that permitted us to undertake this review. And we are grateful for the willingness of the Social Science Research Institute at the Pennsylvania State University, at the time under the direction of Professor Mark Hayward, in providing us with the institutional affiliation necessary to receive the grant.

Special thanks are also due to Professor Gordon de Jong, distinguished professor of sociology and demography and director of the graduate program in demography at Pennsylvania State University, for his generous and helpful counsel regarding the many decisions that grantees must make to conform to University administrative custom. A busy man, wise in the ways of university culture, he never conveyed a sense of being imposed on, although undoubtedly, sometimes he was.

Our editor, Sandra Ward, made us familiar with the rigor of professional editing. While it was always a shock to have to face up to our editorial transgressions, we both slept the better for it. We also appreciate the suggestions received from Sidney Westley of the East–West Center, who drew our attention to a number of points that would have been embarrassing if gone uncorrected.

CHAPTER ONE

INTRODUCTION

Although few, if any, of our political leaders appear willing to face the fact, the greatest test for human society as it confronts the twenty-first century is how to . . . find effective global solutions in order to free the poorer three-quarters of humankind from the growing Malthusian trap of malnutrition, starvation, resource depletion, unrest, enforced migration, and armed conflict—developments that will also endanger the richer nations, if less directly.

—Paul Kennedy, *Preparing for the Twenty-First Century*

International Development Assistance

Since the conclusion of World War II, international economic assistance to the developing world has played an important role in helping to promote economic and social development. It has contributed to slowing the rate of population growth, extending the average length of life, improving the production and distribution of food, enhancing educational opportunities (especially for girls), and promoting greater employment opportunities. The extent to which foreign assistance has brought about these positive changes cannot be measured with any precision. But there is little question that much of the developing world, at least outside sub-Saharan Africa, has advanced considerably over the past 50 years and that foreign aid, especially in areas such as family planning, education, and food production, has had something to do with it.

As the world makes its way into the twenty-first century with seemingly innumerable crises such as international terrorism and security clamoring for attention, the prospects for greatly increased economic development assistance, as opposed to military outlays, appear to be bleak. There has always been considerable skepticism among more conservative constituencies about the effectiveness of foreign aid. In recent years, however, there has also been growing frustration with much development assistance among more traditional supporters and practitioners of foreign aid.

It is widely acknowledged that donor resources are not adequate for addressing priority economic, educational, health, and environmental needs in the developing world. As of 2008, official development assistance (ODA) stood at $119.8 billion, a figure that constitutes an all time high (OECD 2009). However, Development Assistance Committee (DAC) countries still contributed only 0.30 percent of their gross national income (GNI) to international development programs in 2008, a level of support well below the internationally agreed target of 0.70 percent. Only five countries—Denmark, Luxembourg, the Netherlands, Norway, and Sweden were providing at least 0.70 percent of their GNI to international assistance in this year. The addiction of many donor countries to various forms of "tied aid," a sop to domestic political interests, and the overheads charged by their private partners, further bleed resources available for direct application in foreign countries. Stephen Lewis (2005) citing an analysis by the UK-based non-governmental organization ActionAid, concludes that much current ODA never reaches intended beneficiaries.

> Over 60 percent of ODA should be called "phantom aid", aid that is never really availabe for the purposes intended. Where, then, does the money go? To "technical assistance" (otherwise known as overpriced consultants); to "tied aid" (otherwise known as the purchase of goods and services from the donor country's own firms); and to 'administrative costs' (otherwise known as inflated overhead). Furthermore, according to ActionAid . . . a considerable chunk of ODA comes with very particular strings attached – strings knotted by IMF conditionality, especially support for privatization. (pp. 30–31)

The United States supplied only 0.18 percent of its GNI to foreign aid in 2008, along with Japan the lowest of any industrialized Western country. As in past years, much of this assistance was provided for emergency humanitarian assistance, nonemergency food procurement, debt forgiveness, and technical assistance (much of which is money paid out to U.S. firms and consultants). Little funding has gone to nonstrategic counties for investment in basic development. US foreign assistance continues to be directed primarily to "strategic countries"; traditionally Israel, Egypt, and Jordan, with Iraq and Afghanistan joining these priority countries after 2001 (Sachs 2005: 82).

Anemic levels of development assistance are only part of the problem. The bilateral and multilateral channels commonly used to dispense foreign assistance are increasingly seen as ineffective. Present-day development agencies are typically viewed as excessively bureaucratic (seemingly preoccupied with administrative procedure), overly prescriptive in recommending international "consensus" agendas in countries with widely varying priorities and cultural sensitivities, and not sufficiently focused on documenting results.

Whether proceeding with consensus agendas (most recently the poverty alleviation framework of the UN's Millennium Development Goals) or in a more ad hoc fashion, the policies of major donor countries have not always evolved in response to the expressed needs of developing countries. As Perin and Attaran (2003) observe, foreign assistance strategies have largely followed changing donor priorities. They note that aid policies often emerge from the monologues of donors, rather than from productive dialogues with developing countries, despite window dressing to mask this reality (p. 1). New donor-driven policy directions also tend to overreach with respect to program design, host country absorptive capacity, and anticipated outcomes. If this is a fair account of the reality of foreign assistance in general, it appears to have been the case, a fortiori, for the increasingly contentious field of international population assistance.[1]

International Population Assistance

One of the more prominent development issues over the past half-century has been concern over the size, composition, distribution, and growth of the world's population. At mid-century, and for some four decades thereafter, the significance of population growth, especially as related to development prospects in the world's poorer countries, went largely unquestioned and captured much popular and scholarly attention. To be sure, there have been critics, primarily within the ranks of academia, who pointed out the explanatory weakness of demographic variables as predictors of economic growth. But the work of these revisionists, as they are sometimes called, could not dismiss the broadly held conviction, especially in developing countries, that rapid population growth has stood in the way of social and economic advancement.

Initially, the consequences of rapid population growth were portrayed in calamitous terms. Population bombs were set to explode; a demographic revolution was unfolding, which would leave a plundered planet. These alarmist views of a half-century ago have receded from both popular and professional concern. The commentator Ben Wattenberg (1987), for example, plays down the importance of population growth, arguing that the world's population will be shrinking as fertility rates descend to below replacement levels. In his view, rapid population growth is no longer a salient issue requiring programmatic attention. As Wattenberg sees it, efforts to reduce the rate of population growth are not only beside the point but are also one of the main causes of high abortion rates.

On a somewhat different tack, Patrick Buchanan (2002) sees looming catastrophe not in rapid population growth, the specter that haunted past decades, but rather in the differential rates of population growth between developing and developed countries. This, he expects, will generate historically unprecedented migration from poor to rich nations, which in turn will lead to a global demographic redistribution with a concomitant rise in the gradient of economic inequality, one that will present a serious threat to Western cultural traditions and the stability of democratic institutions. For both of these commentators, family planning and reproductive health issues are not of central concern.[2] For Wattenberg they seem to be taking care of themselves and are better left alone; for Buchanan the primary issue is the old fear of demographic inundation from the South that will swamp the North and undermine its way of life.

We cite these two commentators not to approve their views but to demonstrate one aspect of the cracking cake of consensus on population policy. Further crumbling of the cake comes from the other end of the political and social spectrum, where family planning and reproductive health issues are said to have been too narrowly framed and single-mindedly pursued. As a result, it is alleged, they have tended to exclude broader, more basic social issues. This view, which bears the imprimatur of numerous international conferences, is to a major extent an emanation of the movement to give women and their reproductive rights greater attention in matters of policy and action.

From this perspective, concerns about demographic issues, such as the size and rate of population growth, became of secondary interest. The interplay of population dynamics with socioeconomic development, food security, environmental quality, political stability, and national security (the linkages that largely drove bipartisan support for international population assistance in the 1960s and 1970s) are now, in some policy circles, studiously ignored. Instead, there is insistence on empowerment and human rights agendas that are justified primarily in terms of their benefits to women rather than to the welfare of couples, families, communities, and nation states. This focus, rather than the earlier attempt to relate population to development and other macro level outcomes, has become the touchstone of today's "correct" population policy.

There can be no question that women's welfare is a critical factor in development. Indeed, the World Bank has established a Department of Gender to make certain that women's interests are not overlooked in its development work. The problem arises at the operational level, where there is little or no guidance as to the relative importance of interventions that are being advocated in an environment of stringent and faltering resources. Linkages with fertility and mortality decline are also tangential at best. Potts (1997) concludes that "while these broader areas of human suffering and justice represent valid and urgent humanitarian concerns, there is no empirical evidence that their solution is a prerequisite to further fertility decline" (p. 25).

There is also in this definition of the situation, as there is in certain aspects of the conservative position, an unattractive, perhaps largely unconscious, tinge of Western ethnocentrism. It shows through in language that speaks, for example, of "advocacy through social groups and their leaders [that] can provide an enabling context for changes in values and norms that allow individuals to make new decisions about their behavior" (Caro et al. 2003: 14). This may be part of what is meant by "focusing on culture as a resource for change" (p. 7). It is not clear what meaning should be given to the phrase, but it conveys an invasive and patronizing tone. Above all, it replaces policy supported by scientifically based empiricism with social manipulation.

Thus, it is undeniable that population policy, in the sense that the term was understood during much of the last 50 years, no longer enjoys the intellectual stature it once had. In contrast to what Hodgson (1998) has called the period of population "orthodoxy," there is now a more complex understanding of the population–development nexus. Paraphrasing Kelley's (2001) analysis of the decline of population orthodoxy, there have been three significant revisions of the orthodox view:

1. a downgrading of the relative importance of population growth as a factor in economic growth;
2. an assessment of the consequences of population growth over longer periods; and
3. in this expanded accounting frame, the importance of taking account of indirect feedbacks within economic and political systems.

Population growth "still matters," but, as Kelley notes, the justification for family planning shifts from development per se to the "desirability of reducing the large number of 'unwanted' births, the adverse impact of large families (and close child spacing) on child and maternal health, the flexibility and greater administrative ease in managing a slower pace of development, the adverse consequences of population pressures on selected environmental resources, the impact of population growth on the distribution of income and the burden of child-rearing on women" (p. 25).

Further evidence that population assistance is losing its grip on development policy is exemplified by the fact that funding for family planning and reproductive health is falling short of projected needs. By 2006, international population assistance had risen to $7.3 billion, but only 5 percent of this amount was spent on family planning and just 22 percent on basic reproductive health services (UNFPA 2008). The fear is that funding for the core items of population assistance—family planning and associated infrastructure, commodity–logistics requirements, communications, and research—may be severely squeezed by the need to combat HIV/AIDS and support a considerably broadened range of sexual and reproductive health and rights initiatives.

An overriding concern is whether the international community will be able to provide sufficient resources to combat HIV/AIDS while at the same time meeting funding goals for population and reproductive health programs. These daunting future resource requirements tend to affirm the relevance of Seltzer's (2002) concern that "unless funding prospects improve, existing resources will be spread more broadly, and this, in all likelihood, will dilute the potential impact of the reproductive health initiatives, including family planning" (p. 102).

It is currently unclear as to what extent funding for HIV/AIDS has cut into resources available for population activities. In the United States, government funding *levels* for family planning and reproductive health activities fell nearly 20 percent between 1996 and 2008 while resources to combat HIV/AIDS have grown rapidly. One can, of course, always make the case that more funding for reproductive health might not have been available even had there been no HIV/AIDS crisis. A much less ambiguous indication of the resource competition between reproductive health and HIV/AIDS is the redeployment of professional staff previously engaged in reproductive health programs to HIV/AIDS services.

Organizations active in providing reproductive health services have not fared well. The United Nations Population Fund (UNFPA) has been seriously underfunded (especially its country programs), *partly* owing to the withdrawal of US support between 2002 and 2009. The International Planned Parenthood Federation (IPPF), which has traditionally provided 65 percent of its total budget as grants to private family planning organizations in developing countries, has seen its annual budgets fall substantially since 1998, owing in large measure to the cutoff of U.S. government funding following the reimposition of the Global Gag Rule in 2001 (p. 43).

These discouraging trends are unfolding while the demand for contraceptive services continues to grow rapidly in the developing world. Recent estimates based on Demographic and Health Survey data show that 17 percent of currently married women (excluding those in China) have an unmet need for contraception—that is, they are not using contraception, do not want to become pregnant, and are sexually active (Ross and Winfrey 2002: 139). Unmet need tends to be even higher among sexually active young adults (ages 15–24) who have yet to marry, although evidence pertaining to unmarried youth is in short supply and sometimes of dubious quality. The United Nations (2000: 47) reports that future demand for contraception will be monumental, projecting that the total number of users will rise from 549 million in 2000 to 738 million by 2015.

The provision of high-quality family planning services has been shown to be an effective means of limiting abortion and curtailing the number of infant and maternal deaths. By reducing unintended pregnancies, family planning can lower abortion rates—as has been demonstrated in such diverse settings as rural Bangladesh and Russia (see Bairagi 2001 and Centers for Disease Control, USAID, and Measure DHS + 2004). Fewer pregnancies and declines in high-order births to older women and first-order births to young women will contribute to reductions in infant and maternal death rates. Despite these well-documented benefits of family planning services, international support for reproductive health programs is flagging.

Recent evidence of decline in family planning services comes from Kenya. Nicole Itano (2003), writing in the *Christian Science Monitor*, observed the following conditions in a once busy family planning clinic in the Nairobi slum area of Eastleigh:

Just over a year ago, these rooms were packed with women, mostly poor and from the surrounding slums, who came for low-cost contraception, prenatal care, and general reproductive health services. But funding for family planning has been drying up. Groups are starting to feel the effects of Bush administration regulations that ban aid to those who perform or advocate abortion. At the same time, the battle against HIV/AIDS—which includes prevention as well as issues like AIDS orphans—has taken precedence over more general family planning. And because the two efforts are not integrated, family planning clinics are finding they are losing ground. (p. 7)

Substantial financial resources have been diverted from family planning to HIV/AIDS in Kenya between 1995 and 2006. For example, USAID's spending for HIV/AIDS rose from $2 million per year in 1995 to $108 million by 2006, while family planning expenditures dropped from $12 million to $8.9 million (Cleland et al.: 2006:13). Owing to these financial realignments, the availability of contraceptive supplies dropped in public clinics and the percentage of unwanted births in the country rose from 11 percent to 21 percent between 1998 and 2003 (Cleland et al. 13–14).

How we have come to this pass from the days when population policy was clear-cut and widely subscribed to will be a central concern in this review. Equally as important as the shifting focus of population policy is the status of the organizations, public and private, that must find their footing and garner necessary resources in a changing policy and implementation environment.

Certainly, many unresolved population and development issues still haunt the planet. The governments of many developing countries (principally in sub-Saharan Africa) continue to lack the stability and institutional capacity to design and implement effective policies of social action. Many also face uncertain long-term prospects for food and water.

The United Nations Food and Agriculture Organization (FAO) has reported that the number of undernourished people in the developing world has been rising since the World Food Summit in 1996. The number of chronically hungry people in the developing world grew by more than 18 million between 1995–97 and 1999–2001, a reversal of trends that prevailed over previous decades (FAO 2003: 4). The FAO also estimates that 798 million people in the developing world were undernourished as of 1999–2001, a figure exceeding the entire population of Latin America or sub-Saharan Africa. Countries experiencing greater malnutrition tended to be those with higher population growth rates and lower rates of economic growth. With respect to global food security and nutrition, it would appear that population growth still matters.

World food production can be expected to increase somewhat, but if widespread malnutrition is to be avoided and improved standards of living realized, far greater gains in agricultural output will need to be achieved. According to the United Nations' 2001 assessment of the "State of the World Population," in three-fifths of the 105 developing countries surveyed over the 20 years leading up to 1995, food production lagged behind population growth (UNFPA 2001: 15). The FAO (2003: 8) reports that the number of undernourished people in the world increased by 4.5 million per year over the period from 1995 to 2001. Another troubling sign is that between 1998 and 2003, China's annual grain production fell from 392 million tons to 322 million tons—a decline of 70 million tons that equals Canada's current annual grain production (L. Brown 2004: 1). This shortfall, resulting primarily from a reduction in the amount of arable land in production, is causing China to substantially increase its food imports. One recent projection suggests that by 2025, China may need to import the equivalent of the world's current total grain exports in order to adequately feed its population (Wilson 2002: 89). Add to this the problems of land degradation and the failures of land reform, and the burden imposed by population numbers becomes obvious.

The interplay between population growth and natural resource depletion continues to be a major concern for environmentalists. The impact of growing human populations on the availability of clean water, access to cultivable land, the viability of forests, the depletion of fisheries, the growing levels of carbon dioxide emissions, climate change, and declining biodiversity are all critical ecological issues facing the planet in the new millennium. (For a review of the evidence, see Engleman et al. 2000.)

Recent projections indicate that between 2.6 and 3.1 billion people will be living in "water-scarce or water-stressed" areas by the year 2025, compared with 434 million living in such conditions in 2000; the number of people living in land-scarce countries will rise to between 600 and 986 million by 2025, compared with 415 million in 2000; 3 billion people will be living in countries with only 0.1 hectares of forest cover per capita, compared with 1.8 billion people in 2000; and many of the world's main fishing grounds will be largely depleted by 2025 (Population Action International

2002: 1–2). Such numbers and their projection into the future are always debatable. However, given the magnitude and direction of the trends cited earlier, there can be little doubt that we are on a course of collision with nature that in a generation or so hence may reach crisis proportions.

In addition, new international health problems have arisen over the past decade, and we sense stirrings suggesting an ongoing quest for new formulations and an elaboration of the institutional structures that will be involved. Certainly the HIV/AIDS crisis enveloping much of sub-Saharan Africa and rising rapidly in China, India, and other parts of the developing world has refocused attention on the need to strengthen human resources for health service provision, upgrade the accessibility and quality of health delivery systems, and grapple with the growing crisis posed by the rising demand for health services coupled with inadequate levels of international health assistance.

Beyond capturing emerging new directions, new agendas, and institutional revampings, it is important not to lose sight of the fact that there is still important unfinished business with regard to family planning and reproductive health. Out of 133 low and medium income countries in 2000, there were only 20 in which the total fertility rate ranged between two and four children per woman (Ross and Stover 2003: 4). In 33 countries, fertility ranged from five to eight children, and a large proportion of those births were unwanted. Moreover, in a world currently roiling in geopolitical crisis and running short of critical resources, the possible consequences of adding perhaps another 3 billion to the world's population by 2050 is a daunting prospect (United Nations Population Division 2004a). And to stay within that range assumes that the policies and programs now in place will continue to operate with no lessening of efficiency.

Fashionably sanguine views on global fertility decline and the diminution of population growth rates are not well-informed in that (1) fertility remains high in much of sub-Saharan Africa as well as parts of South Asia and (2) population growth remains high in many countries with moderate fertility owing to parallel falls in infant and child mortality. For example, India's official intercensal population growth rate between 1990–2000 was 1.93 percent (which is only slightly below the 1961–1991 average growth rate of 2.13 percent) (Office of the Registrar General and Census Commissioner 2009:4). If unchanged, a growth rate of 1.93 percent will double India's 2000 population of 1.028 billion in just 36 years. We believe this is still a significant demographic circumstance that is cause for concern rather than a signal for complacency and premature declarations of family planning program success.

The argument for "staying the course" in international family planning is well summarized by DaVanzo and Adamson (1998):

> The world's population is still growing. Although the rate of growth has been declining since the 1960s, global population grows each year by approximately 80 million people, or the equivalent of the population of a country the size of Germany. Nearly all of this growth is concentrated in the developing countries of the world, in many of which fertility rates remain high. High fertility can impose costly burdens on developing nations. It may impede opportunities for economic development, increase health risks for women and children, and erode the quality of life by reducing access to education, nutrition, employment, and scarce resources such as potable water. Furthermore, surveys of women in developing countries suggest that a large percentage—from 10 to 40 percent—want to space or limit childbearing but are not using contraception. This finding indicates a continuing need for contraception . . . (p. 1)

In our view, that case needs no further argument. There is in circulation, however, the view that moving from family planning to broadened reproductive health agendas and recasting population policy around gender, women's human rights and empowerment has provoked a revanchist effort in some quarters to return to the policies of the 1970s and 1980s. Then population policy was centered on increasing the prevalence of contraception with the primary justification being the economic, social, and health benefits of lower fertility. George Brown (2002), who has observed this policy divide from close quarters, puts it this way:

> During the past four decades, policies and programs have gradually undergone a shift toward greater sensitivity to women's needs,

improved quality of care, and the incorporation of a user perspective in family planning . . . . But the changes were slow and were sometimes reversed, and the underlying demographic paradigm remained. Improving quality of care was "too expensive," counseling and informed consent "too difficult," and attention to broader reproductive health needs "not feasible." Reproductive rights could not be addressed. Educating girls and improving the status of women were outside the purview of the family planning establishment. (p. xiii)

Brown suggests that such resistance has its roots in "the challenge to authority and tradition posed by women's empowerment" (p. xii). This strikes us as too pat. There is, as Paul Demeny has dubbed it, a "population industry," and it is to be expected that those who work in it would resist what they take to be career-threatening changes, quite apart from the convictions of many that they are engaged in an important activity. So let us be clear about the position taken here: change is desirable, even necessary, in many respects. However, policies, new or old, need to be rooted in empirical reality and geared to feasible programmatic outcomes. In the current jargon, they must involve "evidence-based" assessments of past efforts and empirically demanding evaluations of new programs of action. If for some they also serve ideological ends, well and good, but this should be coincidental, not generative.

There is no returning to the days of coercive birth control and population bomb scares. It is legitimate, however, to demand policies that realistically identify the tasks that need to be addressed and to appreciate that we are far from achieving sustainable positions in many areas such as health-system functionality and sustainability, commodity–logistics management, human resources development, collaborative research, and the transfer of appropriate technology to the developing world. Finally, the vital connections between demographic variables and development should remain an active research and policy frontier and not be treated by elision at international conferences purporting to deal with the subject.

CHAPTER TWO

THE EARLY YEARS OF INTERNATIONAL POPULATION ASSISTANCE: THE STRIVING FOR CONSENSUS

Historically, the meaning of "the problem of population" has varied according to whatever demographic and political alarms have seized popular attention. From the time of Thomas Malthus, population problems were cast in terms of size, growth, and mechanisms for coping with the increase in numbers. Malthus had his own suggestions about how to stem the rate of growth—ideas that have reappeared in the current emphasis on sexual abstinence. Marx dismissed the whole issue by declaring population to be of little consequence so long as society was organized in a nonexploitative manner—that is, if the main object of the economic system were to be something other than the reduction of "variable capital" (labor costs).

In the years before and between the two great wars of the twentieth century, the problem of population quality became the center of debate. Following a period of substantial immigration to the United States and other Western countries, the guardians of the status quo found the changing ethnic, racial, and qualitative compositions of population a worrisome prospect. After a generation or two, immigrants from northern Europe had found a place in American society. Some disappeared underground in the coalmines of Pennsylvania and West Virginia or were plowed into the political landscape of major cities. Others plowed the earth and became, in America's national self-image, the salt thereof. Still others learned to exploit the bounties of the land under the earth and set the course for industrial capitalism and the amassing of great fortunes.

But subsequent arrivals from southern and eastern Europe seemed nothing like former waves. In an age of Social Darwinism, their subaltern status, ipso facto, raised questions about the extent to which they might dilute and debase the native stock. While they provided fuel for the wick of social capillarity distinctive to American society, it was their linguistic and cultural differences that fueled prejudice against them. Of course if the "native stock" would only snap out of its increasing reproductive lethargy, this would relieve the national anxiety. One of the early projects of the Population Reference Bureau, today a charter member of the population club, was an effort to learn whether the graduates of America's elite institutions were steadfast in their reproductive duties. It turned out they were not. The years of the Great Depression in the United States recorded the lowest birth rates in the nation's history, and this was true, a fortiori, among the better-educated, better-off classes.

In Europe, haunted by the specter of "depopulation," totalitarian governments prepared to balance their demographic books through conquest, subjugation, and offering rewards for bearing children. Countries such as France, Germany, and Russia, which sustained heavy loss of life in World War I, favored this latter approach, even though its effectiveness was somewhat dubious. In Europe, besides devastating war losses, there was also widespread concern about the "twilight of parenthood" that accompanied economic recession. The UN Population Commission, established in 1946, stated in its charter that "population policy is generally understood to refer to measures to encourage large families" (Symonds and Carder 1973: 41). For Britain's demographic anxieties over slumping fertility among the "better classes," there seemed no obvious relief other than the spread of birth control among the poorer classes. Despite the fact that immigration had yet to become a significant fact of British life, class differences served the same purpose. The intellectual elite in Britain held strong convictions regarding the importance of eugenics—a view in which Margaret Sanger was swept up during her self-imposed exile to the "sceptered isle."

Sanger's British counterpart was Dr. Marie Stopes, whose legacy in the family planning movement equals her own. Besides her exposure to eugenic thought among British intellectuals, Sanger learned from Stopes that defiance of authority and valorous heroism profited the cause of birth control less than could be gained under the auspices of respected professionalism. After her return to America this realization served Sanger, with guidance from Dr. Robert Dickenson (a highly regarded Ob/Gyn), as she sought to give to family planning the flavor of science and professionalism.

Since the middle of the twentieth century, and for about 40 years thereafter, "the population problem" again became a matter of concern with quantity. To mention "quality" in the same sentence with "population" was to make a professional audience nervous unless it became clear that the quality to which the speaker was referring had to do with acquired aspects of "human capital" and not putative innate abilities. This all-important turnabout in how population problems were defined and addressed owes much to Frederick Osborn, a recognized eugenicist and first president of the Population Council. Osborn stressed that variations in ability *within* presumed qualitative classes—defined by achieved status and indexed by education, income, race, and ethnicity—were greater than variations *between* classes. Even the redoubtable Margaret Sanger, whose work in birth control for a time took on larger personal meaning under the spell of eugenics, had to learn this elementary lesson in the analysis of variance.

The steady increase in international migration over the last 50 years could again touch off concerns about population quality and the dilution of native stock, itself of diverse cultural and ethnic origins. This is the worry that lies at the root of Buchanan's admonitions to prevent further admixture of America's cultural mosaic. The United States admitted 2.5 million immigrants in the 1950s, 4.5 million in the 1970s, and twice that number in the 1990s (La Croix, Mason, and Abe 2003: 2). In Japan, despite its reputation for having a restrictive immigration policy, the number of "registered foreigners" more than doubled between 1980 and 2000. Europe has experienced a similar influx. These shifts in population composition are flammable tinder, especially when complicated by differential rates of natural increase, by questions of legal status, and by attributes perceived as objectionable by the majority population. Although the history of the twentieth century is marred by outbreaks of "ethnic cleansing," tribal and religious conflict, genocide, population partitionings, and other breakdowns of civil order, the solutions are still very much the business of the new millennium.

The other great change in informed discourse after World War II was the internationalization of the "population problem." The sleeping demographic giants of Asia were stirring. Demographers captured this awakening in a conceptualization they called "the demographic transition." Essentially the transition is a depiction of rapid population growth as a function of *differential* timing in the onset and pace of fertility and mortality decline. This was a new and somewhat overlooked phenomenon, although officials in colonial areas had frequently expressed forebodings about the burgeoning populations of Asia. The basic dynamics were clear, but arguments about its causes and consequences would continue for years.

The "theory" of the demographic transition, as simple as it is in its basic argument, nevertheless amounted to an intellectual revolution. It altered the understanding of the dynamics of population growth. It gave a sense of where things were headed demographically. It conferred antiquarian-only status on biological mysteries such as the logistic curve that until the end of World War I had certain credibility as a method of population forecasting. And by separating out the parameters of population growth, it opened the way for advances in research on trends and determinants of fertility and mortality. It introduced new methodologies for making population projections now that the components of growth required separate treatment. These new projection methods were also fallible, but gave greater hands-on control in demographic forecasting than the admitted artistry of curve fitting. Moreover, they had the great advantage of providing age–sex profiles that led to new insights into population dynamics and that enriched the policy yield from population projections.

Demographic projection and estimation became a subspecialty with its own unique history. On an international level, projections pointed to a growing shift in the balance of population between the developed countries of the North and the less developed ones of the South. Governments in the latter regions, many of which had only recently been released from Northern colonial control, were ill-equipped in terms of their stock of human capital, organs of governance, or economic viability of the territorial units left to them to deal with a rapid rise in population. Moreover, colonial power and authority no longer contained the conflict potential inherent in many new states' ethnic and cultural diversity. As subsequent history amply demonstrates, these points of diversity became rallying cries in a sometimes-deadly competition for power and resources.

As viewed by the North, the combination of rapid population growth, strained resources, and ethnic conflict promised to create a degree of instability and humanitarian calamity that it could not ignore. Both self-interest, especially the recognition that global disorder was not good for business, and perceived humanitarian obligation created a vortex of involvement. Thus the population problem came to be regarded primarily as one of slowing population increase in underdeveloped regions. At the time, this seemed to be the most predictable and apprehensible of the factors involved.

Giving point and urgency to development policy at the time was a Cold War paranoia in the West about the ability of democratic, free-market economies to hold their own against planned, "command" economies such as the Soviet Union. In Washington, intelligence analysts buried themselves in the glowing statistics of Soviet five-year plans with their audacious accounts of the heroes of labor, of virgin land slated to be put to the plow, and of rivers to be reversed. India and China were projected as test cases in the race to development with the odds not necessarily favoring the more democratic alternative. And except where Western governments were able, at least for a time, to influence policy, for example in the Philippines and Pakistan, government policy tended to be pro-Soviet. Even India, under the Congress Party, was so inclined in economic planning, with Nehru insisting that India's five-year plans should be guided from the "Commanding Heights."

It is not excessive to say that a sense of peril arose in Western societies from such observations. Population growth, in what might be regarded as adversarial parts of the world, could be expected to strengthen the forces that potentially might be arrayed against us. Western efforts to help control this growth, along with the emergence of a copious literature on development policy were thus a response to this perception of the long-term peril to the West. Moreover, Western economists set about demonstrating that reducing fertility would provide an important assist to development by deepening the physical and human capital that was critical to its success.

There was a humanitarian side to the efforts to limit population growth. Travelers, whether recreational or professional, to Asia, Africa, or Latin America came away impressed with the idea that these places were swarming with too many people. Well-intentioned efforts to do something about it, both by injections of humanitarian assistance, and more subtly by long-term efforts to bring down birth rates, were thought to be appropriate. Where governments, international donors, and policy elites were concerned, the stronger force was probably the recognition that something bordering on the decline of the West and its basic institutions was at stake. Among available policy options an obvious prescription was "birth control."

Institutions of the North, other than the official ones, were eager and willing to help, but not well equipped just then to do so. Their capacity for population assistance was not significantly better than that in the late 1940s when a Rockefeller Foundation mission went to China to test official interest in "population control." The mission, a selection of public health luminaries and academics, was caught flat-footed when the Chinese agreed that they indeed had a problem of rapid population growth and asked what could be done about it. The mission had little to offer. In later years, with the results of their first "census" of the Communist period showing a much larger population than had previously been estimated, the Chinese ultimately shut their eyes to the tenets of Communist orthodoxy and fashioned their own draconian population program. Ironically, as it turned out, one of the first successful family planning programs in Asia was launched in Taiwan without having recourse to the coercive measures adopted on the mainland.

Owing to the state of the art in contraception and the need for resources, the North was increasingly looked to for assistance. As he had for some years, Prime Minister Nehru of India requested international help in slowing his country's high rate of population growth. And in Pakistan, after overturning an ineffective civilian government in the late 1950s, General Ayub Khan, seeking to improve prospects for economic development in his country, came to New York looking for help in bringing Pakistan's high birth rate under control. These requests resulted in the earliest instances of international population assistance on a substantial scale. They involved private sector to government relationships and were somewhat fumbling on both sides.

This account of international population assistance divides, without excessive procrustean trimming, into five decades, with a sixth currently in the offing. A brief review of the central issues and achievements of the four decades leading up to the 1990s sets the stage for the dramatic developments of that decade and for the policy directions that followed.

The 1950s—Organizational Response and Technological Development

We begin our account with the events of the 1950s for this period marks a turning point in the evolution of population activities. It is the time when it might be said population policy came in from the cold. No longer characterized primarily by the heroic efforts of pioneers such as Margaret Sanger and the obstreperous Clarence Gamble, birth control gained top drawer organized backing. The frustration that plagued past efforts over the inadequacy of contraceptive methods came under systematic scientific assault. The underlying energy behind this transformation derived largely from concern over the unsettling implications of rising nationalism in postcolonial Asia and Africa. Instability in these areas was perceived as a coming threat to the favorable terms of trade to which the West had grown accustomed. To add to the anxiety, improvements in mortality dispelled the demographic dormancy that had kept these populations in check. In Ceylon, for example, a campaign against malaria-bearing mosquitoes featuring residual spraying of DDT resulted in a dramatic decrease in deaths. The time was approaching in many less developed countries when it would no longer be necessary to bear four children so that two would survive to adulthood. But until that came to be broadly recognized among ordinary couples sufficiently to affect their reproductive behavior, rapid population growth would necessarily follow.

Two major events of the 1950s reflect this new definition of the demographic situation; namely, the founding of the Population Council in 1952 and the development of oral contraception at the Worcester Foundation for Experimental Biology. The Population Council was the creation of John D. Rockefeller III and his close advisors, with intellectual cover from an illustrious board of trustees drawn from big-name academic institutions. In those days it was advisable to have a strong scientific escort when venturing out into the population arena. Thus it was that the 31 scholars present at the birth of the Council in Williamsburg, Virginia, were overwhelmingly drawn from the scientific community. The head of the Planned Parenthood of America, an ornithologist by profession, and that organization's director of research were there, but the tenor of the meetings was scientific. Research—demographic, social, and biomedical—with action a distant prospect.

The development of the oral contraceptive pill in the 1950s may have been "the single most important medical advance of the century for improving women's health" and "one of the greatest achievements in reproductive medicine" (Segal 2003: 70). Those are perhaps arguable claims, but there can be no doubting the enormous importance of the discovery and development of hormonal control of fertility. Segal estimates that if the "roughly 120 million women" who used the pill between 1960 and 2000 had relied on more traditional methods of contraception and the failure rates associated with them, there would have been "countless unplanned and unwanted pregnancies"—about half of which "would have ended in elective termination, many in countries where abortion was illegal and unsafe" (p. 70).

The pill, like most innovations, has not lived up to the high hopes held for it even though it has been greatly improved over the years since its introduction. A major problem is the high percentage of women who begin to use the pill but discontinue or interrupt its use within a year of adoption, often because of its medical side effects, thus making it a burdensome and costly contraceptive compared with longer-term methods. Nevertheless, the pill and sterilization still provide more protection to couples than other methods (Ross and Stover 2003).

The principal scientist behind the pill's development, Gregory Pincus, was the director of the Worcester Foundation for Experimental

Biology in Worcester, Massachusetts. Other biological scientists and clinicians were crucial to the pill's development, as were the clinicians who tested it under field conditions. Once again, Margaret Sanger, long an advocate of research to develop better methods of contraception, was there with critical help.[1] How she got the heiress of the Cyrus McCormack farm machinery fortune interested in supporting the work on the hormonal control of ovulation at Worcester, by now a familiar story, attests to her catalytic backstage presence in the field.[2]

Underwriting these two developments, crucial support for the Population Council and development of the oral pill at Wooster, was the Ford Foundation. During the early years of the 1950s, the foundation sought to define its role in the new but still contentious field of population research and programmatic activity. Following the arrival in 1958 of Oscar Harkavy, the foundation fashioned a broad conception of its mission with respect to population issues and an accompanying strategy. Donald Warwick, in recounting this formative period, wrote that during the 1950s and 1960s "the Ford Foundation was the largest single source of funds for population activities" (Warwick 1982: 52). This commitment grew until 1966 when it peaked at a level of $26 million. It declined sharply in subsequent years as government funding came on line.

In addition to strong support for domestic research and training and funding for population programs at several universities, the foundation ventured into selected underdeveloped countries where, working in collaboration with U.S. academic institutions, it bankrolled some of the earliest and most ambitious efforts aimed at economic development with fertility reduction always a matter of central concern. As Warwick, a keen observer of this period wrote, "Overall the Ford Foundation was one of the most influential and yet least controversial [of] international donors. It played a leading role in drawing world attention to population questions, preparing the ground for national programs, developing new contraceptives, setting the direction for and actually supporting academic research, developing major training institutions in the field, and facilitating the entry of large donors such as AID and UNFPA into the field" (Warwick 1982: 56).

The decade of the 1950s was much more than the story of a major scientific breakthrough in contraceptive technology and the establishment of the Population Council as a leading institution to exploit it. It was a time when the development of less developed nations was high on the agenda of postwar reconstruction. Underlying much of this interest was the view that underdeveloped countries, if left to their own devices, would sink deeper into poverty and become a troubling source of instability to advanced countries. Rapid population growth was recognized as a crucial impediment to development, a belief that arose not just from common observation, but also from systematic study of the economic consequences of high fertility.

Among population scholars there was fairly pervasive skepticism that birth control would be the sole solution to the problem of population growth. They tended to see fertility levels as responses to social and economic forces and beyond the reach of well-meaning reformers. Thus they took a dim view of policies that aimed to reduce birth rates by putting primary reliance on encouraging the use of contraception. The prominent economist–demographer Frank W. Notestein (1944), who a decade-and-a-half later became president of the Population Council, was of the view that birth control "as a sole solution to the problem of population pressure is of little importance and depends on the social setting" (p. 4). He wrote that "development that would foster rapid population increase would also elicit the economic product to support that increase . . . [and that] in such areas population growth will present no considerable barrier to economic and political development for some time to come" (p. 4). But, he continued, this would not be the case for areas already densely settled—places such as Egypt, India, China, Korea, Taiwan, Java, much of the Caribbean, and to a lesser extent the Philippines.

This was not at all the argument being advanced by the American sociologist Kingsley Davis, who stressed that in general, couples would not be motivated to restrict their childbearing sufficiently to make much of a dent in the rate of population growth at the aggregate level. Notestein was by then aware of Davis' view on the matter, as was Bernard Berelson, his successor as president of the Population Council. They conceded Davis' argument that motivation to reduce fertility might have to be strengthened. Some demand for contraception already existed, and making it easier to obtain family planning services might generate more.

Particularly critical of birth control as a solution to the problem of population growth were demographers with leftist inclinations, such as Alfred Sauvy of the French National Institute for Population Studies and Professor Mahalanobis of the Calcutta Institute of Statistics. They simply denied the validity of the notion of "population pressure." As members in 1950 of the UN Population Commission, both men resisted calls for that body to take a more active role in confronting the issue of rapid population growth. As chair of the commission, Sauvy attacked the thesis, then gaining wide currency, that population growth was detrimental to development. Scholars of this persuasion objected to any suggestion that the advertised consequences of population growth could not be handled by "socialist construction." Injecting much needed common sense into the debate, David Glass, the dean of British demographers at the time, observed with patient reasonableness that the question was not whether birth control or social change was primary, but whether levels of living might not be raised more quickly if rates of population growth were not so high.

In any event, at the time there was a general lack of clarity concerning both the connection of "social and economic forces" to fertility and the more immediate factors through which those forces operated to influence the level of fertility. The second problem was significantly clarified by an analysis published by Davis and Blake in 1956, which provided a systematic account of the variables through which a biological maximum level of fertility could be reduced to an observed level. The first problem (understanding the social and economic factors affecting fertility) continues to lure demographers and social scientists into ever further recesses of methodologically sophisticated inconclusiveness. The second problem of identifying and measuring the effects of the intermediate variables through which social and economic factors must operate—as outlined by Davis and Blake (1956)—has been refined by further demographic analysis, most notably by John Bongaarts of the Population Council.[3]

These finer points of causation and empirical analysis were lost on those who advocated doing something about rapid population growth in developing countries. Protestant churches in America were encouraged to take a clear lead in the matter. The American Conference of World Churches in 1958 adopted a resolution arguing that few problems had greater bearing on the welfare of our fellow men and on world peace than responsible control of population growth. In the same year, the Lambeth Conference of Anglican Bishops declared that the "hand of God" laid on the conscience of parents everywhere the responsibility for decisions about the number of children they should have and when they should have them. It went further to pronounce it a "duty" of better-developed countries to help poor countries become self-supporting in food supplies and health measures. To achieve this goal, they said, population control would be a necessity (Symonds and Carder 1973: 26). There were objections from Rome, but the interventionist tide was rising ever more insistently.

In retrospect, the 1950s can be seen as pivotal in the emergence of the conviction that the developed world owed it to less advanced ones (and to themselves) to help them on the road to economic advance. It was clear to most social scientists that any given social setting was a joint product of environmental opportunities and limitations, social organization, and population structure and dynamics. When it came to development, the population area seemed for many to afford the most obvious openings for effective interventions—and among these birth control had a prior claim.

In this milieu can be found the beginnings of the "population industry." In 1953 the International Planned Parenthood Federation (IPPF) was launched in Bombay, India, with a dual mission of combating poverty through birth control and advancing family planning as an individual right. The UN established demographic training and research centers in Santiago, Chile, and in Bombay. The Pathfinder Fund, which had served as a vehicle for the intrepid birth controller Clarence Gamble, was recommissioned to rejoin the fight for the spread of birth control. The nearly defunct National Committee for Maternal Health, a veteran organization of earlier reproductive health struggles, was revived to become a scientific "safe house" for Dr. Christopher Tietze, a physician and something of a polymath. Numbers aroused in him a fascination for statistical pursuit that was of hound–hare proportions. In the next decade, after the introduction of improved intrauterine devices (IUD), he devised and monitored a protocol for analyzing their "use effectiveness" under field conditions. His assiduous data management and analysis helped establish the IUD as a useful, although far from trouble-free, method of birth control. Tietze was also prominent among epidemiological scientists who demonstrated the value of lactational amenorrhea, extended through prolonged breastfeeding, as an effective means for deferring pregnancy. His analysis of the relative risk of abortion versus full-term delivery, another salient of his abounding scientific interests, gave the jitters to the high priests of population policy.

A famous legal case in Kings County, New York, established the moral legitimacy of medically prescribed contraception in life-threatening situations—a significant policy threshold. The case involved a diabetic woman whose doctor advised her against becoming pregnant and suggested she be fitted with a diaphragm. When it became known, this alleged breach of the legal strictures against the distribution of contraceptive devices aroused the usual religious and legal opposition. The Planned Parenthood Association joined the case in support of the woman's right to be allowed to prevent a further pregnancy and, after a high-profile legal contest, prevailed. Not only did winning this case establish a significant policy benchmark, it also marked a new level of professionalism for the association in its handling of public affairs (Piotrow 1973: 17). It also thrust Alan Guttmacher, one of the physicians involved, to prominence in family planning circles.

Of particular importance were the new books and journals that were published dealing with the factors involved in economic development. Rapid population growth figured prominently in this literature. The economic effect of high fertility, the component of population growth that seemed most amenable to policy intervention, was memorably analyzed by two economists, Ansley Coale and Edgar Hoover. Their analysis, undertaken at the request of the World Bank, not only impressed the academic community, but also strengthened convictions concerning the economic costs of high fertility. It was to have a lasting effect on population policy.

Although in subsequent years Coale readily conceded that economic analysis had moved beyond the approach he and Hoover had taken, their broad conclusions have retained their appeal. They got a second wind during the so-called Economic Miracle in Southeast Asia when the "tigers' " unprecedented rates of economic growth were ascribed, by some analysts, to the high proportion of the working-age population relative to the total population in those countries (see Mason 2002; Bloom, Canning, and Sevilla 2003). The subsequent meltdown of those same economies demonstrated the fragility and simplicity of the Coale–Hoover model with its stress on changing age structures and associated demographic "burdens." It was a lesson not to be forgotten in the dangerous waters of demographic determinism.

In 1953, the Population Division of the United Nations produced a summary of extant demographic knowledge entitled the *Determinants and Consequences of Population Growth*, a volume that for some years was required reading for budding demographers (United Nations Population Division 1953 and updated as United Nations Population Division 1978). In keeping with the circumspection of that time concerning the regulation of fertility and the conservatism of the UN Population Commission, which set the direction and tone for the Population Division, this volume makes no mention of birth control, stressing instead the prospect that economic development would be able to absorb any population increase resulting therefrom. It would be many years until the Population Commission was able to overcome its timidity on the subject of family planning. By that time the field, even other organs of the UN, had moved on.

While all this bag packing was going on, population growth in less developed countries continued apace. Demographers were still coming to terms with the unexpectedly large increase in China's population. In India, the annual population growth rate, which until 1951 had been maintained at a long-term average of less than 1.0 percent, rose above 2.0 percent over the period from 1950–55 to 1970–75—roughly from a doubling time of approximately 70 years to a doubling every 35 years (United Nations Population Division 2004a).

The UN convened the first of what became a decennial series of conferences on population and development in 1954. It was limited essentially to governmental delegates from 58 countries. No advocacy or nongovernmental groups were involved (nor did many exist at the time), although IPPF was permitted two observers.

The following year the first UN regional conference on population and development was held in Bandung, Indonesia. Four years later, the UN's latest population projections were presented to the Population Commission. They aroused concern in that body, but, with the caution that typified official organizations at the time, the commission went no further than to declare itself duty-bound to call attention to rapid growth of the world's population as indisputable fact. Inasmuch as several members of the commission refused to acknowledge the existence of a population problem, this might be viewed as an important benchmark in the evolution of the commission's position. It could also be marked as the beginning of the commission's long descent into irrelevance.

More charitably, it must be admitted that official bodies generally in those days, and even some private ones, were still wary of the subject. The Rockefeller Foundation, having taken some heat for its support of the Kinsey reports on sexual practices in the United States, backed away from further involvement with population—at least through the front door. The Ford Foundation was caught in paralyzing ambiguity, feeling pressure to get involved yet afraid of jeopardizing its projects in other social areas. It eventually came around.

Parenthetically, it was in the final year of the decade that President Eisenhower dismissed the highly influential Draper Report, which, among other things, complained that population growth was hampering development under the Marshall Plan. Nothing, said the president, was less the proper business of government than a husband and wife's decisions on matters of reproduction. Not only did Eisenhower change his mind on this matter after he left the presidency—even accepting a citation from Planned Parenthood for his support of their activities—but so, eventually, did the U.S. government. A foretaste of the pressures on the government to become involved in population matters is General Draper's appearance before the Senate Committee on Foreign Relations in May 1959 in which he said, "The population problem, I'm afraid, is the greatest bar to our whole economic aid program and to the progress of the world" (Piotrow 1973: 39).

The 1960s—Early Family Planning Program Initiatives

The 1960s saw the continued unfolding of forces from the 1950s that were leading to greater acceptance of interventions to reduce the rate of population growth. Opinion polls indicated that an overwhelming majority of Americans favored free access to birth control. The economist Stephen Enke developed a cost-effective analysis of the relative development payoff from investment in family planning as compared to direct investment in development, making a case later used by the Johnson administration to justify its support for family planning assistance (Enke 1960). The Draper Report, which Eisenhower and Kennedy had dismissed as none of the government's proper business, ended up with the Senate Committee on Foreign Relations, where it got a proper hearing.

Subsequently, President Kennedy softened his position, telling Congress that the United States should help less developed countries "understand" their population problems and the U.S. ambassador to India intimated to the government of India that there might be support forthcoming for collecting and analyzing data to do just that. In 1962 the U.S. State Department encouraged support for UN population activities and made exploratory approaches to the Population Council, the Ford Foundation, and the Planned Parenthood Federation. After Kennedy's death, President Johnson promised "to seek new ways" to deal with the problem of rapid population growth. In addition, Congressional hearings on population, which ran episodically from 1962 to 1967, kept the subject in public view. Subsequently, President Nixon (1969) argued that "population growth is a world problem which no country can ignore, whether it is moved by the narrowest perception of national self interest or the widest vision of common humanity" (p. 2).

The United States Agency for International Development (USAID) was created in 1961 out of the remnants of the successor agencies for postwar reconstruction that Harry Truman set loose with his famous Point Four speech. It would be several years before USAID added population as one of its development sectors, but events were moving in that direction. Also in 1961 the UN Population Commission gave its blessing to technical assistance in the population field, a position of high resolve that two years later was rescinded with the explanation that it was never meant to include activities connected with family planning. That would turn out, within the decade, to have been a temporary setback.

Intervention fever was spreading. In 1962 the UN General Assembly passed a resolution affirming that there was no denying the connection between poverty, health, nutrition, literacy, and rapid population growth. At the World Bank, President Robert McNamara, addressing the Bank's governors, announced that the Bank would seek active involvement in the population problem by informing developing countries about the costs of population growth to their potential development, seeking opportunities to finance family planning programs, and joining the search for the most effective means of family planning. In a speech at Notre Dame on May 1969, he declared population growth to be the "most delicate and difficult issue of our era [and] the greatest single obstacle to economic and social advancement of the majority of the peoples in the underdeveloped world" (Symonds and Carder 1973: 17). Although the Bank favored investment in family planning, it took the position that it should not be a "bargain- basement" substitute for development. Otherwise they were on board but, as bankers, were inclined to invest in tangible assets—in bricks and mortar rather than social and human development programs.

By the closing years of the 1960s, USAID also was getting its population act together and Congress helped out by earmarking funds for its activities. In 1967, two congressmen, George H. W. Bush (R. Texas) and Herman Schneebele (R. Pennsylvania) of the House Ways and Means Committee, introduced revisions to the Social Security Act that were concerned in part with maternal and child health (MCH) provisions of the Act. Their amendments provided that 6 percent of the appropriated funds should be made available for family planning. True, this was domestic legislation, not international population assistance, but it indicated how the policy winds were blowing (Piotrow 1973: 141).

Not to be left behind, the United Nations established a Trust Fund for Population Activities in 1967 that on its operational side became the United Nations Fund for Population Activities

(UNFPA)—later simply the United Nations Population Fund—an organization destined to be the largest and most influential multilateral agency in the population field. Two years earlier, at the World Conference on Population and Development in Belgrade, a high UN official told the conferees, heavily weighted with economists and demographers, that the world expected more from these conferences than greater understanding of demographic facts and relationships.

Back at UN headquarters in New York, the UN Population Commission, which functions as a policy directorate for the UN Population Division, recovered from its early recantation and finally agreed that priority should be given to understanding the dynamics of fertility and family planning use. But the Commission was better at expressing sentiments than at taking action, since even if it spoke with one voice, it was required to submit its recommendations to the dilatory procedures of the UN bureaucracy. And in this matter it was not univocal. As expected, two members of the Commission, Alfred Sauvy and Professor Podyachik of the Soviet Union, stood in opposition to these new agendas.

There were other sour notes and spots of resistance. The World Health Organization feared that family planning would divert funds from its broader agenda in public health. It would be better, its members argued, to build MCH facilities first. At the Twentieth Session of the World Health Assembly, there was strenuous resistance to "making family planning part of health." From the left came grumbling that the "cannibalistic" theories of the West would succeed only in diverting attention from the real causes of poverty. The Soviet demographer Boyarski, a member of the UN Population Commission, presented his own population projections, which were heavily skewed by optimistic assumptions regarding a world trend toward socialism and the development benefits assumed to follow from the conversion from capitalism. He projected for the year 2000 a world population of 4.2 to 5.0 billion—a full billion or so below the consensus estimates of the time.

These were some of the surface events of the 1960s. They were propelled by more basic forces such as the failure of the Indian monsoons (two years in succession) during the middle of the decade. The result of that catastrophe was a need for massive grain imports that dispelled much of the optimism that the Green Revolution had inspired. It also resulted in severe strain on donor funds since the Indian government's foreign currency reserves were as insufficient as its grain stocks. Moreover, the Green Revolution was proving problematic, especially with respect to its heavy demand for water; environmental consequences such as soil salinization and water logging; and exacerbated social inequities. Added to these sobering developments were the census rounds of the early 1960s indicating that, as in the preceding decade, population growth had again exceeded expectations.

Moreover, at a subterranean level, Cold War paranoia was rampant during this period. Sputnik, orbiting in space, reminded the West of its deficiencies in scientific and engineering manpower. This realization was reinforced when an astonished world watched as the Soviets launched and recovered the first manned space vehicle. Khrushchev's earlier announced intention to "bury" the West was never convincingly dismissed, and his plans for agricultural bounty from newly opened "virgin lands" of Central Asia were one way of doing it. May Day parades of Soviet military might had their calculated chilling effect as the five-year plans appeared to grind away toward an inevitable hegemonic climax. All of these developments, plus the ultimate failure of Western colonialism, helped socialism find favor in a number of important developing countries. It was understandable that the West, particularly the United States, should adopt a policy of containing the perceived Communist threat and eliminating, through development, the breeding grounds of revolution in those countries. Birth control as a handmaiden to development thus found its place in foreign-assistance policy.

The major foundations, the front line of population action as the 1960s got under way, realized that their resources were inadequate for a build up of family planning programs in countries where they were needed. The first thought of the Population Council in contemplating the U.S. government's newfound commitment to population assistance was to anticipate a manifold expansion of its own activities. At a Population Council strategy meeting in Tarrytown, New York, the prevailing view was that the government would doubtless turn to organizations such as the Council to take the lead in implementing its new resolve to "seek new ways" to help deal with the explosion of world population. Early visits to the Council from Washington officials indeed encouraged that view. Among the documents in the Population Council Archives stored at the Rockefeller Estates in Pocantico Hills, New York, is a 35-page Department of State "Action Memorandum" prepared by Philander Claxton, a central figure in the articulation of U.S. government policy on population. The memo proposes that the government might possibly deploy a staff of six population specialists to be located in Washington and five others in three overseas missions. In other U.S. missions a staff position could be assigned (part time) to a "nonexpert" with responsibility for reporting on the population situation in the country of assignment. To put this deployment into some perspective, the memo goes on to observe that, by contrast, agriculture had 1,100 specialist staff, 35 of them based in Washington.

At the official level, international population assistance, as Claxton suggested, would not require a huge buildup of staff or direct involvement in operations. Rather, he foresaw a linking of private groups such as the Population Council, the IPPF, and the Ford Foundation to provide broad guidance and the creation of various "working groups" that would brief and possibly involve relevant government agencies. He anticipated in his memorandum that private institutions, particularly universities, would provide training in languages, social customs, and the management of family planning programs. To extend family planning programs worldwide, he estimated that an outlay of $150 million a year would be required, and two to three times that amount if incentive payments were included.

On the U.S. government side, USAID started to become involved in international population assistance in the mid-1960s, but didn't really find its direction until the closing years of the decade. While most leaders in the population field welcomed the prospect of additional resources, there were some who expressed concern about being tarred by the brush of U.S. foreign-policy misadventures. The Population Council section of the Rockefeller archives also contains a memorandum from J. Mayone Stycos, the Population Council's man in Latin America, warning of such dangers. He cites the instance of U.S. actions, just then in the Dominican Republic, that risked making difficulties throughout the area for any private organization perceived to be a U.S. flag carrier. This was undoubtedly an important consideration since the Caribbean area in the 1950s and 1960s was the scene of some of the earliest field research into the determinants of population trends. Moreover, early field trials of the oral pill were also carried out there. But the government train was about to leave the station. With few exceptions, most private groups, including the Population Council, were on board or soon would be.

Several years following Lyndon Johnson's call for the U.S. government to seek new ways to deal with the issue of excessive population growth, a member of the medical faculty at the University of Washington in Seattle, Reimert (Rei) Ravenholt, was recruited to organize and lead such an effort. Ravenholt arrived in Washington to take on this assignment in 1966 only to find that he had no budget and no staff. There was also uncertain support from above and numerous bureaucratic and legal handicaps to be faced, the greatest being U.S. government policy banning the procurement and overseas shipment of contraceptives (Ravenholt 1969: 611–613; nd: 6–7). Ravenholt's early efforts were also unfolding in the context of a declining foreign aid budget and the rapid escalation of U.S. military involvement in Vietnam.

After a period of discouragement and questioning the wisdom of having left Seattle, Ravenholt set about with the energy and doggedness for which he was to become famous in finding solutions to these crippling problems. By early 1967 the U.S. ban on contraceptives was removed. And instead of petitioning through channels as usual bureaucratic practice prescribed, Ravenholt made an end run to obtain the help of influential outside advocates, such as General William Draper, to get the authority and funds he needed to build his staff. This, as we shall see, was the beginning of an effort that dominated the field of population assistance for the remainder of Ravenholt's tenure at USAID and beyond.

A few years after USAID accepted population assistance into its portfolio, Rafael Salas, as the first director of the United Nations Population Fund (UNFPA) persuaded the UN General Assembly to grant his agency full recognition and support and thus free it from oversight by the Population Commission. He consolidated his victory by reorganizations at UNFPA designed to make it more responsive as an action agency and adding the position of program coordinator. Named to that position was a Pakistani physician, Nafis Sadik, who eventually succeeded him as director.

UNFPA found what it hoped would be its modus operandi. Rather than involving itself directly in operational activities, it would work through UN specialized agencies whose missions would appear to benefit from a reduction in the rate of population growth. Not only were organizations such as the World Health Organization, United Nations Childrens Fund, the International Labour Organization, Food and Agriculture Organization, and the UN Population Division available to be co-opted, but also a broadening of their activities into population assistance seemed a legitimate expansion of their basic purposes. UNFPA used its budgetary leverage to fund positions in these organizations to do things that a "fund," lacking the necessary staffing and technical specializations, could not do.

This turned out to be an unworkable mode of action. "It produced a legacy of small projects parceled out on something approaching an entitlement basis to UN agencies as a very small adjunct to their main business. The result was a sort of atomization of UNFPA funds among many agencies, few of which were either equipped or committed to deal effectively with population issues" (Sinding 1996: 1). After a decade or so of operating in this manner, UNFPA came to the realization that, as Steven Sinding puts it, "much of its money was being absorbed by agencies which were not able to use it well" (p. 1). Complaints and dissatisfaction also arose from donors and recipient countries about the relative ineffectiveness of UNFPA-funded projects.

Despite such early teething problems, there was a heady optimism about population matters in the 1960s. New methods of contraception, such as the IUD, were coming on line and the high hormonal dosages that caused troubling side effects in pill users were steadily being reduced. Big foundations such as Ford continued to fund biomedical and demographic research and now sponsored some of the pioneer overseas population projects in Asia.

It would be a gross oversight to end this review of developments during the 1960s without mentioning two important developments in contraceptive methods. The IUD came on line in the early 1960s with the discovery that a device made of coiled silastic plastic, which after being straightened to facilitate insertion into the uterus, would return to its original shape. The introduction of a foreign object into the uterine cavity had long been known to prevent pregnancy. The exact mechanism of action was something of a mystery and one that some family planning advocates thought might better not be probed too far since anything that prevented implantation of the fetus would attract the slings and arrows of antiabortionists. It is today a vastly improved device and a staple of many family planning programs. Less widely accepted than the pill (owing in part to its reliance on clinical provision), it nevertheless has the advantage of longer periods of uninterrupted use and eliminates the daily regimen required of successful pill users. The IUD also arouses fewer safety concerns about long-term use than do hormonal contraceptives.

The other significant development in contraception that came into its own in the 1960s was recognition of the antiovulatory effect of postpartum breastfeeding. This is a method that always had a certain standing in the tales of "old wives," just as did the effect of copper, which is now added to the most effective IUDs. What was needed in both cases to turn these notions into an effective addition to the contraceptive armamentarium, were careful observational studies to demonstrate that these effects could be reliably counted upon. Christopher Tietze and other experts in human reproduction were there to do the job.

The 1970s: Heyday of One-Dimensional Family Planning

Insofar as U.S. government policy was concerned, the decade of the 1970s may fairly be called the Ravenholt era in the history of family planning.[4] Ravenholt's unrelenting "supply-side" approach for making family planning methods available throughout the developing world had its incubation period in the late 1960s. It reached full power in the following decade. By the start of the 1970s, USAID had hammered out the kinks in its population policy and under Ravenholt's strong and ambitious leadership, was ready to roll. After some initial dithering and feints toward the big foundations, USAID metamorphosed into an organization bent on putting population control on a war footing.

Ravenholt (1997) believed in a strong, partly latent demand for contraception, which could be activated by making contraceptives readily available. Supply was expected to create its own demand. He summarized his basic approach as follows:

> If one makes contraceptives generally available, one may not know for certain that they will be used, but if one does not make them available, one can be certain that they will not be used . . . Although the availability of fertility control methods is not the only determinant of fertility control behavior, actions to increase availability can ordinarily be implemented more quickly and efficiently than can alternative approaches to fertility control. Furthermore, even when alternative approaches are employed, full availability of the most effective means of fertility control would greatly enhance the effectiveness of these approaches. (p. 4)

Ravenholt believed that increasing availability was an essential starting point, but his focus on expanding new and better means of contraception, his efforts to support new means of measuring program success (or failure), his enthusiasm for critical areas such as training and improved logistics are all tacit evidence of a broader conception than he is usually given credit for. The boundary he would not cross, however, was that which, in those days, was posted "beyond family planning."

Compared to Claxton's mild vision of collaborative, consultative relations between the private and official sectors, the Ravenholt era at USAID was one of command and control. It involved the mobilization of forces in a manner familiar to epidemiologists in confronting an epidemic disease. The basic strategy was based on a simple, many said overly simple, conception of how to go about reducing fertility. He was impatient with the preoccupation of many social scientists who stressed the cultural barriers to the adoption of new, tradition-challenging behaviors such as family planning. While many cheered him on, some demographers and social scientists were distressed by his style of operation and his apparent neglect of the demand side of the equation.

Ravenholt's legacy is a complex matter. He cannot be faulted for failing to put his convictions into practice. He was enthusiastic for new procedures such as menstrual regulation (MR), a disingenuous, don't-ask–don't-tell routine vacuum aspiration of uterine contents with or without the known presence of fetal tissue. MR kits were a staple of USAID programs, even though some believed this initiative was playing with fire vis-à-vis Senator Jesse Helms and other conservative politicians on Capitol Hill. Ravenholt pushed hard for laparoscopic sterilization, a technique that provides access to the fallopian tubes through a small abdominal puncture.

He flooded warehouses with contraceptive supplies, often well in excess of likely need, a practice optimistically dubbed "programming for success." On this he may have gone overboard since the uptake was not always what he expected. (Some of these supplies disintegrated in the tropical heat, others found their way into distributional back channels, and yet others remained as stored monuments to unresponsive logistic systems.) He overcame arbitrary constraints in the government's procurement system to get agreement on a standard formulary and packaging for the oral pill.

As important as anything else, he learned to beat the bureaucracy at its own game. He was able to cut through obstacles that blocked his efforts to secure critical resources for a program that many regarded as dangerously controversial. Ravenholt was forthright in confronting the issue of voluntary sterilization and "developed major programs . . . to train doctors and medical teams and supply them with the technologies to rapidly expand laparoscopic sterilization and later minilaparotomy" (Sinding 2001: 4).

Naturally enough, given his emphasis on contraceptive supplies, Ravenholt turned his attention to logistic management and backed efforts to help developing countries set up systems for estimating their contraceptive needs and for effective, timely, and responsive delivery of products. And finally, beset as he was with resistance to his aims and modes of operation within USAID and under constant pressure to spend the money being appropriated by Congress for population assistance, he resorted to a bit of organizational bypass surgery by working directly with and through private and voluntary organizations. This approach was responsible for the growth of nominally independent "cooperating agencies" (CAs) that now receive over half of USAID's annual spending on population activities (Ravenholt nd: 21–23; Sinding 2001: 3). Interestingly, as Sinding notes, the CAs have become separate constituencies, each with its own political base. In the past this has helped to buffer USAID from administrations unfriendly to population assistance. At the time CAs appealed to Ravenholt as a means of conserving and channeling funds free from the straight jacket of the contract mechanism and the looseness and uncertainty of grants that diluted his control over how the funds were used.

As an epidemiologist, Ravenholt appreciated the need for data on program results, a need he sought to fulfill in several ways. One of these was to contract with the U.S. Census Bureau to produce estimates of birth rates for a selection of countries. Ravenholt was unhappy that these sometimes failed to show the declines he expected and blamed the Census Bureau's estimation methodology, which, he argued, gave too much weight to past behavior and thus missed what was going on "now." He was particularly vexed that in countries such as Indonesia and the Philippines, where USAID hoped to see results of their efforts, the Census Bureau's estimates were stubbornly unobliging. His reaction initially was to modify the Bureau's contract, deleting those countries in which he expected to show results and handing them to a private consultant.

To his credit, Ravenholt subsequently, in what was one of his more important and lasting contributions, undertook to fund a series of sample surveys designed to provide data on fertility and contraceptive behavior for selected countries. This operation, known as the World Fertility Survey (WFS), was funded by UNFPA and USAID through the International Statistical Institute in The Hague. The surveys, now known as Demographic and Health Surveys (DHS), eventually came under direct USAID control. Although USAID's support for DHS helped secure the financial base for this activity, it may also have undermined the international status previously enjoyed by the WFS. Some increasingly view the DHS as an internal USAID monitoring and evaluation tool. However, the DHS has also become the primary source of national data on fertility, mortality, contraceptive use, and MCH in many developing countries.

By many accounts Ravenholt was the man of the hour in resolving the doubts and irresolution of the late 1960s, as USAID moved to launch its population program with a clear sense of direction and commitment. It was a task demanding strong, if somewhat single-minded leadership. A paucity of experience about the course to follow and opposition within USAID stemming from internal rivalries over power and turf required Ravenholt to project firmness in his belief that "demand for contraceptive services both existed and could be created, and that a straightforward family planning approach was a necessary, if not in all places sufficient, condition for rapid fertility decline" (Sinding 2001: 12). For the conditions of the time, Sinding believes that policy was "more right than wrong."

But does this give Ravenholt his full due? However much his single-minded zeal in pursuing supply-side convictions irritated certain influential international donors and alienated those who argued for a broader demand-side approach, the question that can neither be answered nor dismissed is where would matters have stood had he not come along? He injected the 1970s with his own unique dynamism. He brought into the field a loyal following at USAID, which carried on after him, while adapting to the challenges and opportunities that presented themselves. He actively promoted new contraceptive and reproductive health technologies that greatly improved the well being of many women in the developing world. In addition, he encouraged, not always in a hands-off manner, field-based operations research and the evaluation of program achievements. Most importantly perhaps, he made international population assistance a policy issue and a public responsibility that, at least for a decade or so, could not be ignored.

Nevertheless, it can be argued that Ravenholt was also partly responsible for planting the seeds of future contention. Perhaps Sinding sounds the most fitting final epitaph for the Ravenholt era at USAID:

In retrospect, it is unfortunate that Dr. Ravenholt and his more enthusiastic followers adopted so highly aggressive a posture and were so dismissive of those who questioned their approach. The effect was to polarize the population field and to create a resistance in many quarters that remains to this day. It would have been quite reasonable to assert, as many did in the late 1960s, that family planning services are an essential condition of fertility decline and even that their provision and expansion should be the first order of business in population policy. It was not reasonable to imply, as Ravenholt often did, that family planning was the only thing that needed to be done, or that measures "beyond family planning" were distracting and counterproductive. (p. 12)

Ravenholt's aggressiveness as a driving force in USAID's program operations was irritating to many who were involved, but of even greater concern was the fear that his oversimplified strategy would eventually be exposed for its superficiality and bring discredit to the field. His departure from USAID was widely seen by the academic community, and by some international donors, as a move toward greater realism and balance in the official international population policy of the United States.

However, it was also, on the whole, shabby treatment of a dedicated, hard working, creative civil servant who pushed hard for a program he believed in. His style was not to whine over the frustrations he encountered in working against the bureaucratic grain, but to win the battles that stood in his way. While this endeared him to his staff, it also encouraged bureaucratic forces of jealousy and resentment (led by senior USAID political appointees installed during the Carter administration) that eventually cut him down. Less than 15 years after it began, the Ravenholt era came to a drawn-out and, in contrast to its energetic early years of achievement, a somewhat hounded close in 1979.

The decade of the 1970s was not entirely given over to supply-side, top–down, one-dimensional program strategies. New issues were emerging. There was much earnest discussion and field experimentation in addressing the advantages of integrating family planning with other health services (primarily MCH interventions).

Stand-alone "vertical" family planning programs had often been seen as a way to avoid getting involved with inefficient health bureaucracies, often viewed as the graveyard of ministerial ambition. Moreover, experience from the 1960s suggested that providing family planning services as an integral part of health programs did not translate into greater acceptance of contraception. Early attempts to integrate family planning and MCH, for example on the Indian subcontinent, fell short since child survival was prioritized to the near exclusion of maternal health, and contraception held little meaning for couples who could not perceive that their children were now any less likely to die before reaching adulthood. Life tables, the demographic device that captures trends in mortality, are clear to the eyes of the statisticians who create and behold them. Common perception of improvements in life chances may lag behind.

Belief in the value of integration nevertheless persisted as a programmatic ideal. It got a second look in an ambitious project of the Population Council. Known as the Taylor–Berelson Project (named for Howard Taylor, a highly regarded Ob/Gyn from Columbia Presbyterian Hospital in New York, and Bernard Berelson), the project set out to test the belief in the essential complementarity of health and population programs. To determine what synergy there might be in an integration of population and health, study areas in four countries—Turkey, Indonesia, the Philippines, and Nigeria—were organized.

As far as one can tell, the project failed to demonstrate that an integrated approach would lead to greater contraceptive acceptance than one that was more vertically structured. In some settings (e.g., Indonesia and Turkey), the project never really got off the ground in effectively integrating family planning and MCH services. It was also overly ambitious in its initial conception (seemingly trying to do everything at once) and naive in assuming that family planning services could be effectively integrated with the woefully inadequate MCH services that had to be accommodated. Perhaps the greatest fault was in the project's assumption that a standard approach might work in widely varying social settings. Despite the expenditure of considerable resources, no final report summarizing this experiment was ever produced, thus nurturing the suspicion that the outcome, at best, was inconclusive. However, this result did nothing to stay the calls for integration. It is an early instance of the current tendency for careful empirical field-testing of service delivery innovations to give way to advocacy of presumably self-evident truth.

CHAPTER THREE

THE EMERGENCE OF NEW PRIORITIES FOR INTERNATIONAL POPULATION ASSISTANCE: THE YEARS OF GROWING POLICY AND PROGRAM DISCORD

A major event of the 1970s was the UN Conference on Population and Development that took place in Bucharest, Rumania, in 1974. Delegates from developing countries came prepared to do battle with the cost-benefit arguments then being put forward as a justification for family planning. Since Western economists had made the underlying calculations, the delegates sensed a threat to substitute family planning for broader development support. They expressed their concern with the sloganized argument, which gained considerable currency, that "development is the best contraceptive"—a highly distracting argument that led some family planning programs, such as Egypt's Population Development Program (PDP), to undertake ambitious efforts to spur industrial and agricultural growth in an essentially vain bid to reduce fertility (Robinson and El-Zanaty 2005).

Possibly adding to the unease of the delegates from developing countries was USAID's vigorous pursuit of family planning with little apparent thought to development, except as a consequence of success in lowering fertility. In any case, for some who attended the conference, a signal event was a speech by John D. Rockefeller III, chairman of the Population Council's board of directors and an acknowledged champion of international family planning. In addressing a nonofficial forum, which met in a series of parallel gatherings, Rockefeller confessed that he had been misled, by those whose opinions and judgments he had trusted, into believing that family planning activities of the type he had been supporting were correctly conceived. In particular, Rockefeller charged that the Population Council "had become ineffective by focusing exclusively on promoting family planning and contraceptive technology—the supply side of the population effort—and failed to address poverty, health, education, and women's roles, which determine underlying demand for family planning" (Harkavy 1995: 186).[1] It was a dramatic mea culpa and reflected the growing influence of Western feminists and their message that the "patriarchy" simply "didn't get it." In retrospect, Rockefeller's Bucharest address was probably the opening shot in a campaign that 20 years later, as we shall see, decisively turned the population field upside down.[2]

In the meanwhile, family planning in India, a relatively unsuccessful program, received a staggering blow that set it back by several years. Enmeshed in an embarrassing political contretemps, Indira Gandhi sought a way out by proclaiming a State of Emergency, which threw her adversaries off balance and opened the way for a number of high-handed policies, among them a strong-arm family planning effort. Involuntary sterilization, especially for men, became a scourge. The donor community was thunderstruck at this turn of events. The Ford Foundation in India kept its distance from the government's coercive tactics. The former president of the Population Council in New York, Frank Notestein, deplored these measures and predicted, accurately as it turned out, that they would "more likely bring down the government than the birthrate" (Charles Westoff, personal communication). USAID's position was less condemnatory. Caught between its enthusiasm for seeing a rise in contraception in a country that had proven resistant and an uneasy sense that perhaps things were going too far, it nevertheless remained engaged.

The Bucharest conference, which occurred shortly before the breakdown of civility in the Indian Emergency, was a harbinger of the debate that reached its climax 20 years later at the International Conference on Population and Development (ICPD) in Cairo. Instead of a narrow focus on population control as a basic condition for economic development, some delegations (and especially the representatives of the nongovernmental sector) insisted that the principal goal should be the satisfaction of "basic needs." In this process, population control was a mere handmaiden. There was much denunciation of the trickle down mechanism whereby the blessings of development were expected to be distributed. The West was denounced for its lavish and unsustainable consumption habits, which if curbed would do more to benefit the underdeveloped world than all the pills and condoms in Dr. Ravenholdt's warehouses. In the air also were nascent notions that recognized the rhetorical return on arguments cast in terms of presumed human rights—a natural follow-on to the enunciation of basic needs. By the time development theorists tired of the idea of basic needs and turned to formulations such as "community development," the advocates of basic human rights were strong enough to continue on their own tack.

After the Bucharest conference some social scientists decided that the drubbing family planning had received needed a response. Bernard Berelson (1974), with assistance from Ronald Freedman of the University of Michigan, prepared a report stressing the achievements of international family planning and its effects independent of social and economic development. Demographic staff at the Population Council subsequently systematized this line of analysis. Bernard Berelson was the prime mover in developing a measure of family planning "program effort," something that would be necessary for the analysis of the achievements realized by family planning.[3] The work needed to conceptualize and fit data to the idea was taken in hand by Parker Mauldin and Robert Lapham. Subsequently John Ross of the Population Council joined with Mauldin in carrying the work forward.

According to Berelson's conception, measures of program effort should be examined in a range of social contexts. Thus the effect of family planning programs (varying from "strong" to "weak") on an indicator such as contraceptive prevalence could be examined in varying social settings (Ross and Mauldin 1997). It was an imperfect scheme and involved a fair measure of subjective judgment. Critics were quick to point out that program effort is so inextricably embedded in endogenous "social context" that independent cross-national measurement is highly questionable (Schultz 1992: 86). Nevertheless, the analysis convinced many that evidence for the independent action of family planning programs was strong, persuasive, and not readily dismissible. Surveys show a regular increase over time in the strength of program effort. In 1974 nearly one-fourth of 77 countries surveyed had family planning programs that scored either as "strong" or "moderately" so. In a 1994 survey of the same 77 countries, this figure was nearly 60 percent.

An often overlooked but important initiative during this period was the work of the Global Committee of Parliamentarians on Population and Development to mobilize political support for family planning and women's health programs. The first parliamentary committee on population and development was founded in Japan in 1974 by Japan's former Prime Minister Kishi and General William Draper (the first chairman of the Population Crisis Committee, later to become Population Action International). The Global Committee, which was inspired by the successful Japanese parliamentarian model, was founded in 1982 by Senator Joseph Tydings and Akio Matsumura and received funding from Japan as well as from UNFPA, IPPF/London, and various individuals and US private foundations. It later became the main platform from which Congressman James Scheuer, Robert Gillespie, and other advocates engaged world leaders and influential parliamentarians on the importance of population dynamics for national development. This advocacy work proved instrumental in building political legitimacy for family planning around the world and helped prepare the ground for the design and implementation of effective national programs. The Global Committee paid particular attention to the importance of utilizing demographic data in preparing national development plans, identified at the 1974 Bucharest Conference as a priority activity for national governments (see Stamper 1977 for an overview of this work at the time.)

The 1970s also witnessed an important addition to the community of organizations interested in rendering international population assistance. The World Bank, after years of making loans for physical infrastructure, came to the view that high fertility was a drag on development and, as such, merited its attention. This realization came more than a decade after the Bank supported the Coale–Hoover analysis that made the case for the development benefits to be obtained from fertility reduction. The Bank is now the world's largest lender for population activities and a major voice in defining population policy and the conditions required, in its view, for successful program implementation.

In the 1970s, other events with long-term implications for population policy were astir. Chief among these on the U.S. domestic front was the 1973 Roe versus Wade decision of the U.S. Supreme Court affirming a woman's right to abortion. At the time it seemed largely of domestic import and was widely hailed by advocates of women's rights. But as it has festered over the years among abortion opponents and as its utility for political mobilization has become better appreciated, it became, arguably, the most significant population event of the 1970s. It polarized the dispute over abortion between Choice and Life and gave the latter forces a battering ram for their fight against abortion and contraception. Eventually it came to affect not only American women but the unanimity of domestic support for U.S. international population policy as well. Short of war, this is perhaps the most contentious issue in American politics today. Recent advances in abortion technology, which in theory could make pregnancy termination a private matter between a woman and her doctor, appear not to have caught on and thus the practice remains as visible and inflammable as ever.

The 1980s: Programmatic Consolidation and Integration

It can be argued that the 1980s were the best, least troubled years for international family planning. In retrospect it is clear that beneath the surface, developments were stirring that would break through later and redefine the field. But it was largely during the 1980s that countries such as Bangladesh, Egypt, Indonesia, and Thailand became family planning "success stories." The field was moving away from the vertical, stand-alone, target-driven family planning programs of the 1970s. In addition, the integration of maternal and child health (MCH) programs with family planning services was now given greater priority.

In the years when achieving takeoff in contraceptive prevalence was an overriding goal, incentive payments for clients and providers were widely used as a way to jump-start the process. These now came increasingly into bad odor, acceptable perhaps as compensation for time lost in seeking services, but unconscionable when they appeared to exploit women in straightened economic circumstances or when they operated as part of a bounty system for service providers. There were many deficiencies to be remedied, but the field was generally responding positively to the criticisms leveled at it.[4]

The 1980s also saw the dramatic growth of the global women's reproductive health and rights movement as a force in shaping international population policy. These years were marked by several formative conferences that focused attention on women's health and reproductive rights. The first was the 1984 International Conference on Abortion, Sterilization, and Contraception in Amsterdam, which voiced opposition to coercive family planning programs and legal restrictions on access to safe abortion. The 1985 Third World Women's Conference held in Nairobi, Kenya, marked the conclusion of the UN Decade of Women and was notable for questioning demographic rationales for population control and affirming the concept of reproductive rights. The Nairobi conference "was significant because it demonstrated that the global women's health and rights movement could no longer be described as white, Western, and middle class . . ." (Eager 2004: 108). Finally, the 1991 UN World Conference on Human Rights in Vienna was also a pivotal event for the global women's movement in that it affirmed that women's reproductive rights should be considered as indivisible from basic human rights. These three seminal conferences laid the groundwork for more ambitious gatherings that were to follow in 1994 and 1995.

The 1980s were also notable for the emergence of influential women's health and rights advocacy groups, among the more prominent being the Women's Caucus, Development Alternatives with Women for a New Era (DAWN), the Women's Global Network for Reproductive Rights (WGNRR), the Women's Environment and Development Organization (WEDO), and the International Women's Health Coalition (IWHC), which began life as an abortion rights advocacy group funded by Population Action International. The rise of the global women's health and rights movement is recounted by Margaret Hempel (1996) as follows:

> In the early 1980s, searching for alternatives to the narrowly focused government and private family planning programs, women's health

advocates in developing and developed countries started some of the earliest models of comprehensive care, providing women with access to a greater range of choice in contraceptive and other services, including abortion and menstrual regulation. In contrast to the often target driven, sometimes coercive national family planning programs, these services emphasized counseling and attention to interpersonal dynamics, including empowering women to make informed decisions about their health." (p. 74)

As we shall see, many women's health advocates in the 1980s came to the conclusion that "population policies were inherently coercive and could not be reconciled with women's rights" (p. 74). This message was networked around the world with such frequency by women's health advocates that it eventually became decoupled from evidence and ascended to the heights of holy writ.

At the same time that feminists and women's health advocates were becoming more energized, conservative antiabortion activists were also gaining strength. The installation of the socially conservative Reagan administration in Washington in 1981 marked the beginning of a more aggressive morality-driven pro-life campaign. The new policy that was formulated to advance this campaign was announced to the world at the 1984 UN Conference on Population and Development in Mexico City. Known as the US government's Mexico City Policy (and disparagingly referred to by one of its principal features as the "Global Gag Rule"), it featured provisions that at first seemed quirky and such a violation of the physician–patient relationship that many thought they could not stand. In fact, however, the Mexico City Policy has remained the touchstone of America's international population policy between 1984 and 1991 and was resurrected by the second Bush administration in 2000.

The architects of the Mexico City Policy in Washington received intellectual cover from the revisionist "Panglossian"[5] theorizing then sweeping through certain academic quarters. One of the most prominent of the revisionists, the economist Julian Simon, was influential in shaping the position the U.S. delegation took to Mexico City. Their particular brand of argument inspired a debate about population policy that never deserved the attention it got. In essence it sought to demolish extreme forms of Malthusian demographic determinism (exemplified by the still reverberating talk of population bombs). Turning these arguments on their head, the revisionists held that, at least in the short run, larger populations were an advantage since they provided a greater pool of talent that could spur technical innovation and accelerate development.[6] Not content with routing the remnants of Malthusianism with a parade of exceptions to the negative effect of population growth on development, they augmented their argument by using economic models, many of which were suspect on their face. Mainstream social scientists, whose perception of social dynamics recognized the interplay of population, the environment, and social organization, were intellectually immune to such one-sided arguments. They would not be caught out talking about population growth as if it were the only factor affecting the success or failure of development. Unfortunately, for the most part they stood aside from the fray and cultivated their own academic gardens.

On balance, the revisionists' attack on simplistic Malthusianism served the useful purpose of correcting the errant tendencies of the public debate about population policy. At the same time they were a major intellectual distraction and gave aid and comfort to aberrant population policy such as emerged in Mexico City, the effects of which are still evident. In a practical sense, the whole debate was a tempest in an academic teapot, which had little bearing on the family planning movement as it operated in the field or on its ability to attract donor support.[7]

The chief effect of the Mexico City policy has been to deny U.S. government funds to private agencies that provide abortion services or discuss abortion as an option for a pregnant woman. Nongovernmental organizations (NGOs), both American and foreign, receiving U.S. resources have been most directly affected by this policy, it being diplomatically difficult to apply the Mexico City policy to foreign governments. The policy has had a major impact on multilateral organizations such as the United Nations Population Fund (UNFPA). Accusations that UNFPA has been directly supporting coercive abortion services in China are unsubstantiated by firsthand observers (including those chosen by the second Bush administration) but have still resulted in the cessation of U.S. support to UNFPA on three separate occasions—1986–92, 1999, and again since 2002.

Other prominent issues of the 1980s were program quality and concerns about overreliance on attaining contraceptive prevalence targets. As for the question of quality, it has received so much attention that one suspects there may be less to it than meets the eye. That there have been excesses in the recruiting and handling of family planning clients there can be no doubt. However, promoting quality of care as a new family planning "ethos" (Bruce and Jain 1995) or proclaiming "client centeredness" as *the* way forward tends to unfairly characterize much pre-Cairo program effort and possibly misrepresents future needs. And as some observers have pointed out, there is still an inadequate empirical basis upon which to assess the effects of many service quality interventions (RamaRao and Mohanam 2003).

A well-recognized student of quality assessment, Avedis Donabedian (1980, 1988), would not disagree with those who deplore the abuses that at times have marred achievements in international family planning. But he would promote a deeper analysis of the conditions under which these occur. What is needed, he might argue, is a broad conception of health-system performance (both the adequacy of human resources and infrastructure) in relation to social conditions influencing the accessibility and utilization of services (including client acquisition, referral, and follow-up). Economic circumstances influencing the affordability of client services and the cost of competing delivery mechanisms are also essential considerations in assessing overall heath-system performance. His broad functional conceptions of health-system quality have not been widely taken up.

That said, no reasonable person could argue that quality doesn't matter. A case in point is the Egyptian experience. There, as in Bangladesh, acceptance of contraception and a small family-size norm took root despite decades of sluggish economic growth. From a level of less than 20 percent of married women of reproductive age around 1980, the contraceptive prevalence rate rose to 65 percent by the end of the century. The Egyptian program was characterized by the development of a strong service–delivery system. First it developed clinical standards of practice; then it trained providers to that standard, strengthening systems of supervision and management, supplying essential commodities through an efficient logistics system, and effectively monitoring and evaluating program operations. Providing a widened range of methods appropriate for clients with different needs was also a key factor in the success of the Egyptian family planning program. In contrast, interventions geared to improving the autonomy and empowerment of women, nowadays often advanced as the sine qua non of program quality, appear to have played, at best, a modest role (Robinson and El-Zanaty 2005).

Privatization is another issue of the 1980s that has attained virtual ideological canonization as a development strategy. It is a popular prescription in economic planning, especially for lagging economies slowed by the slough of lingering collectivist theory and central-command organization. It has great appeal to donors frustrated by seeing development plans blocked by corrupt, inefficient, or indifferent officialdom. Such situations make the private sector seductively, and sometimes deceptively, attractive. This is the primary appeal of the social marketing of contraceptives and over-the-counter health items. It is the driving conviction of those who put their hopes in NGOs as advocates and as deliverers of services. Nonetheless, social marketing, though a standard off-the-shelf recommendation for family planning and reproductive health programs, has often encountered problems of sustainability, ownership, management, and effectiveness.

The social marketing of contraceptives and MCH commodities such as vitamin A and iron tablets has been quite successful in such countries as Bangladesh and Thailand, but less impressive results have been obtained in India and Indonesia. With the exception of Thailand, most social marketing programs in developing countries still rely in part on donor resources to subsidize their operational and commodity costs. This level of subsidization varies considerably, with some social marketing efforts increasingly able to cover their local costs of operation (e.g., the Bangladesh Social Marketing Company), whereas others are still largely dependent on donors (e.g., recent social marketing efforts in the Indian state of Uttar Pradesh). The dependence on subsidization is something few examine. So long as the subsidy, from whatever source, is cost-effective compared to alternative service delivery systems, there should be no objection.

After this recitation of policy reversals, setbacks, complaints about program quality, what remains of our contention that family planning fared well during the 1980s? Accepting that we are talking about family planning and not everything that in subsequent years came to define population policy, we note that in the 1980s a number of national programs came to maturity; that by the end of the decade the number of countries with strong to moderately strong family planning programs as measured by Ross and Mauldin (1997) increased by 87 percent; and that the decline in total fertility rates was strongly related to the increased level of program effort. In its World Development Report of 1984 the World Bank laid out the argument for the value of family planning in the developing world and a prescribed route to follow in securing that goal. Efforts to build consensus supportive of family planning among political elites from developing countries and, within the United States, among groups and organizations influential in the formation of public opinion were launched with some success by advocacy groups, most notably the Population Crisis Committee (now Population Action International), a legatee of General Draper's vision of population policy. It was, in short, a decade of achievement and a widespread, forward-looking sense that family planning was on an upward trajectory with little need to change the signals.

The 1990s: The Feminization of Population Program Goals and Priorities at Cairo

The 1994 ICPD, held in Cairo, marked a major turning point for international population assistance. The consensus reached at the 1974 Bucharest conference between advocates for population assistance and more broadly based development programs (exemplified by the slogan "no matter what your cause, it's a lost cause without family planning") gave way at Cairo to a more woman-centered social welfare agenda. Without much empirical evidence to support this new prescription, participants at Cairo embraced the view endorsed by feminist activists that a gender-based reproductive rights and empowerment strategy was a necessary precondition for demographic change and sustainable development, and that it should become the central concern of international population policy.

This new policy de-emphasized relationships between aggregate demographic trends and development prospects as a rationale for population assistance. Finkle and McIntosh (1996), long-standing analysts of international population and development conferences, see Cairo as a "turning point in the globalization of the women's movement [but] not . . . a step forward for the population movement, which for many years has given primacy to efforts to limit population growth" (p. 110).

What we have called the "feminization" of the Cairo agenda reflects a major reorientation from previous international meetings on population and development—a change that is often referred to as a "paradigm shift." An analysis of its provenance would suggest that advocates from the feminist movement had a critical part in shaping it. This is not as straightforward as it might seem for many cooks were involved in the preparation of this particular stew.

Preparations for the Cairo conference began with modest ambitions. In some quarters it was even suggested that after the Bucharest and Mexico City conferences, the central issues, some of them fairly contentious, had been laid on the table and that perhaps all that prudence required was a "meeting," not a full-fledged international conference with all the trappings. But that idea was soon overwhelmed by the momentum that developed favoring a full dress conference.

The donors seemed to lack enthusiasm for this course of events. There were no obvious ideas in general circulation relating to population and development that seemed to demand greater attention than they had received at previous conferences. These were expensive affairs and the challenge now was to take action on past recommendations. Besides, who wanted to renew the endless arguments over abortion and other items offensive to some factions. However, this outbreak of donor fatigue was short-lived.

As Joyti Shankar Singh (1998) details in his authoritative chronicle of the "Cairo process," the idea of holding another global conference came into bloom in early 1991 (p. 22). There were to be three so-called PrepComs devoted to discussions of the agenda for an international conference to be held in 1994. In addition there were six "expert" group meetings scheduled for New York, Botswana,

Bangalore, Cairo, Paris, and La Paz. Discussion ranged over an extensive subject terrain, although in general little new ground was opened. These provided grist for the first PrepCom that was convened in March 1991.

For PrepCom II five Regional Commissions were established; these met from August 1992 to April 1993 in Bali, Dakar, Geneva, Amman, and Mexico City and were all charged with formulating a new program of action to displace the one agreed to at the 1984 Mexico City conference. This new Program of Action was to last for 20 years (p. 25). To bring every important player into the process, five round tables of experts and program managers were to be held before the end of 1993 in Ottawa, Berlin, Bangkok, Geneva, and Vienna. At the Ottawa and Berlin meetings family planning, reproductive health, reproductive rights, and HIV/AIDS were taken up (p. 25). In the course of 1993 an additional ten conferences were held in various locations around the world.

PrepCom II became stalled on the issue of abortion and ran out of time. Its files and records were available for PrepCom III, the final step in the Cairo process, which met in New York in April 1994. By then most of the elements that made ICPD distinctive were in place. There were a good many loose ends to be tied up, especially those such as abortion that finally were delivered to Cairo unresolved. But family planning and an expanded definition of reproductive health remained as important agenda items. However, they had to share the stage with the needs and rights of women relative to freedom of choice, empowerment, and equality of treatment.

NGOs were amply represented and became the main force in advancing the feminist agenda. Singh credits the document entitled *Woman's Declaration on Population Policy*, prepared by a group of women's health advocates and circulated for comment to more than 100 feminist groups, with "providing strong affirmation of sexual and reproductive rights for both men and women and calling for their recognition" (p. 40). This initiative not only paved the way for the adoption of broadened sexual and reproductive health agendas, but also elevated women's equality, empowerment, and gender-based violence to prominent positions. All the pieces were there, needing only universal affirmation at Cairo.

A defining moment in the PrepCom process occurred during PrepCom III when NGOs staffed largely by women's health and empowerment advocates were allowed onto the meeting floor and given the green light to participate in the drafting of the final PrepCom III documentation (much of which served as the basis for the final ICPD Programme of Action). The decision to open the PrepCom III meeting to the active participation of women-centered NGOs was made by Dr. Nafis Sadik, the head of the UNFPA at the time. Adrienne Germain, who participated in the PrepCom meetings and who was an active member of the U.S. delegation to the Cairo conference, describes this critical juncture as follows:

> There was a key moment at PrepCom III when Dr. Sadik, who was at the podium and facing enormous opposition from the Holy See, called a recess and allowed NGO lobby groups down on the floor of the plenary to sort things out. It was the women's organizations that hammered on the Vatican and got them to back off. And the way we did it was to assert the high moral ground in the sense that it is our lives and bodies at stake. And Dr. Sadik, along with the family planning organizations and environmental groups in the room, realized that they needed to let women take the lead in the completion of the PrepCom and in the Cairo agenda itself or they were going to loose to the Vatican. (Cited in Eager 2004: 144)

Not only was this dramatic turning point crucial in redirecting the terms of debate within the PrepCom process, but it was also a seminal moment in Dr. Sadik's long career at UNFPA.

Worries about high fertility and rapid population growth were largely dismissed at PrepCom III and later at the Cairo conference as the concerns of demographers, environmentalists, and those affiliated with the "population control movement"—including most governments in the developing world (see, e.g., Dixon-Mueller 1993; Dixon-Mueller and Germain 2000). Such entities were castigated for being preoccupied with high fertility and the effect of population dynamics on development outcomes rather than women's health, equity, empowerment, and human rights. Jain (1998) notes that the demographic objectives considered paramount in past decades were demoted at Cairo.

Contained within the comprehensive document known as the Programme of Action, the main message for improving individual well being comprises two elements: to provide contraceptive methods within broader reproductive health services, and to advance women's equality in education, health, and economic opportunities. The ICPD document does not explicitly link these goals with the reduction of population growth rates. These public policies are justified in their own right, irrespective of their effectiveness in reducing fertility. (p. 193)

The ICPD also represented a significant break with the past in that demographers, family planning activists, development practitioners, and government aid officials, who had largely dominated debates at previous UN population conferences, were largely supplanted by women's health advocates with strong ties to the NGO community. Many government delegations arriving at Cairo were asked to ratify a nearly finalized action plan, which they had little opportunity to consider or help draft. As Caldwell (1996: 72) notes, the United Nations again proved at Cairo that it is a major force for "Westernization" in the developing world.

This major shift in emphasis was marked by the debut in force of "advocacy experts" and feminist anthropologists as well as the marginalization of demography and public health as disciplines considered relevant to discussions of international population policy. This disciplinary tug-of-war was partly rooted in the drive by Western feminists to downgrade, if not disallow, concerns about the impact of population dynamics on development and environmental outcomes. They regarded such preoccupations, which had dominated debates at Belgrade, Bucharest, and, to a lesser extent, Mexico City, as largely irrelevant compared to agendas directly geared to overturning patriarchal power relations, empowering women, and securing reproductive rights.

Family planning programs in the pre-Cairo period came under fire as being excessively driven by demographic targets, overly coercive, and incapable of offering high-quality care. Feminist critics insisted on characterizing pre-Cairo family planning programs as little more than schemes to drive down fertility rates through the distribution of pills and condoms, with little attention given to the provision of a broader range of clinic-based reproductive health services. They argued that the management of contraceptive side effects, the diagnosis and treatment of sexually transmitted diseases, maternal health care, special programs for adolescents, and safe abortion services were either underdeveloped or totally missing components of most family planning programs. Most damming, they contended that efforts to promote the use of contraception and lower fertility rates often employed coercive measures, including the improper use of demographic targets, quotas, and financial incentives.

ICPD-inspired critiques of pre-Cairo family planning effort have been echoed in many quarters. However, they have not always been characterized by unassailable accuracy. A recent example was provided by Sinding and Bouzidi (2002), who stated that the ICPD Programme of Action "consolidated the shift in population policies and programmes from reliance on demographic targets and compulsory family planning services into a rights-based approach, based on reproductive health choices" (p. 323). This statement implies that family planning programs in the pre-Cairo period were typified by the lack of voluntarism and choice, a claim that does not square well with the historical record. The experience of the host country for the Cairo conference, for example, contradicts this view. Commenting on the Egyptian family planning program, Robinson and El Zanaty (2005: 156) observe that "coercion or client-incentive payments have never played a role in the program and it thus has never run the risk of a negative backlash. People have been indifferent to or bemused by the program, but rarely have any significant groups been actively hostile" (p. 17).

Feminist critics tend to rely upon sweeping generalizations and questionable characterizations in describing the failings of pre-Cairo family planning programs. One of the earlier and better documented examples of this genre essentially argues that all family planning programs supported by Western governments in developing countries were motivated by the goal of population control and "typically limit choice of contraceptive method, fail to give adequate information and counseling, neglect screening, follow-up, and the overall health of the woman, ignore the sexual politics of reproduction, and are insensitive to local culture" (Hartman 1987: 56).

While family planning programs have sometimes been guilty of such failings, it is not fair to claim that such deficiencies typified all program effort or that they resulted from intentional programmatic neglect and disregard for women's welfare owing to the misguided priorities of population control zealots. In Hartman's conspiratorially flavored account, family planning professionals are largely in the pay of population controllers, who promulgate "a philosophy without a heart in which human beings become objects to be manipulated" (p. 296). She maintains that population control "is a philosophy of domination, for its architects must necessarily view people of different sex, race, and class as inferior, less human than themselves . . . " (p. 296).

Even reproductive rights have not escaped critical examination by some feminist critiques. For example, Farida Akhter claims that the concept of reproductive rights is just another "slogan" for population control that remains rooted in eugenic, racist, sexist, and other exploitive social tyrannies (cited in Hodgson and Watkins 1997: 505). Hartman concurs with this view, noting that the emphasis given to reproductive rights at Cairo was a "sham," with population control simply being recast in feminist garb and disingenuous talk of new paradigms (cited in Eager 2004: 153).

Other debatable views can readily be cited. For example, Eager's comment that "the manner in which family planning programs were designed, implemented, and evaluated exemplified little or no concern for the individual needs of the developing world's women" is simply at odds with the rationale and practice of most pre-Cairo family planning programs. The first director of the World Bank's Department of Gender, Karen Mason (1996), makes the questionable assertion that "the feminist critique of population programs— that they treat women as uteruses and ignore the totality of their health and human needs—is often correct" (p. 346). Hartman's (1987) critique of the Bangladesh family planning program in the 1980s concludes that the provision of contraceptive services undermined the welfare of women, which would be an incomprehensible proposition for most Bangladeshi women newly able to control the number and timing of their pregnancies. Comments to the effect that pre-Cairo family planning efforts in South Africa were simply part of a white supremacist strategy designed to reduce the size of the black population (Kaufman 1997) constitutes another questionable historical rendering.

The Emergence of Dissenting Views on the New Cairo Paradigm

Few observers have challenged these characterizations of pre-Cairo family planning programs in public forums. One exception is John Caldwell (1996) of the Australian National University. He has voiced skepticism over the charge that pre-Cairo family planning efforts, especially "foreign advisers and their institutions in the First World," were "overly fixated on demographic numbers and so patriarchal in outlook that they decided that women should be the sole vehicle for curtailing population growth, and gave little thought to their comfort, desires or safety" (p. 71). He noted that he knew "few people of this type" during his 40 years of involvement in international family planning programs. The virtually universal view of the individuals and institutions he knew, Caldwell asserts, was that "providing the option to control family numbers and to space births further apart raised the position of women and their future chances in life as well as limiting the reproductive ill-health that threatened them" (p. 71).

Another veteran of international population assistance during the pre-Cairo period, Oscar Harkavy (1995) of the Ford Foundation, shares Caldwell's view of the past. He notes that "most of the workers in the mainstream of the population movement in the sixties, seventies, and eighties were as actively concerned for the welfare of the women served by family planning programs as are their later-day critics" (p. 191). Hodgson and Watkins (1997) maintain that population policy in the decades prior to Cairo was typified by an enduring alliance between "neo-Malthusians" driven by concerns about the deleterious effects of rapid population growth and the international planned parenthood movement that worked to enhance the availability and use of modern contraception and other reproductive health measures in developing countries. They conclude that this alliance promoted the establishment of family planning services "characterized by a voluntaristic and mildly feminist stance," which do not always conform to the unflattering characterizations heard at Cairo (p. 486).

Caldwell worries that Cairo's "attack on concern with numbers and the extraordinary lack of concern about the long-term implications of rapid global population growth" produced a Programme of Action that gave "less emphasis to social, community, and national issues than was warranted" (Caldwell 1996: 72).[8] This outcome may have "eroded the will of donor governments to strain themselves to support family planning programs or the will of Third World governments to give them high priority" (p. 72). He cautions that "First World electorates and their representatives are increasingly unlikely to believe these objectives [the ICPD agenda] to be so important that their incomes should be taxed to achieve them" (p. 72).

The inclusion of recommendations for providing safe abortion services in countries where it is legal and postabortion care where it is not was the single greatest source of contention among the delegations at Cairo. Representatives of the Holy See, conservative Islamic states, and several Latin American countries were most determined to resist calls for the provision of safe abortion. But in retrospect, this was a sideshow to the main event, which was a well-organized, ideologically powered movement to promote a new paradigm.

The ICPD Programme of Action went far beyond embracing a broader constellation of clinic-based reproductive health interventions and services. Schooling for girls (a subject given considerable emphasis in previous decades) and microenterprise schemes for women were also accorded much attention. Domestic violence, female genital cutting, trafficking, and sexuality (including sexual orientation) also received top billing. It was also argued that interventions designed to influence who women marry should become actionable policy in the post-Cairo world (Germain 2000). Formal programs to discourage the practice of prearranged marriage would obviously move the ICPD agenda well beyond family planning and reproductive health into a full-fledged transformation of traditional social customs and culture.

The ICPD Programme of Action argued that these additional sexual, reproductive health, and human rights components needed to be incorporated in future population programs. Family planning was not a priority ingredient in this much-enriched brew, becoming just one component in a broader agenda promoting the status of women. The importance of family planning was acknowledged, but treated parenthetically in relation to the promotion of women's welfare in the realm of sexuality, reproductive rights, and empowerment.

The effort at Cairo to broaden the range of services offered under a reproductive health umbrella has obvious merit, although given existing absorptive capacities in the field and funding constraints, it probably constitutes programmatic overreach. Duff Gillespie (2004), a family planning proponent who has spent much of his career in the front trenches of USAID, offers the following cautionary observation:

> Promoting and implementing it [the ICPD Programme of Action] in its entirety exceeds our existing scientific and programmatic capacity, and potential financial and human resources. Advancing Cairo as an all-or-nothing package may be philosophically comforting, but it will not help the developing world. The Programme is visionary, but not actionable. (p. 36)

What the ICPD Programme of Action achieves in breadth of recommended action, it loses in programmatic coherence, unless, of course, one accepts gender as a logical and theoretically closed organizing principle for programmatic action. In addition, the inability to link the Cairo agenda to specific program goals and performance indicators may have frustrated the ability of implementing agencies to be more responsive to the Programme of Action.

Margaret Catley-Carlson (1998), a former president of the Population Council, notes that the transition from pre-Cairo family planning programs to post-Cairo reproductive health agendas may not be as revolutionary as some have maintained.

> The reproductive health approach, however, is not as new as some would claim—particularly those who insist that all early family planning programs were totally and blindingly demographically driven. Some elements of reproductive health were included in earlier formulation of population policies. The first Kenya population program was focused on reduction of infant mortality and fertility. In fact, as

early as 1952, the Indian Planning Commission thought family planning should be endorsed to improve the health of mothers and children. Program services in Mexico have long been delivered through integrated primary health structures along with infant care and immunization elements. And in Egypt, the link between early marriage and rapid population growth has long been appreciated and was taken account of in setting the country's policy goals. (p. xii)

Similarly, the role of targets in promoting coercive practices was not well documented at Cairo and may have been overstated. It can well be argued that the quality of most pre-Cairo family planning programs suffered more from poorly staffed and equipped facilities, indifferent management and supervision, chronic absenteeism, and inadequate client counseling and follow-up than from an overreliance on performance targets, deplorable as they could be in execution.

It is not clear how the promotion of women's empowerment (e.g., through greater female autonomy, education, and employment) will necessarily bring about desired improvements in MCH. There are some cases in which this may be true and others in which it appears not to be. As Basu (2000), with thinly veiled skepticism, has observed, "it appears that everything that is good for women is good for family health as well" (p. 21). To demand systematic empirical confirmation, not just anecdotal illustration, is to rain on the Cairo parade.

Relationships between women's empowerment and MCH are not well documented, owing in part to unresolved conceptual problems in defining empowerment (see Hobcraft 2000: 161–63). There is also a surprising scarcity of good field research that might clarify the issues involved. Findings that have been reported are not always consistent with preconceptions of the advocacy community, which is no doubt suggestive of the complexities involved.

With regard to relationships between female education and the health status of children, greater schooling in South Asia appears to be associated with more pronounced sex differentials in child mortality, suggesting that education does not necessarily improve the survivorship of girls relative to boys (Basu 1997). For example, Das Gupta (1987) reports that survival prospects for second- and higher-order female births in the Indian Punjab are actually worse in more-educated households. An investigation of the rapid declines in childhood mortality between 1960 and 1990 in the developing world concludes that a change in the proportion of women achieving higher education seems to be a minor factor determining these declines (Cleland, Bicego, and Fegan 1991). Hobcraft (2000) notes that "one unresolved issue is that the effects of maternal education upon child survival seem to be weaker in Sub-Saharan Africa than elsewhere" (p. 165). Knodel and Jones (1996) conclude that inequalities in education by socioeconomic status are even more pronounced than gender-based differentials in schooling, which implies that a preoccupation with the education of girls may do little to address the greater problem of limited access to high-quality education for *both* sons and daughters of the poor or enhance the well being of all children.

Despite such evidence, many observers continue to promote women's education as the single most effective intervention for improving the health and well being of mothers and children. Basu (1997) comments as follows on the primacy given to women's education in reducing child mortality:

> The link between mother's education and child mortality is now being flogged to such an extent that there is hardly any mention of factors such as safe drinking water and hygienic sewage disposal in the academic literature or in public pronouncements on the determinants of child mortality . . . . Such an overstress on maternal characteristics can also have the unwanted consequence of increasing inequalities between the sexes by burdening already burdened women with more responsibilities. (p. 13)

Hobcraft (2000) notes that the effect of maternal age and the tempo (spacing) of childbearing on child survival are equal to the influence of maternal education. He concludes that "it is not uncommon for children born after a very short birth interval to experience a doubling of mortality risks during their first five years of life, net of a range of other factors" (p. 167).

It is also inconvenient for the general ICPD argument that there is evidence from developing countries that greater female employment (especially among poorer women) can result in decreased rather than enhanced child welfare (see, e.g., Basu 1997; Berman et al. 1997; and Sivakami 1996). Other evidence (primarily from developed countries) suggests that greater female autonomy may lead to more instability in partnership formation and marital relationships, which often has a negative impact on the welfare of children from broken homes (Hobcraft 2000: 171). In other words, when examined through an empirical lens, the prescriptions for social transformation through empowerment in the ICPD Programme of Action appear to be more complex and less self-evident than advertised.

A five-country study in Asia (conducted in India, Malaysia, Pakistan, the Philippines, and Thailand) that sampled 56 community sites found inconsistent and generally weak associations between the status of individual women (as measured through such indicators as age at marriage, levels of educational attainment, and employment status) and empowerment measures (including such indicators as control of household assets, power in family decision making, and domestic violence; Mason 2003; Mason and Smith 2003). Mason concludes that "different aspects of women's reported empowerment—for example, their say in important economic decisions within the household versus their freedom to move around outside of the household without their husband's permission—tend to be weakly correlated and correlated differently in different communities" (Mason 2003: 2).

Mason and Smith (2003) also note that in most instances "neither the individual-level nor aggregate proxies of women's empowerment have consistent relationships to the direct measures of empowerment. This suggests that it is risky to employ either individual-level or aggregate proxies for women's empowerment in many settings in the world" (p. 17). However, relationships between women's individual and household characteristics and measures of domestic empowerment do tend to strengthen when relationships are aggregated across communities and countries (a result perhaps due in part to ecological correlation). This outcome allows the authors modest cover in concluding that "multidimensional gender systems" can still be considered salient in accounting for much social behavior in the developing world.

Cleland (1996) notes that while the ICPD Programme of Action was remarkable for the extent to which population and development issues had been recast in a feminist perspective, he finds this reconstruction of the population field to be based on "false assumptions," "biased priorities," and "confusing prescriptions." As such it is likely to have "unfortunate consequences" (p. 107). In his view the principal false assumption behind the plan is the view that improvements in women's status (e.g., educational attainment, reproductive rights, and empowerment) are prerequisites for fertility decline. This position "rests on a very fragile empirical base" and is not convincingly supported by the effectiveness of family planning programs in some developing countries (p. 107).

As Cleland, Phillips, and Amin (1994) have reported, Bangladesh is probably the best example of a country that has achieved major declines in fertility through the widespread adoption of modern contraception without first undergoing substantial socioeconomic development or attaining marked improvements in the status of women. From available census and survey data, the authors are able to find little evidence of widespread socioeconomic change during the years when the Bangladesh fertility decline was most pronounced (roughly 1980–91). They conclude that fertility declines do not appear to be incompatible with gender inequality.

Cleland and Phillips have not been without their critics. Caldwell et al. (1999) argue that Bangladesh was actually undergoing substantial socioeconomic change that enhanced the status of women during the period of its fertility decline. For example, infant mortality declined by 33 percent in the previous 10–15 years and the survivorship of girls under the age of five improved relative to boys. In addition, primary and secondary school enrollment rates for girls rose dramatically over the same period and now exceed male levels. Nonhousehold-based employment for young women, especially in the country's newly emerging urban textile industry, has also created new life choices. A weakness of the Caldwell thesis is that the Bangladesh fertility decline (and the rapid rise in contraceptive use) was well under way before many of the socioeconomic transformations of which he speaks had become widely visible. His tendency to deny the importance of the country's family planning efforts also imparts an incomplete aspect to his line of argument.

Another instance of fertility decline in the absence of marked social change is Egypt's PDP. Before the ICPD Programme of Action came on the policy scene, the Egyptian program invested its hopes in village-level gender-oriented programs featuring measures to increase female education, economic self-reliance, and autonomy with the expectation of increased contraceptive prevalence. Although these programs appear not to have gotten off the ground, fertility still fell significantly and people began calling the Egyptian program a success (Robinson and El-Zanaty 2005). As in the case of Bangladesh, there was scant evidence that rapid socioeconomic change impacting the status of women (or ICPD calls for enhancing reproductive rights and empowering women) had much to do with Egypt's fertility decline.

Curiously, this did not stop some observers from making that attribution. For example, Ibrahim and Ibrahim (1998) reach a conclusion more in keeping with ICPD sensibilities. They maintain that Egypt's family planning success in the period from 1989 to 1994 (following "some 20 years of zigzagging and muddling through") indicates that the promotion of women's education and empowerment strategies, as well as increasing "the freedom available to Egypt's civil society organizations have been key to the country's recent advance and will be most critical to the future success of population policy in Egypt" (p. 51). However, unlike the evidence compiled by Robinson and El-Zanaty, this account makes little allowance for the substantial improvements in Egypt's service-delivery system that accompanied the rapid rise in family planning use over the past two decades.

Despite the empirical record presented by countries such as Bangladesh and Egypt, the ICPD Programme of Action was adamant in insisting that women's autonomy, reproductive rights, and empowerment (priority elements in the new paradigm) should supplant concerns about high fertility and rapid population growth in shaping global population policy. The importance of enhancing the availability of high-quality contraceptive services and reducing unmet family planning need was certainly accorded less attention than in past UN population conferences. But surely these remain for many women and their families, in many parts of the world, goals worth pursuing.

The ICPD Programme of Action was also notable for the relative inattention given to population dynamics and development, the topic of greatest concern in previous UN population conferences in Mexico City and Bucharest. Cleland (1996) notes that in Chapter VI of the ICPD Programme of Action, which deals with population growth and structure, the topics of fertility, mortality, and population growth are "dispatched" in less than one page, with recommended actions pertaining to these issues being accorded only two pages. He writes: "For a conference ostensibly devoted to population and development, there is a perverse sense of priorities" (p. 108). Cleland, argues that the ICPD assertion that improvements in women's status are a prerequisite for fertility and mortality decline "rests on a very fragile base." He posits a different reality:

> Much more consistent with the evidence is the view that the advent of reproductive choice, mass use of contraception and smaller family size represents a giant step on the pathway towards female emancipation and equality. This sense of liberation has always been one of the forces behind the international family planning movement. It is surprising and regrettable that it was not echoed at Cairo. (p. 108)

Moreover, there is little discussion in the ICPD Programme of Action of issues vital to social welfare and development—issues such as employment, job creation, and the role of the state. Instead it is simply assumed that increasing women's labor force participation and career opportunities will produce desirable changes in demographic behavior. As Cleland notes, such faith is undermined by the empirical record. For example, fertility actually fell rapidly in such countries as Japan, South Korea, and Bangladesh during periods when women's employment outside the home and participation in public life were "minimal" (p. 108).

For Cleland, one troubling "unfortunate consequence" stemming from the ICPD Programme of Action is the often-stated conclusion that high-quality family planning services can best be delivered through clinical settings in which a wide range of reproductive health services is also offered. As noted in Chapter VII of the plan, "family planning programs work best when they are part of, or linked to, broader reproductive health programs that address closely related health issues and when women are fully involved in the design, provision, management, and evaluation of services" (United Nations 1995: Chapter 7, Paragraph 7.13:43). It has already been observed that previous efforts to uncover this relationship in the 1960s and 1970s (e.g., the Population Council's Taylor–Berelson Project) largely came up empty-handed, as did earlier research in the Indian Punjab. With regard to the essentiality of clinics and medical control, Cleland believes this to be an unsubstantiated and potentially counterproductive claim:

> The evolution of family planning programs over the past 50 years has often taken the opposite pathway; away from clinics and medical control and towards the community and the marketplace. The contribution of the private sector, of social marketing schemes, and of community-based distribution towards overall contraceptive provision is already appreciable and is growing. These distribution strategies represent greater choice for clients, better access, greater convenience and often, greater confidentiality. None of them, however, is very amenable to the concept of integrated reproductive health services, with their stress on clinical skills and diagnostic procedures. (Cleland 1996: 109)

Despite such reservations, ICPD recommendations have been widely heralded as a significant reordering of international population policy and a major breakthrough for the social welfare of women around the world. The agreements reached at Cairo and reaffirmed a year later at the 1995 Fourth World Conference on Women in Beijing have been summarized by Dunlop, Kyte, and MacDonald (no date). They assert that the importance of attaining gender equality is no longer open to debate and that all forms of coercion, discrimination against women, and gender-based violence must be eradicated. They conclude by stating that the Cairo vision is now "truly global policy" and that "governments and non-governmental organizations must now deliver, and the women of the world, working in partnership with men, will hold them accountable" (Dunlop, Kyte, and MacDonald n.d.: 9).

With allowance for its Western ethnocentric content, many of the provisions of the ICPD Programme of Action are meritorious insofar as they attempt to address forms of discrimination and human rights abuses that undermine the welfare of women. But to suggest that the Cairo vision of population and development is now truly global policy is to make policy by proclamation, and that is often an unprofitable course to follow.

How was it that the development rationale for family planning programs was so thoroughly swept aside at the Cairo conference? Demeny (2003) offers one explanation. He notes that by 1994 only West Africa and West Asia had population growth rates that were similar to those prevailing more widely in developing countries during earlier decades when the population industry was in its infancy. He concludes that "the development rationale of family planning programs was gradually dropped and replaced by the argument that the programs [should] satisfy important health needs and help people exercise a fundamental human right. The Cairo conference formalized this shift . . ." (p. 15). This appears to us to be an intellectualized garnish applied to a situation that was, in reality, a policy lurch with overtones of a coup, rather than a smooth and logical transition. It was the culmination of the determination adumbrated at Bucharest 20 years earlier by feminists and human rights advocates to effect what they were fond of hailing as a paradigm shift. However loose that usage, it captured the sense of a policy revolution and a determination that was not to be denied. It guaranteed feminists and women's health advocates a dominant place at the population policy table.

And, we would agree, a rightful place. But as with any successful social movement there were points to be scored. It was necessary to have a credo, a victimized past, and a claim to social restitution. For that, the boilerplate dictum from the feminist movement's broad challenge to "the patriarchy" could be appealed to. With women far more readily entering the labor force, with the steady, admittedly incomplete, extirpation of sex discrimination a socially sanctioned goal, and given that family planning and reproductive health have been framed and approached largely as "women's issues," the claim to be heard and listened to is undeniably just and overdue.

More puzzling is the acquiescence of institutions (e.g., the Population Council, the Ford Foundation, and UNFPA) that at one time were heavily invested in the promotion of family planning, in converting to the new ideology. Some honest conversions there undoubtedly were. But with institutions there is always the primal matter of survival to consider. The sociological literature is replete with analyses of institutional reorientations once the original rationale appears to be getting threadbare. In this sense, Demeny may have provided the clue. With only mopping up to do generally and faced with uninviting recalcitrance in places such as Pakistan and West Africa, the continued focus on family planning would lack appeal for institutions on the lookout for new challenges. A new mandate, a new mission, would be just the thing. The trouble is, who is to take care of the dull business of putting existing family planning programs on a sustainable basis and undertake the rough slogging in countries where, as yet, there is little to sustain? And are there resources enough to do those things and still chase the array of butterflies released into the garden of sexuality and reproductive rights?

USAID, which only belatedly sought to cope with ICPD recommendations, maintained its family planning orientation, while others saw its future in a "new paradigm." Did this persistence on the part of USAID mean, as some have suggested, that the family planning community was unaware of the policy shift that had been unfolding even ten years before Cairo? That seems unlikely. Or was it that USAID, with its entourage of cooperating agencies locked to it through long-term contracts, was not sufficiently limber to change course quickly? A more likely explanation may be that USAID, by often operating closer to field programs than other donors, was somewhat immune to abrupt changes in policy fashions. As a Pakistani physician involved in his country's family planning effort once put it when lamenting USAID's departure from Pakistan in the early 1990s, USAID, unlike other donor agencies, "knew the nitty-gritties of the program."

In any event, no matter whether ICPD is viewed as a logical transition in a field some regard as essentially played out, an outbreak of regnant feminism, or merely a reflection of the need to survive among drifting institutions matters little. Cairo is a policy fact. The field has evolved from family planning (FP) in the 1960s and 1970s, to family planning and MCH in the 1980s (FP/MCH), to family planning and reproduction health in the early 1990s (FP/RH), to just reproductive health (RH) in the immediate post-Cairo years of the 1990s, to sexuality and reproductive health (SRH) in the late 1990s, and most recently to sexuality, reproductive health, and reproductive rights (SRHR) in the early years of the new millennium.[9]

Family planning is a well-understood health intervention and, according to the protestation of its supporters, does not include abortion as a method. Likewise, MCH has been around awhile and contains no dark mysteries, other than the fact that maternal health has been underemphasized relative to child health in past decades. An expansion of program agendas into areas of sexuality and "rights," given their very diffuseness and elasticity, invites attack from opponents of anything that goes beyond the bounds of the familiar in the population field. It is also disconcerting to empiricists who are attentive to program designs and operational definitions when trying to sort out causal relationships and measure results.

The claims made for the correctness and efficacy of the human rights approach are fairly extravagant. A recent statement released by the Program for Appropriate Technology in Health (PATH) asserts:

> A rights-based approach [to reproductive health care] can provide tools to analyze the root causes of health problems and inequities in service delivery. By emphasizing fundamental values, most notably respect for clients and their reproductive decisions, a rights-based approach can shape humane and effective reproductive health programs and policies .... In three landmark international meetings in the 1990s, the [women's empowerment movement] succeeded in forging a new consensus on reproductive rights and made them central concerns for health programs and policies around the world. (Kols 2003: 1)

For PATH, a nonprofit, international organization interested in promoting the health of women and children, achieving "20 years of providing health information worldwide" is cause for celebration.

And its description of events does capture the tone and content of the sexuality and reproductive rights "movement."

However, to assert that "women's rights are human rights and should not be subordinated to cultural or religious traditions" (p. 1) will no doubt be viewed as confrontational in some settings. It may have made the term "sexuality and reproductive health" a red flag for those who, given their cultural and religious proclivities, oppose what they take to be its central meaning. Moreover, to hard-bitten empiricists, the claim that concentrating on rights provides adequate tools "to analyze the root causes of health problems and the inadequacies in service delivery" constitutes an instance of egregious causal underspecification.

In short, although population growth and its consequences invades virtually all aspects of social policy, those who make development policy and those who clamor for its change have lost sight of that cardinal fact. The agendas that have guided recent international meetings purporting to be concerned with "population and development" give scant attention to that subject as such. Rather they often become entangled in argumentation about various wrongs that should be righted and canonized as universal rights. Little concern is given to their relative priorities, the feasibility of dealing with them, or their roots in social structure. Those with the special knowledge and skills who could probe the subject at a deeper level are often notable by their absence.

CHAPTER FOUR

THE NEW MILLENNIUM: THE ASCENDANCY OF ANTIABORTION POLITICS AND MILLENNIUM DEVELOPMENT GOALS

Large international conferences sponsored by the United Nations over past decades have provided the marching orders for international population policy and so we necessarily give them considerable attention. Strong currents have been running through these policy discussions. One rises from the very legitimate demands of women for recognition of their grievances over the second-class treatment they often receive in societies in which their importance as members of society is slighted. Another flows from the supposed high ground claimed by conservative forces opposed primarily and most openly to abortion and modern methods of fertility regulation—as well as a general resistance to social changes they are not happy to accept.

In recent years, development debates are also coming to be dominated by efforts to deal more effectively with poverty alleviation and questions of program feasibility. Presented in 2000 as an effort to define development goals for the new millennium, poverty reduction was identified as the key to human betterment with respect to a variety of social problems. Known as the Millennium Development Goals (MDGs), they prescribe modes of attack on some eight major problem areas.

On the subject of population growth and reproductive health, the MDGs were essentially silent. Among the specific issues that touch on population-related matters, only maternal mortality and child survival were recognized. A full treatment of these two areas, of course, would be expected to involve birth spacing and limitation, but this falls far short of recognizing the interplay between population growth, reproductive health, and poverty reduction. However, because of their salience in current development policy debates, the utility as well as shortcomings of the MDGs deserve careful consideration.

The Counter-Reformation: The Growing Power of the Christian Radical Right

Before it was really possible to pass judgment on the success of implementing the International Conference on Population and Development (ICPD) agenda, a major bump was encountered on the road from Cairo. The start of the new millennium saw the growing power of the Christian radical right and antiabortion activism. With the ascendancy of extreme conservative politics in the United States, personified in the "election" of President George W. Bush in 2000, the population debate was recast yet again. Driven primarily by a zealous determination to curtail the use of abortion both at home and abroad, there was a-none-too-subtle campaign on the part of the Bush administration to both limit and circumscribe the use of public funding for reproductive health. As we shall see, the effect of this policy shift influenced the position of the U.S. government in its external dealings, in particular in its participation in the multinational effort to enunciate goals for the new millennium.

This hard turn to the right constituted a serious challenge not only to family planning and reproductive health programs, but also to the proclaimed international consensus on population and development reached at Cairo. It appeared to argur a growing softness of support for ICPD and determination to interfere with domestic social policy in developing countries. One organization representing the religious right, the Catholic Family and Human Rights Institute, even launched an assault on the United Nations Children Fund on the grounds that UNICEF has become too enamored of feminist agendas and has strayed from its primary mission of improving the welfare of children (Crossette 2003b).

It would be a mistake to see the evangelical substratum in which these conservative values are embedded entirely in the crass terms of electoral politics or as a moral fog that will necessarily lift after a change in the power alignment in the United States. It is, rather, an emanation of a well-rooted social movement replete with martyred believers and persecuted churches. This evangelical substratum is a well-articulated, interactive movement that includes alliances between persons of varied political and religious stripes. Robert Putnam, a sociologist who has made much of the decline of social connectedness and civic engagement in contemporary society, nevertheless recognizes this significant exception to the trend toward social withdrawal. He writes: "Religious conservatives have created the largest, best-organized grass roots social movement of the last quarter century" (Putnam 2001: 162).

The first decade of the new millennium opened in the United States with a comprehensive and concerted campaign of disparagement, disinformation, and the partial demolition of reproductive health programs. It was fueled by, among other things, moral indignation compounded by confusion as to the underlying facts and relationships and, of course, by the proven potential of the abortion issue to arouse and mobilize conservative political sentiment. The campaign was thoroughgoing, aimed not only at abortion but also, in its extreme reaches, at family planning as a partner in crime.

The basic argument advanced by those who would like to see the end of international population assistance was both sociological and, at its center, moralistic. It saw the integrity of the family as essential to the stability of society.[1] Since contraception (and most egregiously abortion) was thought to encourage sexual adventuring outside the bounds and bonds of sanctified marriage and was therefore threatening to the fabric of social organization, it was held to be wrong. Wrong not only for its disruptive effects on social relations, but also because, in an absolute sense, many believe it involves moral transgression that needs no further social explication. For many this *was* simply a "gut issue" and an effective hook for political manipulation—some of it sincere, some disingenuous, much of it uninformed.

Further strengthening the case against legally permitted abortion was a seemingly willful confusion of the relationship between contraception and abortion. Although the two may move in parallel, especially in the early phases of a family planning program, research shows that contraception is the most effective way to prevent unwanted pregnancies and thus reduce the demand for abortion. It is true that couples faced with contraceptive failure may turn to abortion, but this is not at the heart of the matter. In most settings it is unclear to what extent abortion results from contraceptive failure as opposed to a rise in the demand for abortion services for other reasons. This is a difficult empirical question, yet the argument over the link between contraception and abortion rages on without this essential knowledge.

The *New York Times* (2003) called it "The War against Women." The reference is, first and foremost, to the Bush administration's effort to reverse that most irritating of liberal Supreme Court rulings sticking in the conservative craw, the Roe versus Wade decision affirming a woman's right to abortion. And this could still happen if the composition of the court shifts to include another justice who takes a negative view of a woman's right to decide what to do about an unwanted pregnancy. There is no shortage of such candidates.

But much more than picking judges for their views on abortion was involved. The legal basis for a challenge to Row versus Wade was also pursued by attempts to confer "personhood" on the fetus (and if possible the fertilized egg) so that abortion could be open to the charge of murder. This legal Trojan Horse was first hinted at in an action of the Department of Health and Human Services when it extended health benefits to the fetus while doing nothing to assist the mother with prenatal care. A substantial share of fertilized eggs, perhaps verging on one-third (not counting recognized miscarriages), vanish without a trace before any obvious signs of pregnancy show up. Abortion in the sense of the unaided evacuation of fertilized ova is a natural phenomenon and a fairly common one at that.

The personhood doctrine has succeeded in some state courts in bringing charges of homicide against defendants other than the mother, who through "violent action" bring about the death of a fetus. Paradoxically, this position leaves the legal right to voluntary abortion untouched.

In line with this incremental strategy, which chips away at legal abortion short of a direct challenge to Roe versus Wade, was the attack on a recognized and sometimes necessary medical procedure commonly known as "partial birth abortion" (a nonmedical label bestowed on it by antiabortionists).[2] As part of the attempt to criminalize abortion, it places the attending physician in the double bind of facing litigation for performing the procedure or the possibility of being charged with malpractice if the patient dies for lack of it. Seemingly, this could be a strong inducement to abortion providers to quit the practice. Compared with the petty annoyances of waiting periods, mandatory counseling, gag rules, and the proposed restrictions on adolescents seeking abortion, this change constitutes a serious violation of the canons of good medical practice. Not all doctors, however, take exception to this intrusion on their medical judgment. A spokesman for former Republican Senate Majority Leader, Dr. Bill Frist, noted that the Senator had long supported a ban on so-called partial birth abortions (Toner 2003). A ban on partial birth abortion was passed by Congress in October 2003 and signed into law by President Bush shortly thereafter. [3]

The assault on the gains celebrated just a few years earlier by pro-choice advocates was more far-reaching than the attempts to criminalize abortion, challenge the autonomous judgment of medical practitioners, or violate the supposed sanctity of the doctor–patient relationship. While abortion tops the list of concerns, there were other actions that together with the antiabortion campaign revealed a deep-seated determination to defeat any and all programs that tamper with things as they are. How else, for example, to explain the confused policy on stem cell research.

To call these measures conservative is a disservice to that respected term. The intention was not responsible stewardship. Rather it was an effort to root out anything that might upset a political constituency that opposed government meddling in matters they feel should not concern it. The methods employed in this effort grew out of a vigilant and punitive absolutism of a type not unfamiliar to other periods of history. It was an ideological search and destroy operation on a comprehensive scale and involved the tactics of misinformation, denial of information, and the imposition of arbitrary prohibitions. It reflected a largely unarticulated resistance to change that broods, cicada-like, in large swatches of the American population.

This is not a passing phenomenon that is likely to be extirpated at the polls. It has been around since the days of Margaret Sanger and before. The Reagan administration tapped into it for its Mexico City policy and it served as a policy touchstone for Bush-era policy overlords. The much advertised ABC policy under which U.S. government agencies and those they support had to operate (where A stands for Abstinence, B for being faithful to one's partner, and C for Condoms, which may be used as a last resort if all else fails) was an illustration of how moral imperatives can result in policy prescriptions that, however ineffective and unrealistic, survive on their appeal to a conservative political base. Moral absolutism was evident also in the opposition to the morning-after-pill that many see as an undeserved escape from personal responsibility.

The tactics used may not necessarily be aimed at issues so obviously "objectionable" to some as a morning-after-pill.[4] For example, the Bush administration at a conference on the subject voted against agreeing to the "right" to mental and physical health apparently fearing that this could open a back door to abortion. While fixated on the problem of abortion with its potential for political arousal, the administration nevertheless was not supportive of the one demonstrated way to reduce its prevalence—modern contraception.

The chipping away at the abortion rights guaranteed by Roe versus Wade continued throughout the years of George W. Bush's administration. It became a felony to transport an adolescent across a state line for an abortion without written parental permission. In addition, a previously passed statute that requires all feasible measures be taken to sustain the "life" of an aborted fetus showing any sign of life was more rigorously enforced.

Possibly most distressing was the resort to misinformation (such as the abortive attempt to link abortion with breast cancer), the denial of information, and the general denigration of the condom as useful in the prevention of HIV transmission. Nicholas Kristof, writing in the *New York Times* (2003), cites evidence for what he calls the "Secret War on Condoms." In addition to a stepped up campaign of misinformation about the effectiveness of condoms ("they don't work") and the purported erotogenic effect of providing information about them ("it encourages sex"), the U.S. Centers for Disease

Control removed its informative condom "Fact Sheet" from its web-site and replaced it with a message explaining that condoms may not always work. Apparently in line with this disparagement of the con-dom, Kristof notes that the United States donated only 300 million condoms annually worldwide by 2002 compared to 800 million at the end of the first President Bush's term.

Though Kristof does not make the point, such comparisons can be tricky, depending on the fullness of supply pipelines, the diversion of condoms into black-market channels (not an unknown phenom-enon), and, with respect to the condom's use as a contraceptive, a loss of market share to better methods. But with contraceptive use rising in most countries, with a growing population of potential customers, and a raging HIV/AIDS epidemic, Kristof's straightforward inter-pretation is hard to dismiss.

The U.S. government also put conditions on its support of preventive programs to combat HIV/AIDS. For example, U.S. assis-tance for the Brazilian HIV/AIDS program, one of the most success-ful of such prevention efforts, was made conditional on the Brazilian government's willingness to pledge that it would condemn prostitu-tion (Phillips and Moffett 2005). A key feature of Brazil's program is its success in working cooperatively with sex workers to increase knowledge of the spread of the disease and the value of condom use in its mitigation. For this intrusion into its health policy, Brazil refused proffered funds from USAID.

Not all of these observations are of equal value in demonstrating the case for the Bush administration's drive to turn back the clock on reproductive freedom. Some are merely eyebrow raising, such as the presence of persons with ties to the Vatican in official U.S. del-egations to international meetings on sexual and reproductive health. Others, such as the disappearance of contraceptive informa-tion from government websites were of unknown provenance (and, if one is inclined toward generosity, could be due to something as innocent as cost-cutting or routine replacement of web-page con-tent). Scientists applying for research grants on HIV/AIDS and reproductive health at the National Institutes of Health reported that their applications were less likely to be accepted if they dealt with issues that were sensitive to the Christian right and political conservatives (e.g., topics pertaining to sex workers and homosexuality). In addition, government employees who wanted to undertake consultancies with the World Health Organization occasionally had to be vetted by the Executive Branch of the U.S. government. Taken together, these actions displayed a coherence of purpose and grimness of determination to revise U.S. population policy, especially as it affected individual choice. The human side of this was reflected in the replacement of civil servants experienced in the administration of international population and health programs by political appointees of confirmed political loyalty and correctness on reproductive health issues.

This moralistic sea change could also be seen in the greater involvement of religious and faith-based organizations in international development work. Funding of religious groups for international health programs (e.g., the Seventh Day Adventists and Catholic Relief Services), either through USAID or U.S. embassies, reflected the Bush administration's goal of channeling more American overseas development assistance through "faith-based organizations." It was a radical departure from past practice that had substantial effects on the directions of U.S. foreign assistance. The administration's requirement that abstinence be given priority in addressing the HIV/AIDS crisis in the developing world is a tragic case in point. President Bush was of course correct when he asserted that when it comes to preventing pregnancy abstinence "works every time," but this essentially meaningless truism has little relevance in the real world of sexual interaction.

The United Nations Millennium Declaration

Beyond the Bush administration's assaults on family planning and reproductive health, there was perhaps an even larger threat that the whole subject might enter a policy black hole. In September 2000, the United Nations convened 189 heads of state in a Millennium Summit in Monterrey, Mexico. Out of it came the Millennium Declaration, which set forth eight goals to be achieved by 2015.[5]

Of the eight main goals, two call for the eradication of extreme poverty and the development of a global partnership for development.

The other six goals are concerned with education (universal completion of primary education for all boys and girls), the promotion of gender equality, environmental stability, reducing child maternal mortality, and controlling the spread of HIV/AIDS. There are eighteen specific objectives within this framework, and still more are under discussion. Working out the details of implementation has involved a breathtaking array of committees and task forces. In order to achieve the MDGs, it has been estimated that an additional $70 billion in development assistance would be required by 2006 and $130 billion by 2015 (Sachs 2005: 84).

The original declaration makes no mention of family planning or reproductive health. Steve Sinding (2005), the current president of the International Planned Parenthood Federation (IPPF), found this situation "deeply disappointing" and as evidence that sexual and reproductive health had been "relegated to a lower status in development priorities by developing countries" (pp. 140–141). However, it was still possible that objectives enunciated at Cairo could eventually make an appearance as guests of one of the health goals. For example, the explicit goal of reducing the mortality rate of children under age five might implicitly recognize the effect of birth spacing on the survival of children.

Similarly, the goal of reducing the maternal mortality ratio by 75 percent would, one would think, be obliged to take account of birth spacing and the differential risks to a mother associated with parity and age patterns of fertility. The empirically more demanding maternal mortality rate, which involves not merely the ratio of mothers who die from causes related to childbirth but also the prevalence of pregnancy in a given population, was not initially considered among the goals to be achieved. To do so would have raised concerns about unintended pregnancies, family planning, and other aspects of reproductive health.

Halting and reversing the spread of HIV/AIDS, another health goal, should involve effective condom use and distribution—a problem with which family planning programs have a great deal of experience. But there is reason to believe that overlooking family planning and reproductive health among the explicit goals was not entirely accidental.

Equally conspicuous in its absence is the role of population dynamics (the composition, distribution, and growth of human numbers) in achieving the MDGs. In earlier decades, rapid population growth was seen as a major impediment to development prospects in poorer countries. Despite the fact that the United Nations currently predicts that the world's population will grow from 6.1 billion in 2002 to 9.1 billion by 2050 (with much of this increase concentrated in the developing world), little mention is made of this dynamic in the Millennium Project's "Practical Guide" for achieving the MDGs (United Nations Millennium Project 2005). It is acknowledged in one abbreviated bullet that unplanned births and rapid population growth can contribute to the impoverishment of people living in rural areas (p. 19), but little else is said on the subject.

Scant recognition is given to the fact that the attainment of MDGs relating to such areas as education, health, extreme poverty, hunger, and the environment will be difficult to attain in many of the world's more impoverished countries still experiencing annual population growth rates of 2–3 percent a year (rates that typify many sub-Saharan African countries). A Global Health Council Report (2004) recently highlighted the role of population growth in achieving the second MDG pertaining to the attainment of universal primary education by 2015.

> Meeting this goal (the second MDG) would require thousands of new schools and teachers. In most heavily indebted poor countries, due to rapid population growth and population momentum, the increase in schools and teachers is barely able to keep pace with the increased number of students. Furthermore, in 2002 alone, nearly 1 million African children lost a teacher to HIV/AIDS. This fact strikingly illustrates the intersections between population growth, health and education, and highlights the need to create positive rather than negative synergies between them if the MDGs are to be met. (p. 20)

The eight MDGs, along with their targets and indicators, were "agreed to" by senior officials from the United Nations Secretariat, the IMF, World Bank, and Organization for Economic Co-operation and Development (OECD). Little in the way of consultation with developing nations was undertaken during the MDG design effort. There are certainly other possible goals that might have merited attention in drafting the MDGs had that task begun with a tabula raza and not been limited by the bounds of the UN secretary general's Millennium Declaration. For example, such issues as food production and agrarian reform (especially in dry-land agriculture), housing, transportation, the conservation of nonrenewable energy sources, pollution abatement, support for displaced refugee populations, and security are conspicuous in their absence from the MDG framework. Another conspicuously absent initiative, championed notably by Stephen Lewis, is the elimination of school fees for primary and secondary schooling (Lewis 2005: 71–107).

The basic UN document on which the MDGs were based was the secretary general's Millennium Development Report published in April 2000. While it recognizes that women are often subject to poor treatment, the Report makes no mention of their needs in the area of family planning and reproductive health. As Crossette (2004) states, "the fact remains that there is no direct mention of a woman's rights over her reproductive life, and why that matters in the battle against poverty" (p. 6). Stalwarts from the NGO community and government experts who favored family planning and reproductive health "were barred entirely from the process of drafting the [Millennium] declaration" (p. 4).

The drafters of the MDGs were determined not only to side step needless controversy but to avoid upsetting members of the G77 countries among whom unanimity on matters of family planning and reproductive health was fragile indeed. As Bernstein (2005) notes, "the United Nations, in putting together a development framework for the twenty-first century to provide coherence . . . does not want debate" (p. 129).

Contentious or not, it seems shortsighted not to include issues that are at the center of a woman's existence, her sexual and reproductive life. Failure of the Goals in this respect may reflect the UN Secretariat's lack of resolve when it comes to commitments to women's reproductive rights. Interviews with leading figures involved in drawing up the MDGs strongly indicate a firm desire to avoid the overreach of the ICPD Programme of Action (Crossette 2004). The aim, apparently, was to set goals that appeared to be feasible and clear as to their operational definitions and programmatic requirements. Certainly such a disciplined approach was not characteristic of the ICPD Programme of Action.

Appraising where matters stood in 2003 with respect to progress on the Millennium Goals, Kofi Annan concluded that "the best that can be said is that there is increased global awareness of issues affecting women's rights, although at the country level, there is little progress and in many cases even the rights that have been achieved are under threat" (p. 7). Ambassador Gert Rosenthal of Guatamala, one of two diplomats asked early on by the president of the UN General Assembly to take the lead in drafting the Millennium Declaration, told Crossette:

> Why reproductive health wasn't put up as one of the seven domestic policy goals—I think is obvious. It's a very contentious issue, just as it is domestically in this country [the United States]. A lot of Islamic countries and countries that are close to the Holy See prefer not to talk about the subject, in spite of the Cairo declaration. I think the calculation of the Secretariat was let's not sacrifice the greater coherence and get involved in these highly controversial issues. (p. 10)

The Secretariat apparently saw a backlash against the gains of Cairo, and with an eye on the Bush administration in Washington had no inclination to reopen what some were calling "the mess of Cairo." This is of a piece with the decision to mute Cairo plus ten festivities in 2004 for fear of a rollback of those putative gains if the issues were to be revisited. For the first time in 50 years, the United Nations did not convene its decennial international conference on population and development.

Such contentiousness has not dampened efforts to reaffirm the supposed complementarity between the MDGs, the ICPD Programme of Action, the Beijing Platform of Action, and the 1979 Convention on the Elimination of All Forms of Discrimination against Women (CEDAW). A seminar on the achievement of the MDGs organized by the United Nations Population Division in 2004 was notable for its attempt to reconcile seemingly disparate

UN development agendas competing for attention and resources. It concluded that "there is ample compatibility and coherence between, on the one hand, the goals and objectives of the ICPD Programme of Action and the key actions for its further implementation and, on the other, the MDGs and their associated targets" (United Nations Population Division 2004b: 2). This conclusion appears somewhat disingenuous given that the MDGs make no mention of the role of population growth in affecting development outcomes and did not initially include goals or indicators with respect to reproductive health programs. There is also no mention of reproductive and human rights for women, core components of the Cairo and Beijing conferences.

Beyond the question of how the MDGs came to be are questions as to their content and feasibility. The eight major goals were the product of seven months of effort by a working committee that included representatives of UN specialized agencies [the World Bank, the International Monetary Fund (IMF), United Nations Population Fund (UNFPA), WHO] plus the OECD. Rosenthal has described the result as a grab bag of ideas drawn from various UN sources including the Millennium Declaration itself (Crossette 2004: 7).

In an effort to acknowledge the deficiency of the MDGs with respect to reproductive health, the Millennium Project, chaired by Professor Jeffrey Sachs of Columbia University, has included the expansion of access to "sexual and reproductive health services" as one of 17 "quick wins" for promoting the MDGs. However, given the growing shortfalls of resources for family planning and reproductive health commodities and services in the developing world, it is unclear how "quick win" results can be generated by 2015.

Closer to the road–rubber interface, WHO's Commission on Macro Economics and Health, a 15-member body headed by Jeffrey Sachs and economists from the World Bank, the International Monetary Fund, UNDP, the OECD, and the Economic Commission on Africa, does not include family planning in its estimates of funds needed. Similarly, in estimating the money required annually for child health activities, nothing is provided for birth spacing, and funding for maternal health appears woefully inadequate. There are other exclusions that, as one informed UN official observed, are "too bizarre not to be intentional." In any event, by the year 2015, all 185 UN member states have pledged to meet the eight broad MDGs irrespective of the struggles over specific indicators, program elements, and implementation strategies that surely lie ahead.

As of this writing these are not closed issues. The World Bank, which now includes the contraceptive prevalence rate as one of its health indicators, wants reproductive health to be included as an achievement indicator for the Millennium Declaration. The Department for International Development (DFID), the British development agency, appears to be of similar mind, although its position on such matters is currently in flux. The IPPF in London has promoted the idea of adopting a ninth MDG in 2005, which would explicitly address reproductive health needs. Sinding (2005) notes that "the ICPD goal of universal access to sexual and reproductive health information and services is the vital missing ingredient of the MDGs" and that "a 'universal access' indicator should be adopted and used to hold governments accountable for progress on sexual and reproductive health and rights" (p. 142). However, this initiative has recently been replaced by the more modest goal of incorporating sexual and reproductive health indicators as part of the MDGs pertaining to maternal health and HIV/AIDS.

Perhaps the goals should be looked at from the perspective of the history of health care policy. Perin and Attaran (2003) observe that "while donors' health policies and strategies have evolved over time, there is no corresponding evidence that health needs in developing countries were changing in ways that justified these policy shifts" (p. 1217). One might amend their statement to recognize the change in health needs in countries where HIV/AIDS has become a major cause of death, but their larger point remains valid, namely that "donors' shifting policies may not be related to recipients' needs, but fit the contemporary political, economic or managerial ideology of the donors." Thus they "operate from the top down, with donors shaping the organization, management, priorities, and rules of access to aid, and very seldom from the bottom up, with the recipients making these choices" (p. 1217).

Basu (2005) echoed this view in noting that "changing donor priorities have appeared almost out of thin air" and that "the health needs of developing countries certainly have not changed as rapidly as have donors' priorities" (p. 134). Do the MDGs constitute broadly accepted redirections in health policy or, as Perin and Attaran (2003) put it, "another trend indulged for the sake of donors rather than recipients?" (p. 1217). This leads one to wonder whether the MDGs, good intentions aside, are capable of generating broad support, meaningful resources, and successful outcomes.

CHAPTER FIVE

INTERNATIONAL POPULATION ASSISTANCE SINCE CAIRO: TRENDS IN POLICY AND PROGRAM ACTION

Over a decade has passed since the International Conference on Population and Development (ICPD) Programme of Action became a favored operational paradigm for international population assistance. How well have donors, nongovernmental organizations (NGOs), and recipient countries delivered on the promise of the Cairo agenda? Evidence to date suggests that the record has been mixed in terms of financial commitment, program action, and policy direction.

It should come as little surprise that donor funding for international population programs has disappointed since 1994. There had been, as we have noted, ample warnings that the ICPD Programme of Action would be a hard sell both to donors and the health, finance, and planning ministries of many developing countries.

Since the 1994 ICPD in Cairo, international assistance for population has fallen well short of projected need. However, owing to rapidly expanding outlays for HIV/AIDS programs, overall population assistance has been rising significantly in recent years. In 1994 (prior to the explosive growth in the HIV/AIDS epidemic) it was estimated that an annual budget of $18.9 billion would be required by 2006 to meet global needs in four ICPD program areas: family planning, other reproductive health services (e.g., safe-motherhood interventions and adolescent services), sexually transmitted diseases and HIV/AIDS, and research. Other key ICPD program areas (e.g., emergency obstetric care, adolescent services, education, women's empowerment programs, and reproductive and human rights advocacy work) were not included in the $18.9 billion estimate. Of that amount, $12.7 billion was to be provided by national (domestic) resources and $6.2 billion from donor countries.

By 2006, a total of $30.4 billion was allocated for population and reproductive health activities (with STD/HIV/AIDS funding accounting for over two-thirds of this amount). The United Nations Population Fund (UNFPA) and the Netherlands Interdisciplinary Demographic Institute (NIDI) estimate that national resource contributions amounted to $23.1 billion and donor funding came to $7.3 billion in 2006 (UNFPA 2008: 9, 29). Unfortunately, there is some uncertainty about the reliability of these estimates, particularly the accounting of national private-sector resources dedicated to population programs.[1]

While total population assistance has risen substantially between 1995 and 2006, there has been a major shift in the composition of this assistance. Resources for family planning have declined substantially in relation to other major components of population assistance. Family planning expenditures fell from 55 percent of total outlays in 1995 to 5 percent in 2006 (an absolute decline from $729 million in 1995 to $365 million by 2006) (UNFPA 2004b: 29, UNFPA 2008: 27). The most substantial expenditure gains have been for STD/HIV/AIDS programs— reaching 70 percent of all Development Assistance Committee (DAC) population funding by 2006—a trend that looks set to continue (UNFPA 2008: 27). These compositional shifts do not bode well for efforts to insure universal access to family planning and other reproductive health services in developing countries by 2015.

Post-Cairo Programmatic Realignments

The ICPD Programme of Action is an ambitious gender-based agenda for international population assistance, which places the social welfare of women at center stage. A broad range of programmatic initiatives are proposed as part of the ICPD reform package, the most notable being the following:

1. Improving access to high-quality family planning services.
2. Integrating family planning with a broader array of reproductive health services (e.g., diagnosis and treatment of sexually transmitted diseases and reproductive-track infections, post-abortion care, and postpartum services).
3. Developing special reproductive health programs for adolescents and young adults.
4. Adopting more client-centered strategies in the delivery of reproductive health services.
5. Converting to target-free managerial systems and removing demographic outcomes as the justification for program activities.
6. Partnering with NGOs and local community organizations as a means of promoting greater client choice and pluralism in service delivery.
7. Decentralizing reproductive health budgets and field operations to local government units (LGUs), NGOs, and community organizations.
8. Encouraging integrated rather than vertical program structures for family planning and reproductive health activities.
9. Providing commodities and services for family planning and reproductive health as part of clinic-based essential services delivered by primary health care providers.
10. Supporting "male involvement" activities.
11. Promoting women's empowerment through education, microenterprises, and legal reform.
12. Enhancing the human and reproductive rights of women.
13. Incorporating greater sexuality awareness and sensitivity in reproductive health activities.

Largely left out of this new formulation are more traditional considerations related to the impact of demographic dynamics on development prospects and concerns about family and community welfare as opposed to the well being of individual women and men. It is noteworthy that much family planning literature in the pre-Cairo period focused largely on the needs of couples, whereas in the post-Cairo period women's individual requirements have largely displaced couples as a unit of concern. Men now only enter the picture, seemingly as an afterthought, under the rubric of male involvement.

In 1998 and early 1999 UNFPA held a series of meetings in the Hague to review progress in implementing the 1994 ICPD Programme of Action. Recommendations from these gatherings (the Hague Forum) were presented at a Special Session of the UN General Assembly during the summer of 1999. The ICPD + 5 Special Session was notable for its rhetorical reaffirmation of the ICPD agenda, but sparing in the presentation of evidence on how the Programme of Action was being implemented. There was little discussion on how to provide the comprehensive reproductive health package advocated in the ICPD Programme of Action or how to establish programmatic priorities in resource-poor settings.

The final report of the ICPD + 5 Special Session stated that good progress was being made in implementing the Cairo agenda, although it was noted that financial resources were still inadequate for implementing the full range of ICPD-mandated initiatives. Results from a 1998 UNFPA field inquiry, conducted mainly in developing countries, reported "concrete results" in implementing the action plan (United Nations 1999c: 37). These achievements were cast largely in terms of improving gender equality (e.g., promoting women in policy decision-making roles, advocating the protection of girls, and outlawing violence against women, most notably the practice of female genital mutilation). Little mention was made of family planning, other than to say that progress had been made in transforming family planning programs into "comprehensive reproductive health packages available at the primary health care level" (p. 38). The UN secretary general, reporting on the field survey, recognized several constraints to the achievement of the ICPD goals. In brief, these were: a serious lack of donor country resources; impeded efforts to generate necessary resources at the national level; and continued hindrance to the achievement of gender equality (United Nations General Assembly 1999).

How these reorderings were actually unfolding and whether they were producing results got little attention. For example, it was simply assumed rather than demonstrated that the accessibility and quality of family planning services were being enhanced through an integrationist approach emphasizing clinical service provision over more informal, less medically dependent distribution mechanisms (e.g., the provision of contraceptives through doorstep and community distribution schemes as well as social marketing through pharmacies and other commercial establishments).

Other assessments of progress in implementing the ICPD Programme of Action have been less triumphal in tone. For example, a survey of government officials and NGO representatives in developing countries undertaken by the Futures Group for USAID found considerable confusion on the best way to address Cairo objectives (Hardee et al. 1998a). While generally supportive of those objectives, respondents were often uncertain how to go about setting programmatic priorities and implementing the new reproductive health agenda. The authors of the study drew the following conclusion:

It will be impossible for countries to make significant progress in implementation if they do not rank their reproductive health interventions and develop well-conceived plans for introducing or strengthening delivery of those services. . . . The key to progress is setting priorities and phasing-in interventions, including making improvements in existing services. (p. 59)

Luke and Watkins (2002), analyzing the same survey data, report that there does not appear to be universal agreement on the advisability of implementing all elements of the ICPD reproductive health agenda. A more selective approach appears to have been the norm. Family planning and maternal health services have generally been accorded high priority, whereas interventions more directly focused on sexuality and gender issues have been downplayed:

The lack of interest in promoting gender equity is striking. Opposition to the new agenda is primarily in terms of its conceptions of gender rather than the narrower health agenda. Many respondents portrayed their culture as one in which men are in control, and they claimed that health has nothing to do with gender. A few made use of the rationalistic language of science to justify dismissal of gender issues: health priorities have to be determined by data, by indicators of the prevalence of a problem—but there is too little data on domestic violence and sexual coercion to warrant attention to these issues. (p. 722)

Respondents also mentioned that elements of the new reproductive health agenda (such as its focus on gender-based violence and adolescent services) were culturally sensitive and did not necessarily have high priority in their countries. The concept of reproductive health was deemed "complex," "difficult to understand," and "too broad." In addition, there was considerable confusion about how to respond to the Cairo action plan given the limited financial resources typically available for reproductive health.

Respondents in such countries as Bangladesh, Malawi, and Senegal expressed frustration at having programmatic agendas imposed by donors. A typical comment was the following: "The donors are trying to impose their own agendas on Bangladesh and their agendas keep changing" (p. 728). In general, opposition to the ICPD recommendations was less pronounced in countries where donors had more influence. Employees of NGOs, which often depend on donor funding for their continued existence, were found to be more supportive of the Cairo agenda than were many government officials.

Given the broad agenda articulated at Cairo, it is difficult to assign priorities to programmatic goals. Five goals that seem to be core operational elements are (1) the broadening of programs from family planning to reproductive health; (2) the promotion of more client-centered services; (3) the abolition of provider performance targets; (4) the elevation of NGOs and "civil society" as key actors in advancing the agenda; and (5) the promotion of decentralized program strategies as a means of empowering local communities and women. We review these five goals here in light of recent program experience in several developing countries with long-standing population and reproductive health programs.

The Transition from Family Planning to Reproductive Health

The ICPD Programme of Action recommended that family planning programs offer a broader array of reproductive health services to enhance the quality of care and address the health needs of women more effectively. As part of this revamped vision, family planning services were to be integrated with maternal and child health care (MCH) and other primary health services. The vertical program structures that typified many pre-Cairo family planning programs (not to mention other infectious disease programs) were to be transformed in favor of more integrated structures.

The extent to which developing countries have been able to expand the range of reproductive health services (and provide the additional staff and infrastructure needed to provide such care) and field more integrated service delivery systems is far from clear. Despite the readiness of many developing countries to reaffirm the central tenets of the Cairo agenda, current evidence suggests that most have failed to meet ICPD's ambitious goals for reconstituting reproductive health service delivery. Resource and program absorption constraints (including weak primary health care systems) have been major impediments. In addition, many donor projects still require "vertical accountability," which tends to frustrate "funding, management, commodities, logistics, reporting and so on" in support of integrated service delivery systems (Mayhew 2002: 221).

One of the better examples of attempts to respond to Cairo has been in Bangladesh, a highly donor-dependent country. Among the countries surveyed by the Futures Group, Bangladesh is credited with having made the greatest progress in "grappling with the issues of setting priorities, financing, and implementing reproductive health agendas" (Hardee et al. 1998a: 58).

Bangladesh had been an instructive case study prior to Cairo. Over the previous two decades it had succeeded in implementing a national family planning program that was a unique partnership between the government of Bangladesh, the NGO community, and an effective national social marketing program. Between the early 1980s and 2004 the percentage of currently married women using any form of contraception rose from less than 20 percent to 58 percent (NIPORT 2005: 67). The gain in contraceptive use was associated with a fall in the total fertility rate from around 6 births per women in 1980 to 3.0 by 2003 (NIPORT 2005: 32–33). This dramatic change occurred in one of the poorest countries in Asia and at a time when Bangladesh apparently had not experienced major socioeconomic transformations, particularly in relation to the status of women (Cleland, Phillips, and Amin 1994).

The delivery of family planning services in Bangladesh prior to 1998 did not depend heavily on clinics and medical staff. The government supported a vertical program that provided contraceptive services, limited MCH care, and referral support through a network of fieldworkers called Family Welfare Assistants (FWAs), local-area clinics (the Health and Family Welfare Center), and regional hospitals (the Upazilla Health Complex). The backbone of this program was the doorstep delivery of services through the FWA, an indigenous strategy that has been shown to be effective in providing family planning services to rural women with little or no access to clinics or medical doctors.[2] A network of donor-supported NGOs, working primarily in urban areas, and a widely dispersed social marketing program offered additional channels for obtaining affordable family planning commodities and services.

With the arrival of the ICPD Programme of Action, the donor community (most prominently the World Bank) argued that the structure of the Bangladesh family planning program was not conducive to providing a broad range of high-quality reproductive health services. It claimed that a doorstep delivery system reliant on fieldworkers was not cost-effective and could never offer women the range and quality of reproductive health services mandated under ICPD. It also criticized the Bangladesh program for being overly vertical (not sufficiently integrated with primary health services), too driven by demographic objectives and service-provider targets tied to the recruitment of new family planning acceptors, and not sufficiently attentive to gender equity.

The World Bank therefore recommended that domiciliary service delivery and fieldworkers be phased-out and that a community clinic-based delivery system be instituted instead. These community clinics would offer an "essential services package" combining four elements: childcare, reproductive health (including family planning), communicable disease control, and limited curative care (World Bank 1998: 10). This required a forced marriage of two divisions of the Bangladesh Ministry of Health and Family Welfare that was justified largely on the grounds of quality enhancement and cost, despite the absence of a thorough-going analysis of the cost savings expected to be realized in transitioning from fieldworkers to a clinic-based "one-stop-shopping" primary service system.

This programmatic sea change was in no small measure the result of strenuous lobbying by the donor community, which for more than 30 years has provided a substantial percentage of the total public-sector budget for health and family planning in Bangladesh. The World Bank was the first major donor in the 1990s to propose a clinic-based reproductive health approach for Bangladesh—ironically returning to its earlier failed strategy of the 1970s. This approach was first articulated by Germain (1997) and later formally outlined in the World Bank's Project Appraisal Document (World Bank 1998).

Despite reports of considerable misgiving on the part of the Bangladesh government, it accepted a new "target-free approach" with priority given to clinic-based reproductive health care as the new model for family planning (Government of Bangladesh 1997). The World Bank provided $250 million over five years to support the new concept through its Health and Population Program Project (World Bank 1998). USAID, through its support for NGOs, was actually the first donor to implement the new clinic-based approach in Bangladesh.[3]

Although the donor community and ICPD advocates have hailed these programmatic reorderings, convincing evidence is lacking as to how successful they have actually been. In NGO service areas, early qualitative research has apparently found considerable client approval of the new clinic-based delivery system (Schuler, Bates, and Islam 2001; Schuler, Islam, and Bates 2000a, b). This analysis notes, however, that the abrupt removal of fieldworkers in NGO service areas initially compromised access to family planning services for some women and generated greater reliance on husbands for supplying contraceptives—and presumably for basic information on reproductive and child health as well as referral services for the treatment of chronic conditions, both functions previously provided by fieldworkers. New user fees at NGO clinics, not always administered on an ability-to-pay basis, may have also imposed barriers to access among lower-income clients (Schuler, Bates, and Islam 2001: 197).

At present, some government fieldworkers in rural Bangladesh appear to have stopped making regular visits to clients in their homes. The community clinics that were to replace doorstep delivery either have not been built or, if built, not adequately staffed and equipped in many areas of the country. Since fieldworkers were supposed to be reassigned to the still nonfunctioning community clinics, and since many of them no longer provide door-to-door service provision, it is not clear how they are currently being deployed. Doubtless there is considerable regional variation. The present confusion is not helped by the uncertainty about whether the Bangladesh government is still committed to the community clinic concept.

Some ICPD advocates have maintained that the problem of implementing Cairo agendas in Bangladesh is the continuing adherence to a discredited service delivery "culture" (Schuler, Bates, and Islam 2001). Schuler and her coauthors claim that progress has been impeded in NGO service areas by service providers' remaining committed to the recruitment of new acceptors (the "motivation mentality"), by their continuing to promote provider-preferred contraceptive methods in a "paternalistic" manner, and by their sustaining the expectation among clients that family planning services should be offered free of charge as part of a "national fertility reduction agenda" (pp. 198–99). As long as these impressions persist, it will be difficult, these critics say, to implement a clinic-based service system.[4]

Rather than moving too slowly to implement the new clinic-based reproductive health strategy, the transition may in fact have occurred too quickly. In the public-sector program, phasing out doorstep delivery before having the new network of community clinics in place—that is, built, staffed, and equipped—is evidence of poor planning and suggests the possibility of undue donor interference.

Evidence from the 2004 Demographic and Health Survey reinforces these concerns. Between 1993–94 and 2004, the percentages of modern method family planning users obtaining services from government fieldworkers fell from 41.8 to 22.7 percent (Mitra et al. 1994: 60 and NIPORT 2005: 67). In 2004, only 1.7 percent of all users of modern methods obtained services from community clinics, while 7.1 percent utilized satellite clinics or EPI outreach sites (NIPORT 2005: 67). Commercial distribution of contraceptives through pharmacies instead became the favored source of supply as domiciliary delivery faltered. Between 1993–94 and 2004, the percentage of modern method clients using social marketing outlets rose from 8.2 to 29.3 percent. Non-clinical methods (pills, injectables, and traditional methods) account for much of the gain in contraceptive use between 1996–97 and 2004.

Despite these changes in the source of supply of family planning services, a prominent enthusiast for ICPD recommendations, Adrienne Germain, has asserted that the Bangladesh program has not "faltered" as the result of efforts to integrate reproductive health services and further empower "civil society" (Germain 2005: 3). If faltering refers to a decline in the contraceptive prevalence rate (CPR) this view is correct, but much of the credit for the modest gains in CPR in recent years must be given to social marketing rather than, in a post hoc fashion, service integration and NGOs. Germain also implies that improvements in ante-natal coverage, maternal and child mortality, and life expectancy between 1998–2002 can be attributed to "strong" government support for reproductive health service integration (Germain 2005: 7). However, these improved health outcomes constitute long-term trends that largely predate efforts to integrate reproductive health services in community clinics. It is also worth noting that most Bangladeshi women did not have access to clinic-based essential services programs in their communities during the period under review by Germain.

The government of Bangladesh has reservations about many of the policy and program changes promoted by the donor community. In the spring of 2003, the government decided to abandon efforts to restructure the country's health system and instead reassess the advisability of proceeding with numerous "sector-wide" reform initiatives (e.g., the move to integrate health and family planning program structures and the continued devolution of line authority to local program staff). It also formally reinstituted doorstep delivery of family planning and basic MCH services throughout the country and decided to reconsider the merits of relying upon community clinics for all primary service delivery needs. These programmatic shifts were justified on the grounds that too many rural women were now underserved owing to the partial cessation of doorstep delivery and the lack of functioning community clinics in much of the country.

There is no doubt that women in Bangladesh would benefit greatly from a wider range of high-quality reproductive health services. And certainly if the acceptability and cost-effectiveness of an exclusively clinic-based system can be demonstrated (which has not yet been the case), it would be wise to proceed in that direction. But in doing so, the government needs to resolve major constraints peculiar to the situation in Bangladesh.

These are not problems that yield readily to the imposition of donor "conditionalities." They include problems associated with civil service reform and personnel policy; program design and service-delivery restructuring; and the mobilization of local government officials in support of culturally transforming agendas. Lush (2002) remarks that the preconditions for enacting health-sector reforms are often not in place and can frustrate efforts to quickly transform service-delivery systems. She notes that integrated service delivery systems usually cannot be quickly established owing to the lack of adequate administrative and legalistic frameworks; insufficient technical expertise and guidance (e.g., in providing effective STD screening and treatment), and deficient health system infrastructure.

> Integrated service delivery is further inhibited by problems in health facilities, particularly the low pay, poor morale and lack of motivation among providers, and the lack of appropriate physical infrastructure and equipment for expanding services . . . Integrating HIV and STD services with maternal and child health and family planning services requires these cadres to undertake a whole new range of activities without concomitant improvements in salary and working conditions. (p. 74)

The problems involved in implementing donors' reform agendas cannot be laid squarely at the door of government intransigence and an unwillingness to provide "an enabling environment strengthening the role of autonomous civil society advocates" (Jahan 2003: 190). Rather, if countries are to achieve real, sustainable advance, reforms need to be realistic with respect to the absorptive capacities of recipient countries, sensitive to local cultural beliefs and traditions, and respectful of national priorities and needs. In addition, health-sector reforms should be more than exercises in cost cutting and the rationing of care. Lush and Campbell (2001) note that "many reforms have been driven more by the need to cut costs and increase efficiency than to improve quality of care or local accountability. This has taken place in an environment of declining funds for health care among both low-income country governments and donors" (p. 184).

In the case of Bangladesh, the donor community appears to have been guilty of pushing for major structural reforms too quickly (especially with regard to the disorderly phase-out of doorstep service delivery), imposing culturally sensitive agendas (e.g., gender mainstreaming and women's empowerment) that were not always well understood or seen as programmatic imperatives, and at times demonstrating a disregard for the opinions of senior government health officials.

The Promotion of Client-Centered Services

Another key recommendation from Cairo is that reproductive health services become more "client-centered" and less driven by demographic imperatives. Since Cairo, there has been a rush among leading donor organizations to institute reforms that make clinic services more responsive to clients' expressed needs. Management tools such as COPE (client-oriented, provider-efficient services) and GATHER (greet, ask, tell, help, explain, and return) are examples of efforts to enhance clinic services and client satisfaction.

Orienting service delivery to the needs and preferences of clients is of course essential for good quality of care. The ICPD affirmation of this central tenet is a welcome contribution. Many country programs still have a long way to go in providing an agreeable clinic experience and high-quality of care. Although undoubtedly a valid conclusion, the vast majority of studies on client satisfaction report that women are usually happy with the services they obtain—even when objective criteria demonstrate that provider– client interactions and clinic facilities are substandard.

Research on the quality of care and client satisfaction often enters into very subjective territory. Identifying deficiencies in service quality that matter to clients is not a straightforward matter. An example of these difficulties is provided by an operations research study on the quality of family planning services in Davao del Norte on the southern Philippine island of Mindanao. The authors of the study identified numerous deficiencies in the quality of care "typically" provided by *barangay* health workers (BHWs) in two service sites, the most egregious being that "many BHWs attempt to convince women to limit their fertility and often promote a particular contraceptive method—without inquiring about the client's health status, reproductive intentions, or needs" (Jain et al. 2002: 102). Despite this shortcoming, a previous inquiry undertaken in Davao del Norte on the need for client follow-up visits reported client dissatisfaction to be only 2 percent among all respondents (p. 109). This tells us little about quality-of-care issues except that client satisfaction is a more elusive concept than a priori standards of quality often assume.

National survey data in the Philippines are limited with respect to information on the quality of care, and what there is may be misleading. Such information as does exist suggests that clients are generally satisfied with the quality of family planning services on offer. According to the 1998 Philippine Demographic and Health Survey, only 2.1 percent of clients using modern methods of contraception were unhappy with the quality of care they received. This finding suggests that Davao del Norte may be quite typical of national patterns. Among the small number of dissatisfied users, having to wait too long at clinics was the most commonly cited reason for displeasure. The vast majority of clients interviewed in the survey also knew about the full range of modern and natural methods provided by the Philippine family planning program, which seems somewhat at odds with the authors' assertion that BHWs don't offer clients information about all available methods (Philippines National Statistics Office, Department of Health, and Macro International 1999: 49). They may not, of course, but clients get their information somewhere and it is unreasonable to exclude health workers as a likely source.

The study of client centeredness in Davao del Norte also raises questions about the ability of clients to make informed choices about contraception. The authors complain that instead of listening to clients' perceptions of their reproductive health needs, there is a tendency for providers to tell clients what they need in order to minimize the health risks of pregnancy. This, they say, is inconsistent with the goal of client-centered care. First, it uses general predictors of risk derived from rates of maternal and infant mortality and morbidity rather than relying on a client's clinical history, current health status, and reproductive intentions. Second, it undercuts the spirit of Cairo's client-centered philosophy in that it overlooks the client's childbearing intentions (Jain et al. 2002: 103). However, it strikes us as irresponsible not to advise clients on the reproductive risks they may face in fulfilling their reproductive plans and disingenuous to suggest that such counseling constitutes subtle coercion.

The topic of client-centered care is important and deserves priority attention in field research. Considerable care needs to be taken in documenting the manner in which clients' expressed needs are articulated and acted upon by service providers. In many developing countries, is poor service quality largely due to inadequate client-centered care and uncaring health staff, or are other supply-side failings (e.g., poor facilities and shortages of essential drugs and supplies) more to blame? Actually, as Shelton (2001) notes, little is typically known about service providers: what skills they possess, what social and cultural constraints they may face in providing care, and how they might be more effectively mobilized to provide a higher grade of care. Future research on the quality of care might profitably give more attention to upgrading the effectiveness of service providers rather than focusing primarily on client's identification of need.

Women's health advocates also often argue that client-centered care must incorporate sexuality and "rights-based approaches" geared to transforming reproductive and social behavior that meets clients' needs. Jacobson (2001) summarizes this view as follows:

A rights-based program is part of the process of establishing new social norms that encourage partnership, communication and cooperation . . . Because the proximate risks of sexual relations are indivisible—most women seeking family planning services simultaneously face the risk of sexual coercion, unwanted pregnancy, and infection—the rights-based approach should address all risks. Concerns about sex, power, gender and rights should therefore be considered intrinsic to each aspect of programming—research, range of methods, service delivery, education, communication, and client-provider interaction—and not be compartmentalized. (p. 59)

The agenda of women's health advocates clearly entails a much broader reach than typically embraced by public health professionals struggling to improve the accessibility and quality of clinical services. Integrating reproductive health services with a human rights approach entails the enactment of interventions that go far beyond the clinic setting and the dynamics of client–provider interactions (the traditional locus of situation-analysis studies dealing with the quality of care). It is doubtful whether any country, developed or developing, has been able to meet the standard proposed by Jacobson.

To ask whether it might be unrealistic to expect often overburdened service providers to also assume the role of social reformers and human rights activists in no way abnegates the importance of human and reproductive rights. However, moving beyond the rhetoric of integrating health and human rights into effective field-based programmatic action is a daunting task, particularly in many sociocultural environments that may not be in step with the transformational agendas of Western feminism. At the very least, models for how traditional health delivery systems might be transformed into rights-based systems in various settings need to be carefully weighed before passing judgment on their advisability or practicality.

The Abolition of Performance Targets

Pre-Cairo era family planning programs have been harshly criticized for being excessively driven by demographic objectives (e.g., lowering rates of population growth and fertility) and by performance targets that emphasized the recruitment of family planning acceptors. Such concentration on narrow results, the critics have argued, ignored concern with satisfying client needs and improving the quality of care. They have indicted targets as the major impediment to providing high-quality reproductive health services. The origin of targets is obscure, but one source in a position to know credits the Ford Foundation in India with their early appearance in the 1960s as a device whereby family planning objectives could be better directed and results more reliably measured (Jain 1998).

Targets have been widely blamed for the failures of family planning programs in which they were used. There is certainly evidence that performance targets were sometimes abused in recruiting and retaining family planning clients (e.g., see Warwick 1982: 197–99). However, how widespread and enduring these practices have been is debatable. The vast majority of developing countries implementing family planning programs over the past 50 years have officially embraced voluntarism, contraceptive choice, and concerns for women's health. In any event, the perceived widespread abuse of demographic targets led delegates at Cairo to recommend in the Programme of Action that "demographic goals, while legitimately the subject of government development strategies, should not be imposed on family planning providers in the form of targets and quotas for the recruitment of clients" (United Nations 1994: Paragraph 7.12).

However, the extent to which targets compromised the quality of services as compared with other common programmatic failings is debatable. Not all family planning programs that used targets actually implemented them with much efficiency, and some programs (e.g., the Indonesian Family Planning Program after the mid-1980s) evolved in the direction of using targets to evaluate national and regional program performance rather than as punitive administrative controls for assessing the success of government officials in reducing birth rates and health providers in recruiting clients. As a programmatic deficiency, it is difficult to rank target setting against such competing problems as inattentive program administration, inadequately trained service providers, poorly maintained clinical facilities and equipment, the unreliable provision of essential drugs and commodities, inefficient client counseling and referral mechanisms, and limited choice of contraceptive methods.

Despite the existence of competing deficiencies in many pre-Cairo family planning programs, since 1994 much attention has been given to abolishing demographic rationales for family planning and instituting "target-free approaches" in country programs. Whether such reforms have actually led to substantial improvements in the quality of reproductive health care still has not been convincingly demonstrated. India provides one instructive example of where efforts to incorporate target-free strategies in reproductive health service delivery actually may have triggered greater administrative confusion and compromised service delivery.

Since its inception in 1952, the Indian Family Planning Program has been noted for its reliance on method-specific provider targets, with emphasis given to the recruitment of female sterilization clients. Female sterilization was a method for which there was significant demand and one that, as compared with methods that involved continuous recommitment, required relatively simple administrative procedures.

In 1997 the government of India decided to abolish provider targets in favor of a target-free approach. The new strategy was designed to reorient service provision to the fulfillment of client needs rather than centrally administered targets. Contraceptive needs in new localities and among individual clients were to be identified through surveys conducted by community health workers. These surveys provided data essential for calculating workers' "expected levels of achievement," primarily to guide local health workers, female auxiliary nurse midwives, and male multipurpose workers in laying out their activity rounds. Expected levels of achievement were to be established through the identification of local client needs using survey information rather than centrally established quotas.

At the time this major administrative reform was enacted, the Ministry of Health and Family Welfare provided little guidance on how states and districts were to carry out the target-free approach. Therefore, there was little uniformity among individual states in the extent to which the new mandate was carried through. In the short-run, results were less than might have been hoped for.

Most states lacked operational methodologies to assess community needs, develop realistic performance goals and plans, and institutionalize quality in service provision, especially at the district level and below. [The target-free approach] at the operational level was even misinterpreted in some states as "no targets means no work" . . . The formats introduced to estimate community needs and expected levels of achievement were too complex to be followed by the workers . . . The training provided to health workers in the use of these formats was inadequate and lacked uniformity . . . and many did not understand the philosophy behind the new approach. The formats provided were complex and many workers could not understand how to calculate the ELAs [expected levels of achievement] based on sample surveys. (Narayana and Sangwan 2000: 2–5)

After the introduction of the target-free approach, family planning use declined substantially in many states, most notably in Bihar and Uttar Pradesh. The decline may have been due in part to earlier inflated performance data resulting from the zeal to meet targets (Murthy et al. 2002: 32).

Given these difficulties, the government of India decided to drop the target-free approach. A strategy of community-needs assessment was adopted instead that emphasized the role of health workers in defining and meeting community needs for family planning and reproductive health services. Community-needs assessment was essentially an effort to establish community performance "goals" rather than centrally defined "targets." The extent to which this new strategy was an improvement on the target-free approach, to our knowledge, has not been demonstrated. There is, as one might expect, considerable confusion on how to proceed. Commenting on the implementation of community-needs assessment, Narayana and Sangwan (2000) conclude that "some states have blended the old approach with the new approach and designed new monitoring systems, some have tried to implement the new system, completely replacing the old system . . . and a few others have neither the old nor the new system in place" (p. 6). When the center relinquishes control of a national program, it is naïve to think that local authorities will necessarily put program goals ahead of local interests.

An assessment of the new community-needs assessment system in Karnataka and Tamil Nadu found that it had not been successful in achieving a target-free approach. Health workers had to achieve more targets under the new procedures, and workloads actually increased substantially (Murthy et al. 2002: 53). In the Karnataka districts of Dharwad and Kolar, 15 reproductive health targets came into force under community-needs assessment as opposed to just one family planning target in the period preceding its introduction. These new targets were often judged to be beyond the capacity of the local health delivery system. For example, women's "expressed need" for oral hydration packets for the treatment of acute diarrhea was four times greater than the packets available locally, and new treatment targets for acute respiratory infection were five times higher than previous treatment rates (p. 38).

Furthermore, local district health officers and supervisors often set targets arbitrarily irrespective of the levels derived from community-needs assessment surveys of women's expressed need. This may be a carryover from an old administrative practice in India whereby local administrators would raise the performance ante to spur greater effort. Most disturbingly, "overall, women did not notice any improvement in the quality of services" under the new regime (p. 40). Despite such short-term disappointments, however, there remains considerable optimism that India's community-needs assessment mechanism will eventually improve the morale of health workers, lead to less arbitrary and punitive management systems, and make reproductive health services more responsive to women's needs.

While family planning provider targets clearly had their drawbacks, the superiority of the presumably more client-centered and decentralized approach still has not been demonstrated under real field conditions. Until such evidence is available, developing countries will not be confident on how to respond to ICPD calls for implementing target-free management reform and client-centered services.

The Rise of NGOs and the Private Sector

Another feature of the 1994 ICPD Programme of Action has been the call for greater involvement ("partnering") of NGOs and civil society[5] and the private sector in implementing the reproductive health, social welfare, and human rights objectives identified at

Cairo. The program highlights the newly elevated status of NGOs at several junctures, most emphatically in paragraphs 15.1–15.6.

> To address the challenges of population and development effectively, broad and effective partnership is essential between Governments and non-governmental organizations (comprising not-for-profit groups and organizations at the local, national and international levels) to assist in the formulation, implementation, monitoring and evaluation of population objectives and activities . . . In many areas of population and development activities, non-governmental groups are already rightly recognized for their comparative advantage in relation to government agencies, because of innovative, flexible and responsive programme design and implementation, including grass roots participation, and because quite often they are rooted in and interact with constituencies that are poorly served and hard to reach through government channels. (United Nations 1994: Paragraphs 15.1 and 15.2)

The elevation of the private sector is seen as a means of providing greater choice to women in selecting service providers, strengthening the quality of services, and more effectively advocating for the rights of women. In addition, the twin goals of promoting civil society and "grassroots community participation"[6] are viewed as being dependent on partnerships with NGOs. The fact that many NGO representatives were active participants at Cairo (both on official delegations and in unofficial parallel meetings) helped to ensure that their interests were well recognized.

The promotion of the private sector as an efficient mechanism for the provision of family planning and reproductive health services predated the ICPD and more recently has become a centerpiece of health-sector reform. Introducing greater pluralism and choice in service delivery may help improve cost recovery and efforts to enhance the quality of care in many settings. Nevertheless, the call for central governments to greatly reduce or abandon the task of service provision seems inconsistent with the priorities of most developing countries. Two experienced commentators on international reproductive health service provision typify this view by maintaining that "central governments should focus on health care financing and social security programs" and delegate "service provision to organizations that are closer to communities" (Hardee and Smith 2000: 18).

Over the past decade, NGOs have become a widely favored mechanism for channeling foreign aid resources to developing countries. In some cases, such as Somalia, they are the only organizations with which donors can work, although apparently to mixed effect (see, e.g., Maren 1997 for unflattering accounts of NGO performance in Somalia). According to *The Economist* (2000), "NGOs now head for crisis zones as fast as journalists: a war, a flood, refugees, a dodgy election, even a world trade conference, will draw them like a honey pot" (p. 130). It has been estimated that there were nearly 29,000 international NGOs and a vastly greater number of domestic ones as of 1995, including around 2 million in the United States and 65,000 in Russia. Developing countries are acquiring their fair share of NGOs as well. Around 240 new NGOs are created every year in Kenya (pp. 130–32).

The popular perception of NGOs as altruistic, independent, and idealistic is accurate in many instances. They will continue to be an important constituency in designing and implementing development programs. But it is worth noting that NGOs have often competed with government programs for human and financial resources. Picazo, Huddart, and Duale (2003) comment on the situation in sub-Saharan Africa as follows:

> The proliferation of NGOs in the 1990s certainly caused a discernable exodus of health workers from the government service, either as direct health providers, program managers, or consultants. NGO health projects attract a wide range of government health professionals since the pay is much better and the work is similar to that of the civil servants; hence very little retraining costs are needed. (p. 10)

Experience in dealing with Third World governments has led some observers to view them with extreme skepticism as partners in development. One of the more negative appraisals views governments as "hopeless" and argues that "we must do everything we can, individually and collectively, to ignore them and work around them" (van den Berghe 1994: 29). This is a position that resonates strongly with many veterans of the development trenches. NGOs that try to work through governments, says Professor van den Berghe, risk being "so thoroughly plucked and parasitized by ruling elites that most of their resources [are] drained away from the intended recipients" (p. 29).

As NGOs become more closely involved in the business of development by offering donors a way around governments in which inefficiency, corruption, and nontransparent dealings can be rife, they begin to lose their independence. Whether it comes to that, at the very least the "upward accountability to donor assistance has skewed NGO activities towards donor-driven agendas for development rather than at indigenous priorities" (Hashemi 1996: 103). One observer attributes the popularity of NGOs with donors to the fact that "NGOs have adapted to the goals of donor groups, rather than donors adapting to NGOs" (Cross 1997: 9).

A variation on this theme of donor absorption is offered by Robert Chambers, a development guru of long standing, who notes that as more NGOs become agents for Northern donors, they increasingly encounter pressure to report "good" results, which in turn promotes superficial or even dishonest reporting.

> The patronage of funds, pressures to disburse . . . and accountability upward . . . give rise to top–down standardization of packages, with misfits between central programs and local needs. Prudent staff then provide misleadingly positive feedback. The more the need or desire for funds [by the NGO], the greater the danger of deception . . . The deceiving and self-serving state has long existed; it is now being joined by the deceiving and self-deceiving NGO. (Chambers 1996: 211)

There is wariness on both sides: NGOs often do not trust the governments to which they are accredited and governments are wary of some NGOs that may be seen to bear silent witness to the public sector's failure to do its job. In Southeast Asia, spokespersons for the Asian-Pacific Resource and Research Centre for Women assert that "the policy environment is not enabling, with many governments hostile to advocacy-oriented NGOs and NGOs [are] . . . almost universally absent from committees to oversee ICPD implementation" (Dasgupta and Sen 1998: 22).

Annis (1987) offers a long list of possible pitfalls faced by NGOs. These include questions relating to forms of governance and problems associated with "upward" and "downward" accountability. Sustainability and performance evaluation are also questions that frequently are left in a marinade of lip service. It does not help matters that many NGOs are essentially shells, set up by government officers as a means of supplementing their household income with outside money. This state of affairs is in sharp contrast to the view that saw the rise of voluntary associations as the most significant development since the rise of nation states in the nineteenth century.

Before proceeding too far in this direction, let us acknowledge that there are some exceedingly fine NGOs and that, in any case, many are here to stay. Our objection is to the canonizing view of them that crops up, almost mantra-like, in discussions of development policy. The best approach would seem to be an eyes-open pragmatism in making policy and deciding on modes of implementation. This usually will involve a firsthand look around.

In the Indian state of Gujarat, for example, a young Indian doctor did just that (Mavalankar 1996). He found that NGOs supplying family planning and reproductive health services helped to dilute the overwhelming predominance of surgical methods that characterize the public-sector program. They were more dependable in providing nonsurgical contraception, in part because they found a way to become independent of the government's creaky logistics system. With respect to MCH, they were able to provide the progesterone-only pill, appropriate for breastfeeding women, which the government program did not supply. NGOs were also free to offer other modern contraceptive methods such as injectables and implants. But Mavalankar shies away from an absolute position. He acknowledges that "not many NGOs have done any special efforts to widen the choice of contraceptives" (p. 10). Overall, he concludes:

> NGOs . . . have more flexibility and sometimes do employ more committed and qualified staff. Better supervision may also encourage workers to provide more information. They have better training programmes and hence their workers may be more updated with information than government workers . . . The overall picture in the

Indian programme, both in the public and private sectors, seems to be one of scanty information to the clients and to the public. (pp. 13–14)

A main point in our discussion of NGOs, and in our review of recent donor efforts to restructure the Bangladesh Family Planning Program, is that imported ideas should not be subscribed to as absolute dicta. Intimate knowledge of context is essential for success. Innovations need not have the imprimatur of large international conferences, and can also profit by the scrutiny of experienced, on-the-ground observers such as Dr. Mavalankar in his consideration of the operation of NGOs in Gujarat. Donors, in particular, need to temper their enthusiasm for ideas that sound good with the realities they are apt to face in execution.

To further cement this obvious, but often-ignored point, we might consider USAID's large "flagship" project in Uttar Pradesh, India (USAID 1992). Here an abstract enthusiasm for privatization and NGOs as a means of circumventing underperforming government family planning efforts (inspired in part by USAID's productive association with NGOs in Bangladesh) was given a full dress rehearsal. A ten-year project entitled "Innovations in Family Planning Services" was organized under an all-embracing NGO known by the mouth-twisting sibilant (SIFPSA), or State Innovations in Family Planning Services Agency. The legal basis for the organization came from the Societies Registration Act, a carryover from the British colonial period when charitable groups sought legal cover for their activities.

The time seemed right for constructing a project along these lines. Not only were donors enamored of private initiatives, free from bureaucratic palsy, but also in 1987 the Indian National Institute of Health, a satrapy of the Ministry of Health and Family Welfare, proposed a set of nine recommendations for improving government–NGO relations. According to the recommendations, family planning and health projects should be free to operate "outside the government" under the direction of an approved agency with a private governing board. The board was to be granted a fair degree of operational autonomy, but with ultimate responsibility to the government. Outside funds would flow to projects so organized through government channels, but with some relaxation of procedures. The boards of these moderately constrained NGOs were authorized to sign contracts with or to make grants to private voluntary organizations. The private voluntary organizations in turn would be subject to fewer restrictions than those in force for government-run projects. All this was seen at the time as real liberalization (Narayana and Kantner 1992). It was not a total victory for private agencies, however. Local officials did not immediately stop trying to control all aspects of activities in their districts, but it seemed a step in the right direction.

The project began its organizational life in 1992 in the northern state of Uttar Pradesh. USAID planned to deploy its battery of cooperating agencies to provide specialized services to the project. The idea was to demonstrate the efficacy of various service-delivery innovations, some of which were in the air in the run-up to Cairo, in selected districts of Uttar Pradesh. The experience in these districts would then provide a platform for an improved, statewide family planning and reproductive health program.

There were early signs that the government would not let matters stray far from its control. The governing body (SIFPSA) was to include representatives of the government of India, Uttar Pradesh, USAID, the corporate sector, the media, and NGOs—in today's organizational patois, the major "stakeholders." Since NGOs were something of a rarity in northern India, the reference here is to USAID's participating cooperating agencies. As for the private voluntary organizations, the project would either have to find or, more likely, create them.

The primary goal of the project was to reduce the total fertility rate in the state of Uttar Pradesh from 4.8 children per woman to 4.0 through doubling of the use of modern contraceptives. As for the "innovations," they were to promote family planning by "broadening support among leadership groups, increasing the public understanding of the health and welfare benefits of family planning, creating a better image of the program and providing information . . . on the availability of services and methods" (USAID 1992: 2).

A panoply of service delivery approaches would increase access to family planning through hospitals, clinics, rural practitioners, household and community-based distribution channels, social marketing, and commercial retail sales. The quality of family planning services would be improved by expanding the choice of contraceptive methods, improving the technical competence of personnel, ensuring informed choice through effective counseling, strengthening management and follow-up of client services, and enhancing contraceptive logistics. It had everything, including a ten-year price tag of $325 million, funded entirely by USAID.

A final end-of-project assessment was conducted in 2002–03 by a team of consultants assembled by POPTECH, an organization under contract to USAID to undertake project design and evaluation activities. The team (screened and approved by USAID) was unable to prepare a final report that all members of the team could endorse or that was acceptable to USAID. A 32-page summary report entitled "Assessment of the Innovations in Family Planning Services Project" (dated April 2003) was posted on the POPTECH website (POPTECH 2003). No authorship was indicated, and an inquiry to POPTECH revealed that nothing further by way of a full report had been approved for release by USAID.

The summary report provides few quantitative data beyond two tables showing a modest increase in contraceptive prevalence for "modern methods" between 1992–93 and 1998–99 and a breakdown of changes in method use. In the 28 districts included in the "Innovations in Family Planning Services" project, use of modern methods increased over the six-year interval from 18.4 to 22.4 percent. Extrapolating this rate of increase to the end of the ten-year project duration yields an estimate of 26.5 percent of married women of reproductive age as current users of modern methods. The goal at the outset of the project was to "double" the prevalence of modern methods, which would have meant raising it by more than 10 percentage points above projected achievement levels.

As for the major "innovation" of the project, the establishment of a "registered society" with operational autonomy subject only to relaxed government oversight, the project amply illustrates the difficulty faced in the Indian situation by a supposedly "apex" NGO in securing real managerial autonomy in collaboration with the public sector. The present case provides a general caution worth heeding.

Not only did SIFPSA have to clear many hurdles to be reimbursed by the government for its work, but also from the outset the government ensured its control over the project by appointing Indian Administrative Service officers as executive and additional directors. In addition, four out of five general officers were seconded to the project from the public sector.

An outside observer might reasonably suspect that the government had hijacked the project. Indeed the mid-term review cited problems associated with the inflexibility deriving from government procedures and expressed the fear that over time, because of the preponderance of government officials in its senior management, SIFPSA might come to prefer working with the public rather than with the private sector. These concerns are echoed even more strongly in the summary report. Although the project was created to avoid the trammels and burdens of government bureaucracy, the culture of bureaucracy is deeply imbued in those who come from it and may one day return to it.

Problems are to be expected in a large, complex undertaking of this sort. The summary report points to serious management shortcomings: virtual abdication of an elaborate performance-based disbursement scheme, failure of certain basic project components (communications, operations research, specialized technical assistance, logistics, and use of the private sector), and the inability to reduce the per acceptor cost of NGO community based distribution to levels competitive with public sector service delivery (POPTECH 2003: 16–17). Also noted was the high NGO dropout rate from the project (nearly 50 percent after the first three years of implementation), the failure to expand the coverage of community-based workers, and the inability to identify the level of family planning and reproductive health service provision among NGOs participating in the project (p. 16). Perhaps the unkindest cut of all was the inability to operate the project smoothly, free from the restrictive bureaucratic cultures of both the American and Indian governments. In short, although the summary report points to some accomplishments,[7] it is hard not to see the project overall as having failed to live up to expectations.

On reflection, however, the single greatest reason for the project's limited success, we would argue, was its reliance on imported ideas and institutions together with the lack of significant local input. USAID personnel in Washington and in New Delhi were the project's chief architects. Hardworking, of serious purpose, and experienced in the procedures and modalities of USAID, this group, even with the help of consultants, could not have been expected to make it safely through the bogs and pitfalls of a society that has become expert at bending the schemes of outsiders to its own interests. The specialized technical assistance supplied to the project by USAID's cooperating agencies often fit less like a tailored jacket than an oversized pullover.

We have gone into this amount of detail to show the downside of proceeding on the basis of policy nostrums. They can be seriously misleading, especially when they involve assumptions about operational modalities that turn out not to fit the local political and administrative culture.

USAID does not always fail to appreciate the limitations and opportunities of local culture and find effective ways to operate with respect to them. For example, in Peru a contraceptive-use and reproductive health project, operating in six regions of the country in cooperation with USAID, appears to have attained impressive traction in a relatively brief period for a cost of $20 million. The secret to the success of ReproSalud, as the project is called, seems to be that women were asked about their families' and their own health problems and participated in designing activities to address them (Rogow and Wood 2002). Although Rogow and Wood give major credit to the "mandate of Cairo," such attribution comes close to being a post hoc fallacy since the operative principle here appears to be finding a good fit to local conditions and encouraging real local participation, out of which emerges a strong sense of ownership. If specialized assistance is needed, it is obtained from an appropriate local source. Although presumably available to it, USAID did not deploy its cooperating agencies or allow them undue influence in the project's design or operation.

But here is the rub and the basic dilemma of all projects that attempt to elude government control. By its own admission, after six years of effort and "notwithstanding its remarkable achievements, ReproSalud does not have the authority or influence to improve the accessibility and quality of services on a large scale. Meeting donor interests in increased family planning and use of reproductive health services, therefore, lies beyond the project's control and ultimately depends upon parallel efforts by the Ministry of Health and local health care providers" (p. 389).

As we have seen repeatedly, project ideas based on imported notions of what should work or on ideological predilections can go badly astray. The innovations and the modes of implementation that were featured in the Uttar Pradesh project, unlike those in ReproSalud, enjoyed little indigenous design input. The designers in Washington and at the cooperating agencies, for the most part, had only a spotty knowledge of India or one of its least pliable states. Self-deception may also have flowed from the conviction that programmatic advance depended largely on reducing the role of government and relying primarily on the private sector and NGOs for solutions.

Decentralization of Reproductive Health Services

Cairo stressed the importance of promoting the decentralization of population and health programs. As advocated in the ICPD's Programme of Action, "governments should promote much greater community participation in reproductive health-care by decentralizing the management of public health programs and by forming partnerships in cooperation with local non-governmental organizations and private health care providers" (United Nations 1994: Paragraph 7.9)

The push to decentralize appears to be a global trend that reflects the priorities of the donor community. UNFPA's Office of Oversight and Evaluation accounts for decentralization as follows:

Decentralization has emerged as a result of a global trend to local autonomy and self-determination, and as a result of a trend to reduce reliance on centralized planning of economies and be more responsive to market forces as well as local needs and characteristics. Countries receiving international assistance have also been pressured by donors to improve the delivery of public services in terms of responsiveness, effectiveness and efficiency through decentralization. (UNFPA 2000: 2)

Health-sector decentralization strategies are often justified on the grounds of their potential to promote services that are more responsive to local needs, that allow for more effective program implementation and client or community-centered approaches, that encourage greater collaboration between public and private-sector providers, that reduce inequities between urban and rural services, and that stimulate greater community involvement and financing of health services. Unfortunately, there is a paucity of evidence that the wand of decentralization has been able to impart these alleged advantages.

A comprehensive summary of evidence from the 1990s concludes that central governments have often been unwilling to transfer sufficient responsibility (especially for planning local health systems) and resources to local governments or community organizations to make decentralization work (Hardee and Smith 2000: 3). There is also a substantial body of information that suggests that poorly implemented decentralization may frustrate governance and poverty-alleviation goals (Litvack, Ahmed, and Bird 1998; Prud'homme 1994) and may undermine the effectiveness of health service delivery (see, e.g., Bossert, Beauvais, and Bowser 2000; Collins and Green 1994; Gilson and Mills 1995, Kolehmainen-Aitken 1999; Zheng and Hillier 1995).

Three commonly cited factors that can limit the effectiveness of decentralization are the difficulty of implementing national policy objectives and enforcing program standards when local government officials and program managers have competing agendas, the inability to adequately fund and effectively manage financial resources at local levels, and the overloading of local facilities and staff with too many activities and competing responsibilities. Regional inequities can be exacerbated if local governments and community organizations do not secure central funding commensurate with their needs. Mayhew (2002), commenting on decentralization experience in several sub-Saharan African countries, notes that "if decentralization of decision-making and management powers occurs before the capacity at district level is actually in place . . . poor service implementation and human resource management may result" (p. 222). In addition, Hardee and Smith (2000: 5) argue that decentralization efforts can frustrate attention to women's health issues because local government officials are usually men.

In an assessment of decentralized reproductive health services in seven developing countries, UNFPA (2000) observes that it is difficult to judge the success of decentralization since there has been little consistency in how countries are proceeding with it. For example, in Indonesia, the Philippines and Nigeria, decentralization is characterized by the devolution of all health facilities, staff, and program responsibilities to local government entities. In Bolivia, Ghana, India, Mexico, and Vietnam, some administrative tasks have been "deconcentrated" to local officials, but central authorities are still largely responsible for policy formulation, the setting of program agendas, and budgets. The report concludes that "in many countries the decentralized structure is not yet mature, but rather is in a state of evolution" (p. 4).

According to the UNFPA study, efforts to decentralize reproductive health services in these seven countries have been mixed. Although each country's circumstances are unique, the authors identify several common barriers to successful decentralization. For example, the push to decentralize rural health services has often occurred too quickly, with the result that "decentralization has been unsettling and confusing for the dislocated personnel involved, and caused a certain amount of demoralization and a decrease in productivity" (p. 6). The allocation of resources to local administrative units is often inadequate, and there is insufficient capacity at the local level to implement national program agendas. As the UNFPA report notes, "decentralization of responsibilities has been overzealous and decentralized units are either too small or too under-resourced to take on their obligations, especially at the secondary level of the health system" (p. 5). Local capacity is frequently "characterized by insufficient staff, inadequate training, and poor administration as well as insufficient management systems and procedures" (p. 5). Another hazard is political instability in countries where successive governments have passed contradictory laws and regulations affecting the transfer of national programs to local officials, as for example, in Bolivia and Ghana. New management challenges, for both donors and host countries, are an inescapable aspect of decentralization. Prior to decentralization, donors usually work with just one central authority in developing reproductive health policies and programs. Having to interact with several subnational levels of bureaucracy vastly complicates this task. According to the UNFPA study, decentralized program formulation and implementation place greater demands on advocacy efforts and pose new challenges for ensuring the commitment and accountability of program staff and resources at local levels. They also place unaccustomed demands on local staff for the timely flow of resources to local officials and service providers, the collection of local-area project data, and coordination with donors (pp. 9–15). There is considerable evidence that decentralization substantially increases the workloads of UNFPA field offices in monitoring and evaluating project activities:

> Country offices have had to maintain a heavy schedule of field visits—sometimes covering great distances—to a large number of decentralized projects not only to maintain a close control of resource utilization, but also to resolve program and technical issues at the local level. Moreover, the increased number of projects has multiplied the number of review meetings the country offices have to manage. (p. 14)

For central authorities, decentralization does not necessarily relieve them of the responsibility of monitoring local activities since it is essential that they know what is going on. It is moot whether such monitoring is easier under decentralization than when programs are centrally administered. Matters may become so removed from central authority that problems uncovered locally may be difficult to rectify. A former UNFPA official told us of a China state family planning "boss" who complained that decentralization could lead to local abuses that central authorities could not correct once people at the local level had been given the authority and resources to run their own show.

It is still much too early to determine whether the push to decentralize reproductive health services will achieve the benefits that proponents hope for. In countries such as India and Indonesia, where comprehensive health-sector reform and decentralization have been attempted only recently, anecdotal information suggests that all may not be going well.

Writing about Indonesia's 1999 autonomy law, *The Economist* (2003b: 38–39) asserts that "devolution isn't working as planned." In an effort to strengthen community participation in development programs and forestall secessionist political agitation in several Outer Island provinces, the Indonesian government has begun devolving primary responsibility for many development programs to provincial and local district (*kabupaten*) government units. This heightened responsibility has coincided, however, with a marked reduction in resources for such sectors as education and health. The government now sends one-quarter of its central budget to provincial and *kabupaten* government units for the support of programs that were previously fully funded from Jakarta. A portion of the revenues generated from the exploitation of local natural resources (e.g., oil and forestry products) is also now being made available to local government officials. This newly devolved wealth is having unintended consequences, as is apparently on view in the Sumatran province of Riau. *The Economist* reports as follows:

> Signs of Riau's new riches are everywhere: shiny new four-wheel drives clog the roads, flashy shopping malls are springing up, and the city's main mosque is getting a facelift, complete with six new minarets. . . . But Riau is also a showcase of the many unexpected tensions the new system has brought on. The province's 15 regents (district heads) exercise their new administrative and financial clout so imperiously that locals refer to them as "little kings." Stories abound of reckless extravagance or outright corruption. . . . Tabrani Rab, a Riau native and member of the central government committee overseeing the devolution system, claims that the Riau government has spent 10 billion rupiah ($1.1 million) on an as yet invisible stadium, and another 37 billion rupiah on a phantom cultural centre. . . . The provincial government, meanwhile, is making controversial forays into the oil and airline business, to name a few. In other parts of the

country, regents have simply seized companies belonging to the central government, or imposed arbitrary new rules on businesses. (p. 38)

The Economist concludes (p. 38) that "fears of decentralization run amok are beginning to replace fears of Indonesia's disintegration." Advocates of health-sector decentralization in Indonesia are attempting to bypass both central Jakarta and provincial-level administrative control and work directly with district-level (*kabupaten*) officials in formulating policies, providing services, and evaluating and monitoring program performance. Responsibility for implementing health activities (including family planning and reproductive health) previously fell primarily to provincial officials from the Ministry of Health and the National Family Planning Coordinating Board (BKKBN). With less booty to divert for unintended purposes, one might hope that local health authorities would be less likely to stray into the paths of temptation. Perhaps so, but there is still plenty of opportunity for health-sector devolution to go off the rails.

Directly engaging *kabupaten* officials with little past experience in devolved self-government constitutes a radical departure from past practice. We question whether this strategy can prove effective throughout much of the country, especially when it is expected to unfold without the intensive donor-supplied technical assistance that is currently on offer to several decentralized pilot *kabupatens*. Will district officials give the same priority to family planning that had been a hallmark of Indonesian national health policy during the Suharto years? Will district officials be able to resist the temptation to invest in prestigious new hospital construction projects when what may really be needed are better-staffed and better-equipped community clinics? Will they, in a climate of pervasive, freebooting governance remain true to a higher calling?

India has traditionally had one of the most centralized health delivery systems in the developing world. Efforts to decentralize the provision of health services from the Indian Ministry of Health and Family Welfare in Delhi to individual states and districts have coincided with the push to abolish demographic targets and promote greater NGO involvement. In much of the country, decentralization does not appear to have progressed very far. While state and district-level planning boards have been widely established, decentralization still suffers from the lack of stakeholder participation in the planning process, the inadequacy of reliable local-area data for planning and evaluation, and a lack of clarity in the delegation of central authority to state and LGUs (Cross, Hardee, and Jewell 2000: 10–11).

The SIFPSA project in Uttar Pradesh has assisted in developing district action plans as a means of promoting decentralization, achieving greater "integration" of public and private service providers, and strengthening community involvement in reproductive health programs. These planning activities entail the identification of local programmatic needs, the specification of required human and infrastructure resources, and the collection of data needed to formulate and evaluate the implementation of district plans. This requires that *panchayat* (village council) officials be trained in the promotion of reproductive health services (pp. 17–21).

An additional concern is that India's health decentralization policies may have frustrated efforts to reform discredited program strategies from past decades. A recent article in the *International Hearld Tribune* (May 5, 2005) notes that coercive measures to reduce the birth rate, similar to those discussed before Indira Gandhi's Emergency of 1977, have reemerged. The State of Maharashtra, the country's wealthiest, has recently adopted a law requiring farmers with more than two children to pay a 50 percent surcharge on irrigated water. Across India other jurisdictions are taking up similarly brusque ideas. In some places, couples with too many children are now disqualified from holding local government posts. In Mumbai, hospitals will deliver two babies without charge but require payment for the third. The feeling that something needs to be done to curb population growth reflects the fact that since independence in 1947 the population of India has tripled to more than one billion and is still growing yearly by around 1.8 percent. There is, at the same time, a feeling of pride in some quarters that India, on its way to becoming the world's largest country, will enjoy greater stature on the world stage—provided, of course, that it can avoid being the world's largest poor country.

Although promising, there has been little evaluation of these efforts in the Uttar Pradesh districts backstopped by SIFPSA. Despite the unceasing clamor of decentralization advocates, who tend to represent the interests of donors and NGOs, it is still far from clear whether decentralization has significantly enhanced the accessibility and quality of reproductive health services in Uttar Pradesh or in any other state in India. Certainly worries that the primary effect of decentralization may be to undermine the implementation of centrally mandated standards, services, and financial resources have not been put to rest.

Evidence from the Philippines indicates that the decentralization of reproductive health services has not proven to be a clear step forward. Nearly ten years of experience with health-sector decentralization has not demonstrated much clear benefit, especially with regard to the provision of reproductive health services. A recent appraisal by Lakshminarayanan (2003: 96) concludes that decentralization has not enhanced the "efficiency, equity, and effectiveness" of the Philippine health system. The evidence presented suggests that the quality of clinical services, client referral mechanisms, investments in preventive health services, and the morale and remuneration of service providers have all degraded since the onset of health decentralization in 1991. In particular, family planning and other reproductive health services appear to have been compromised owing in part to the reluctance of local government officials to support reproductive health services. As Lakshminarayanan notes,

> when some local government units succumbed to local pressure and stopped providing contraceptive services, the centre was unable to compel them to do so, even though these had been identified as priority services under the Health Care Agreement . . . The national government should have defined a core package of reproductive health services to be made universally available and accessible, irrespective of whether the system was decentralized. The absence of such a nationally mandated package allowed local government to ignore reproductive health services if they chose to, exacerbating an already fragile situation. (pp. 99, 105)

Experience to date suggests that local governments in the Philippines prefer to invest in infrastructural projects rather than in social services. Quite often, local social service budget mandates have neither been followed nor enforced. Efforts to promote health insurance through local-government-unit matching grants (an approach championed by USAID) have also not been very successful. Since a significant proportion of the labor force is in the informal sector, health insurance premiums are often difficult to collect (as well as unaffordable). Moreover, the middle class balks at paying the health insurance costs of the poor. Compounding this problem is the fact that tax collections are notoriously incomplete in the Philippines, posing serious constraints in funding public-sector social services.

Another recent review of health-sector decentralization in the Philippines notes that national objectives in the areas of family planning and child health have not always received sufficient attention from Local Government Units (LGUs) (Chemonics 2002: 18). In addition, resources available to LGUs from the national budget were generally not sufficient to cover local costs for providing newly devolved reproductive health services (p. 23). The decentralization of health services may have made it more difficult to adhere to national standards of service accessibility and quality of care. For example, the review notes that local governments have adopted inconsistent and often inhibitory policies regarding contraceptive service delivery. Some have imposed minimum-age and minimum-parity requirements for sterilization clients. Acceptors of oral pills are sometimes required to return to clinics every month for additional supplies and checkups for side effects. Some local units do not allow BHWs to provide community-based distribution of contraceptives, and unmarried women can be denied access to contraception at clinics providing diagnosis and treatment for sexually transmitted diseases (p. 23).

The Select Committee on International Development (2003), Parliament of the United Kingdom, sounds a warning about decentralization and broader heath-sector reform efforts in its Eighth Report on International Development:

> Health sector reform in many developing countries has negatively affected the provision of sexual and reproductive health (SRH) services, particularly where reform has involved decentralization. This has often led to insufficient supplies of sexual and reproductive health

care commodities, the introduction of cost recovery and user fees and, in some cases, the exclusion of sexual and reproductive health services from local portfolios. (26, paragraph 51)

Our aim is not to make Cassandra-like pronouncements on the problems of decentralization. It is too early for that. But it is the better part of wisdom to recognize that, as with other imported program innovations we have discussed, they rarely come "ready to serve" and may, in some cases, result in serious programmatic indigestion if not properly prepared by cooks familiar with local tastes and ingredients. An important corollary is that donors should avoid being swept away by program fashions or ideologically inspired imperatives. While decentralization may be easier than "nation building," it nevertheless presents, on a smaller scale, similar perils. In any event, once a genie such as decentralization is out of the bottle, attempting to put it back, if that is deemed desirable, could be as messy as returning toothpaste to its tube.

CHAPTER SIX

AN OVERVIEW OF MAJOR DONOR ORGANIZATIONS CURRENTLY PROVIDING INTERNATIONAL POPULATION ASSISTANCE

Multilateral and bilateral organizations are the major channels for international population assistance. Nongovernmental organizations (NGOs), while often dependent on the resources of these organizations, may also receive funds directly from donor countries and from private philanthropic foundations. For example, an NGO such as the International Planned Parenthood Federation (IPPF) may, after covering its own administrative costs, serve as a pass-through to its affiliates for donor funds it has received. Embassies of foreign donor countries may sometimes provide funds to recipient-country NGOs, but most donors prefer to vet and channel requests through NGOs in their own countries. With the rising importance of private philanthropic foundations for international population assistance, expanded partnerships with NGOs appear to be in the offing. Another route for philanthropic funds is the United Nations Foundation, which provides an entrée for donors to population activities in the UN system.

The two major multilateral organizations providing resources for population programs are the United Nations Population Fund (UNFPA) and the World Bank, while the largest bilateral organizations (in terms of total disbursements) receive their support from the governments of the United States, the Netherlands, the United Kingdom, Japan, and Germany. In recent years major private philanthropies such as the Gates, Packard, Hewlett, and the UN Foundation have also provided significant support for international population and reproductive health programs. A brief review of the administrative and programmatic approaches employed by these major donor organizations is useful for charting the way forward.

United Nations Population Fund (UNFPA)

In 1967 a new agency—the UNFPA—became an administrative reality. It began life as a fund rather than as an operational agency. This mechanism was instituted in the hope of promoting population issues and channeling support for programs through some of the UN's key development agencies. A few years later UNFPA sprang into action under the direction of Rafael Salas.

Under the determined leadership of Dr. Nafis Sadik, who succeeded Salas as head of UNFPA in 1987, annual expenditures rose to around $300 million by the time of the 1994 International Conference on Population and Development (ICPD) in Cairo. Except for the World Health Organization (WHO) and the UN Secretariat, other UN specialized agencies now receive very little funding from UNFPA. A variety of expenditure channels, including national governments, NGOs, and UNFPA's own direct project expenditures, are currently its principal funding outlets. It operates in 150 countries, providing project support and technical assistance.

UNFPA relies principally on government contributions. In recent years pledges from donor governments have exceeded their actual contributions by a significant margin—something in the vicinity of 40 percent. While serious, such shortfalls are less of a problem than the sudden changes in funding levels that can disrupt programs and undermine partnerships and commitments. The United States is a prime offender in this regard.

Sinding's (1996) assessment of UNFPA, now almost eight years out of date but still on target, concludes that the organization suffers from tired blood in its senior staff as a result of the glacial rate of personnel changes in its New York headquarters, limited interchange of staff between the field and headquarters, and resistance to recruiting experienced professional staff from outside the agency. And it can still be criticized for having too many small projects and country programs that are inadequately funded and poorly coordinated.

Over the past decade, UNFPA's organizational structure has become more centralized, with its New York headquarters staff exerting more control over broad program strategies. Recently, there have also been hopeful signs of greater proactive engagement by its field missions, but these are not yet characteristic of the organization. In Pakistan, for example, UNFPA took a leading role several years ago in sending, along with other donors, an open letter to the government demanding that it reform certain of its practices that were effectively nullifying donor projects as well as projects of the government's own agencies. This represented an unprecedented break from UNFPA's usually reticent diplomatic behavior. Elsewhere, as for example in Bangladesh, UNFPA has been an active partner in the coordination of donor activities. In India, the agency has been willing, under strong leadership, to break the chains that have confined it to a government-to-government mode of operation by encouraging some of its staff to get out of its Lodi Estate offices for a firsthand look at programs in the field.

UNFPA has invested considerable staff time and financial resources in international conferences—the 1994 ICPD, the 1995 Beijing conference on the status of women, and the 1999 ICPD + 5 being the latest and most declamatory events in this series. It has also supported regional meetings and global advocacy efforts in the post-Cairo period. This has led to worries that these activities may have squeezed UNFPA's budgets for country programs. UNFPA has never provided a public accounting of the costs of its large international gatherings or the extent to which such ventures may have drained resources from its country programs.

Since Cairo, UNFPA has been very much in step with efforts to bring a feminist cast to its activities and put gender and women's empowerment at the center of everything it does. This can be seen in the organization's advocacy efforts to promote the status of women, "gender mainstreaming," and reproductive rights. The provision of family planning services appears to have been somewhat demoted in UNFPA's eyes—from a gleam to a glimmer. Nearly gone are efforts to strengthen demographic statistical capabilities through support to censuses, surveys, and vital statistics registration systems; support for country-level operations research in reproductive health; and assisting developing countries to anticipate and plan for the impact of population dynamics on long-term development outcomes.

It is unclear how effective UNFPA's technical support for the design, monitoring, and evaluation of projects has been in recent years. During the 1980s, technical backstopping for its projects was based mainly in New York (e.g., at the Department of Economic and Social Affairs, and the now-defunct Department of Technical Cooperation for Development). In the 1990s, these New York based operations, funded by but not directly under the purview of UNFPA, were replaced by regional country support teams (CSTs) based in Bangkok, Kathmandu, Amman, Harare, and Santiago. The teams functioned as fully integrated operational units within UNFPA.

Curiously, the role of UNFPA's CST offices has never been clearly articulated or made coherently operational. Initially, CST regional staff appeared to spend much of their time providing technical assistance in project implementation and evaluation. In more recent years, CST staffs have become increasingly active in country programs and the design of project activities, at times seeming to supplant UNFPA's country representatives in this regard. In addition, falling budgets and staff reductions have raised new concerns about the future viability of the CST mechanism.

CST staff positions were created to cover many of the new program areas identified in the ICPD Programme of Action. It became de rigueur to have technical advisers working on advocacy and gender issues in CST offices to complement more traditional areas. Owing to budgetary constraints, however, many key CST positions have been vacant over the past decade.

A recent attempt to reorganize the CST system does not appear to have been well managed. As part of this reorganization process, the number of professional positions has been substantially reduced. Informal observation suggests that UNFPA has recently come to place greater weight on advocacy skills in gender and reproductive rights than on technical proficiency in the population and health sciences (e.g., training and experience in public health and reproductive health care) when promoting existing staff and recruiting new personnel. In any event, there is currently a surprising underrepresentation of scientific and technical staff at UNFPA headquarters.

UNFPA's current financial difficulties are just one cause of concern about the future of the organization. Its programmatic orientation also appears increasingly unfocused, with a broad array of new agendas competing for too few resources. If UNFPA is to become a more effective presence (especially at the level of its country programs), it will have to set priorities more aggressively and be more diligent in defining its unique comparative advantage within the UN system. It might attain a greater sense of coordinated purpose by refocusing on priority needs in family planning (including contraceptive commodity support) and other reproductive health initiatives (e.g., the management of STDs, postabortion care, and the treatment of obstetric complications). With the millstone of ICPD around its neck and with declining resources, the degrees of freedom for new policy initiatives appear to be restricted.

To the extent that funding allows, UNFPA's earlier support for demographic data collection (e.g., censuses and surveys) and programmatic research should be reconstituted as part of a more focused agenda. Although the agency should rightly pursue certain advocacy activities in support of what it does and to explain why it exists, competing with the United Nations Development Fund for Women (UNIFEM) in becoming the UN's principal source of advocacy for women's social welfare, empowerment, and human rights issues may actually be compromising its own mission.

By far the largest policy wrangle for UNFPA involves the agency's role in China. In 1979–80 China adopted a population control policy that subjected couples of reproductive age to harsh measures to limit their childbearing to one child. Known as the one-child policy, it is credited by Chinese officials for averting more than 300 million births since its inception (Greenhalgh 2003: 163). Between 1949, when the communists took power in China, and the adoption of the one-child policy, China's birth rate and population growth rate declined by more than 50 percent and its fertility rate moved to within one-half birth of the replacement level of 2.1 births per woman. For most developing countries this would have been a source of considerable satisfaction. China was clearly on its way to achieving a modern demographic regime.

But for China this was not good enough. Even though the number of births in 1979 was the smallest in its modern history (baring the years of turmoil in the mid-1960s when Mao-Zedong's Red Guards roamed the land), population growth came to be regarded as the major threat to the country's modernization and to the recognition by major powers to which it felt entitled. Limiting population growth was seen as the route to achieving the "four modernizations"—of industry, agriculture, national defense, and science and technology— that formed the foundation of Chinese development policy.

Less Draconian measures promoting later childbirth, longer spacing between births, and smaller families were advocated in the early 1970s (p. 167), but the rise of Deng Xiaoping opened the way for stronger medicine. As Greenhalgh spells it out, the one-child family was devised out of an unquestioning adoption of models depicting interrelationships between population, capital, food, nonrenewable resources, and pollution developed by Meadows et al. (1972) for the Club of Rome. Applying these projections uncritically and simplistically, with variable fertility rates and other inputs remaining constant, yielded a set of demographic scenarios to various "optimum" conditions between 1980 and 2080. A path leading to a substantial reduction in population by 2080, which appeared to be the best to follow, was selected. It produced "optimal" results with respect to capital, food, nonrenewable resources, and pollution by the end of the period. It also entailed a substantial decline in the size of the Chinese population. The fertility rate that produced this result was an average of one child per family. From that point on it became a matter of sticking with crude scientism and imposing an iron will in execution.

The abuses and lack of humanity in this policy have been widely chronicled and justly condemned. Chinese officials insist that the program has been softened and made voluntary. Critics, especially such groups as the Population Research Institute, have been unrelenting in adducing anecdotal evidence to contradict these official claims. Delegations have been dispatched by the U.S. government, by UNFPA, and by Catholics for a Free Choice to review the status of China's program. By and large these groups have cleared the official program, as it now is attempting to operate, of the charges against it. They are even clearer in their conclusions that UNFPA has used its funds only in an attempt to promote voluntarism and provide alternatives to the harsher aspects of the one-child policy. Where, as in this case, the issue of "fungibility" is involved, closure is almost impossible to achieve. The position of the current U.S. administration is to withhold congressionally authorized funds, a relatively modest $34 million, from UNFPA. Though a small amount, it puts a significant dent in UNFPA's program resources.[1]

Before leaving the question of China and UNFPA, we should take notice of Robert Kaplan's (2000) point that "it is a misconception that China has gotten its population under control. Large-scale population movements are under way from inland China to coastal China and from villages to cities, leading to a crime surge like the one in Africa and to growing regional disparities and conflicts . . ." (p. 26). It would not violate UNFPA's mission to turn attention to this problem, and by so doing reduce contention over what it does in China. The prospects are good that China will continue with its birth-planning program, hopefully endeavoring to make it more humane in response to both external and internal criticism.

The United Nations Children's Fund (UNICEF)

The acronym no longer fits. The United Nations Children's Fund began its life as the United Nations International Children's Emergency Fund, or UNICEF. Since 1953 UNICEF has been a permanent agency in the UN's family of specialized agencies. Until the early 1980s, UNICEF concentrated on improving child health, nutrition, and such related matters as the provision of clean water and children's educational needs. Beginning in the 1980s, under the leadership of its executive director James P. Grant, UNICEF articulated a much-admired program of selected, "do-able" health interventions for the benefit of children, which addressed their major causes of mortality. It was widely hailed as a revolution in policy, one that aimed to cut global child mortality in half by the end of the twentieth century. To reduce infant mortality by half, Grant anticipated that it would be necessary to reach four–five hundred million children living in the developing world plus annual additions approximating one hundred million.

As with other UN declarations, such goals are largely for psychological uplift, maybe a bit of handkerchief dropping for interested donors, and a hortatory platform for subsequent regional and world conferences. UNICEF is not the only organization to engage in the practice. The famous slogan of the Alma-Ata conference of yesteryear, "Health for All by the Year 2000," one of the more ambitious overreaches, partakes of the same P. T. Barnum quality.

In the case of infant mortality, few countries in the developing world have come close to achieving Grant's expectations. Some countries have done well, for example Thailand, Egypt, Bangladesh, and the Philippines—countries that by the early 1980s had already begun a transition toward lower infant mortality. The UN Population Division, in its 2004 revision of global demographic conditions, estimated levels and trends in infant mortality rates (IMR) for the period from 1980–85 to 2000–05. For sub-Saharan Africa the IMR is thought to have declined by 19 percent; for South–Central Asia by 36 percent; and for Southeast Asia by 48 percent (United Nations Population Division 2004a). But enormous differentials remain. For example, IMRs for sub-Saharan Africa are nearly 140 percent higher than those in Southeast Asia.

Current evidence suggests that there may have been some slowdown in the rate of decline in infant and child mortality in recent years. In South Asia, diphtheria, pertussis, and tetanus immunization coverage appears stalled at less than 70 percent coverage; and in sub-Saharan Africa coverage declined from 60 percent in the early 1990s to 46 percent in 1999 (Bellagio Study Group on Child Survival 2003: 324). Immunization against bacterial meningitis among children under five (mainly haemophilus influenzae type B—Hib bacteria) is also quite low in many settings susceptible to meningococcal meningitis epidemics (principally in sub-Saharan Africa and South Asia). In some regions of Africa fewer than four in ten infants are breastfed exclusively for six months, partly because their mothers are unaware of the protective effects of the practice (Bryce et al. 2003). Recently polio has also reemerged in India, Indonesia, and Nigeria.

It is unclear how much of the improvement in infant mortality during previous decades can be attributed to UNICEF programs, however well conceived and executed they may have been. A large share of the credit must surely go to improved sanitation, safer water, and other environmental and public health measures. Nevertheless, Grant is entitled to enormous credit for devising intervention programs focused on the factors in child survival that were low-cost, feasible in execution, and amenable to improvement through increased knowledge and enlightened policy. The program that UNICEF adopted, introduced under the acronym GOBI, was strongly pragmatic. Growth monitoring (the G) would target those children in most critical need of help, primarily through better nutrition. The O stood for the administration of oral salts to children who were the victims of dangerous diarrheas, a treatment innovation that was receiving great attention. The same was true of breastfeeding (the B), which not only was safer than formula preparations made with unclean water but had other advantages, not the least of which was the contraceptive protection conferred by extending the period of a mother's lactational amenorrhea and thus increasing the interval to her next pregnancy. The I was for immunization against preventable causes of childhood mortality: TB, polio, diphtheria, whooping cough, and measles. Anecdotal evidence suggests that UNICEF data on completed immunizations were sometimes exaggerated, but in inception the effort was fully justified. This was the basic UNICEF program until new leadership was installed in 1995.

Since then UNICEF has undergone an expansion of its program that some say echoes the agenda enshrined in the ICPD Programme of Action and subsequently endorsed in Beijing. Douglas Sylva (2003), in a publication of the International Organizations Research Group sponsored by the Catholic Family and Human Rights Institute, flatly charges that pressure for UNICEF to "alter its traditional child survival programs and . . . add new and ever-more controversial programs" comes from "the ideology of radical feminism" (p. 1). He seeks to show that UNICEF is deeply implicated in supporting reproductive health activities and that it has broadened its mandate from child health to concern with the welfare of women over undefined stretches of the life course. He argues that this change in policy is a reflection of the feminist cast that has descended more generally on the policies of many specialized development agencies of the UN system.

It is a point–counterpoint situation. Sylva charges, UNICEF officials deny the charges. Sylva does not conceal the fact that he represents the Catholic Church's opposition to "artificial" birth control and abortion, but insists that UNICEF has abandoned its early position on child survival, and in the course of so doing risks losing the backing of the church for its programs. UNICEF stoutly denies that it has wandered from its commitment to child survival or that it has become involved with reproductive health. The debate rarely rises to a level much above that of a schoolyard argument over irreconcilables.

Less contaminated by philosophical subtext and free from polemics is a *Lancet* article by the Bellagio Study Group on Child Survival (2003) entitled "Knowledge into Action for Child Survival." Written by a committee from the World Bank, the Packard Foundation, WHO, and two developing-country research centers, the article documents the decline in resources for child-survival programs and the difficulty of tracking the flow of funds to that area.

Excluding those countries with high prevalence of HIV/AIDS, the authors conclude that "the main killers of children today are diarrhoea, pneumonia, and malaria, just as they were in 1980" (p. 324). But they complain that the current tendency toward disease-specific health initiatives, while expanding resources in general, results in "a set of fragmented delivery systems . . . that makes it hard to engage in cross-disease planning, implementation, and monitoring" (p. 325). In such a policy environment, it is maintained that efforts to serve the needs of children and their families will come up short.

Further distractions from efforts to address the needs of children and families are the sector-wide approaches (SWAPs) favored by the World Bank and other development agencies and, in particular, poverty-reduction strategies that link health and other development outcomes to macro-level policies and finances. In theory this policy orientation need not squeeze out concern for children, but the reality is that few poverty-reduction strategies have a strong health component (p. 325). The Bellagio group worries also that efforts to promote privatization compromise the long-term goals "of defining needs, generating resources, managing programmes and people, delivering cost-effective services, and gathering and using data to improve the effect of their efforts" (p. 327). This is admittedly a tall order, but perhaps more readily accomplished by a rational division of labor between the private and public sectors.

What all this means for UNICEF and reproductive health is a bit unclear. Essentially the Bellagio Study Group on Child Survival has issued a call for getting back to basics in the effort to improve child health, not necessarily to GOBI as originally projected but rather to an updated version with the same pragmatic aims and philosophy. It is certainly within UNICEF's basic mandate to expand into the area of maternal health. In doing so, however, it should hew closely to implementable strategies and measurable outcomes. If GOBI constitutes a policy revolution, the ICPD Programme of Action is a siren song tempting UNICEF's leadership onto the shoals of reproductive-rights advocacy. The Bellagio Study Group has stuffed its ears and lashed itself to the mast of epidemiologically guided action and mensuration. "Application of what we know," they say, "can reduce child mortality by two-thirds and achieve the ambitious millennium development goal" (p. 327).

Unlike Sylva's frontal assault on UNICEF leadership, the Bellagio Study Group merely observes that as "strong and unified leadership was the hallmark of the child survival revolution of the 1980s, [it must now] be re-established at international, national and subnational levels. At present no institution or individual is out in front pioneering responses to recognize failures and needs, influencing technical and political agendas, directing investments, and producing credible evidence that child mortality is decreasing as a result of specific actions" (p. 326).

The World Bank

The World Bank, another major multilateral organization that provides population assistance, is the largest lender for that purpose and as such claims the right in many developing countries to lead donor community dialogue with host governments. During the course of its work in development, the Bank has given increasing attention to population growth and health. In fact, it was the World Bank that requested Frank Notestein, then director of the Princeton Office of Population Research and later the president of the Population Council, to prepare an analysis of the population-development nexus. The result was the study by Coale and Hoover (1958), which at the time was one of the most influential contributions on the economic consequences of high fertility.

In the Bank's early days following World War II, it gave priority to the building of infrastructure—dams, roads, electricity systems, and buildings. In health, the Bank also embraced a "bricks and mortar" approach to enhancing physical infrastructure. Around the mid-1980s, however, loans for social and environmental projects (education, health, nutrition, water supply, and sanitation) began to receive greater emphasis. By 1969 there was growing realization at the Bank that its infrastructure projects, for dams and irrigation particularly, were encouraging the spread of certain water-borne diseases. In the interest of pulling the appropriate resources together, the Office of Environment and Health and the Population Project Department at the Bank were merged to form the Department of Health, Nutrition and Population.

Subsequently the Bank issued a health-sector policy paper laying out the mission of the new department (Preker, Feachem, and De Ferranti 1997). After expressing misgivings about the lack of political will in developing-country governments to institute and carry through basic health policy reforms, uncertainty about the feasibility of low-cost health care, and questions concerning the Bank's proper role vis-à-vis the WHO, the paper went on to advise against direct lending for health infrastructure and advanced curative care. Rather, it espoused primary health care at the community level as a more efficient course to follow. In the background was the worry that direct lending for health might imply a shift in emphasis away from family planning and population goals, then dominant priorities among international donors.

At about that time, the Bank had in hand a commissioned commentary by Bernard Berelson, one of a parade of reviewers over the years, in which he recommended "overt lending" for health in programs that would include family planning. Insistence on demographic targets as criteria for lending, Berelson argued, "resulted in lost opportunities for broad based health programs with likely demographic consequences" (Stout et al. 1997: 39)—a view out of step with his later demonization as a demographically driven family planning zealot. In any event, from then on the Bank was enlisted in the business of service delivery to which it became a major contributor.

The recognition that delivering population and health services was a proper and significant concern of the Bank was but a momentary policy-resting place. By 1980 the Bank had overcome its objections to direct support for health. It approved lending for health infrastructure at the local level, training for community health workers, strengthening logistic systems, and the supply of essential drugs. It also gave the nod to the provision of maternal and child health services, disease control, and improved family planning. Taken together these were seen as "essential elements" for the alleviation of poverty. The Bank conceded that the pursuit of these basic ingredients would offer a forum for the "discussion of population issues and support for family planning services delivered through the health care system" (p. 39).

Since then the World Bank has made significant amendments to its policy position. The 1984 *World Development Report*, an annual Bank publication, presented evidence to demonstrate that public policy can and has played a role in reducing fertility, presumably by providing good family planning services (World Bank 1984).[2] Advancing into ground that in theory could be dangerous, the report held that governments should take their responsibility as custodians of society seriously, to narrow the gap between private and social perceptions of appropriate family size.

In the Bank's continual search for a more effective policy posture, 1987 was a pivotal year. It was also a time of generally sluggish economic growth accompanied by mounting government deficits. So it should not be surprising that a Bank policy study conducted in that year on the topic of financing health services in developing countries stressed the problem of funding the recurring costs of health programs (World Bank 1987). It proposed that user fees for drugs and curative care and premiums for health insurance might be considered as ways of mobilizing resources. It also recommended more effective use of nongovernmental resources and the decentralization of planning, budgeting, and purchasing. The study left it at that, offering little guidance on how these ambitious policy innovations were to be achieved in specific situations.

At about that time, the Bank embarked on a reorganization that gave greater control over project lending to its country departments. As a consequence, a number of the Bank's specialists in population and health were reassigned to country program offices, where interest in population and health issues would depend on how forcefully the case was made for them in country reports.

Today "soft" projects focusing on meeting social and environmental objectives make up a much larger part of the Bank's lending portfolio than in the past. In some years lending for these sectors has equaled or surpassed support for more capital-intensive infrastructure projects in areas such as electric power, oil and gas, industry, telecommunications, and transportation (Stevenson 1997).

The Bank continues to provide substantial loans for population and reproductive health activities in many developing countries. However, it is not clear what priority such efforts currently have within the Bank. There is still a senior technical adviser in population and reproductive health (a holdover from the Bank's earlier functional mode of organization), but the position is advisory and not geared to the Bank's day-to-day operations.

In 2000 the Department of Health, Nutrition and Population released a lengthy document entitled "Population and the World Bank: Adapting to Change." Its purpose was to describe the Bank's current activities and future priorities in health, population, and nutrition. The document's rendering of unfinished business amounted to a rousing endorsement of the ICPD agenda (World Bank 2000: 6–13). However, the report carried a disclaimer by the Bank's senior management with respect to the views expressed in it.

Population and health activities remain the province of the Department of Health, Nutrition and Population. The published goals and objectives for the Bank's new Department of Gender, a natural ally one might suppose, make little mention of family planning or reproductive health (World Bank 2002). Instead, they place emphasis on broader empowerment agendas such as women's education, employment, access to microcredit, and human rights—all worthy in their own right. But amidst all the talk of program synergies, one might expect greater attention to women's health and child survival in an agenda meant to address the priority interests of women. At present the Bank is giving much emphasis to SWAps that address health-sector reform, poverty alleviation, and the attainment of Millennium Development Goals. The rapid expansion of funding and the redeployment of professional staff to combat the HIV/AIDS epidemic appear to have diminished the visibility of reproductive health as a program priority. An assessment of World Bank assistance by the Global Health Council (2004) concludes that the Bank's rhetoric in support of reproductive health has not been matched by the commitment of program resources. The report notes that the World Bank's share of international population assistance has fallen from 25 percent in 1994 to just 10 percent in 2002 (p. 43). In addition, International Bank Association (IDA) credits for population and reproductive health programs have fallen to their lowest level since 1997.

On balance, the Bank's policy evolution in population and health has contributed to collective thinking on the interconnections of development goals and the problems of project design and execution. While not without its critics (see ACHR 1996), the work undertaken by the Bank in the early 1990s on the cost-effectiveness of competing health delivery strategies through the development of the DALY (disability adjusted life years) methodology, which measures the efficiency of competing health investments, comes to mind in this respect. However, there also appears to have been declining interest in relationships between population growth and development outcomes at the Bank in recent years. The Global Health Council recently noted that "few Bank documents from the past decade pay heed to stabilizing population growth—whether in relation to environment, urbanization, expansion of social sector infrastructure and services or poverty reduction" (Global Health Council 2004: 43).

It is not that the Bank has learned little from its efforts in the population and health areas. It has learned much and that knowledge has nurtured thinking about policy. However, the Bank's recognized problems in health programming are still numerous. Project designs are often too complex and thus difficult to evaluate. There is often inadequate supervision at the field level, especially for projects directed toward institutional reform. Resident missions typically lack appropriate sector specialists. Often there is poor implementation of projects, especially those aimed at capacity building and institutional development. In addition, monitoring and evaluation capacity within the Bank's health sector is weak. As noted by the Global Health Council "an ability to demonstrate effectiveness of its investments through sound monitoring and evaluation has not been a core strength of Bank projects" (p. 38).

United States Agency for International Development (USAID)

The United States Agency for International Development (USAID) is the leading U.S. agency for administering humanitarian and economic assistance to about 160 countries. The USAID administrator reports to the secretary of state and, in theory at least, receives overall foreign policy guidance from that department. Its foreign assistance programs operate from its offices in Washington, D.C., and from missions and offices around the world (U.S. General Accounting Office 2003: 4).

Despite stormy political seas in Washington over the past decade, USAID continues to be the single largest bilateral donor for population and reproductive health activities, eclipsing even the World Bank and other large multilateral organizations. It directs its population assistance to countries that are eligible to receive U.S. foreign assistance. The bulk of U.S. population assistance goes to Bangladesh, Egypt, India, Jordan, and the Philippines. The agency tends not to provide assistance to middle-income developing countries such as Malaysia and Thailand or to smaller developing countries (primarily in Africa) that do not have operational USAID missions.

USAID's Global Bureau for Health coordinates all population and reproductive health assistance. Three substantive offices fall under the Global Bureau for Health—the Office of Population and Reproductive Health, the Office of HIV/AIDS, and the Office of Infectious Disease and Nutrition. In recent years, funding for the Offices of Infectious Disease and Nutrition and HIV/AIDS has risen relative to the Office of Population and Reproductive Health, but annual funding levels for population assistance for the three years prior to 2003 remained roughly constant at around $450 million. USAID continues to provide substantial support for family planning services, in particular funding for the procurement of contraceptives. Within the Office of Population and Reproductive Health, budget allocations for family planning services have declined in relation to support for other reproductive health initiatives (e.g., the diagnosis and treatment of sexually transmitted diseases and postabortion care).

Under directives handed down from the Bush administration, USAID's programs in population and reproductive health had to adhere to the limitations imposed by the Mexico City policy and its infamous gag rule as well as the so-called ABC policy. Much of this prescription was so obviously out of touch with behavioral reality that it amounts to abnegation of sensible policies that experience suggests would be effective and widely accepted.

There is growing concern that USAID may be losing its autonomy vis-à-vis other federal agencies, particularly the Department of State. Recent reports suggest that U.S. embassy staff have increasingly been advising USAID field missions on which projects and activities to fund and which organizations to support. This practice may disrupt USAID's ability to address agency goals, especially if political appointees assigned to U.S. embassies are allowed to exert decisive pressure on USAID program decisions and contracting mechanisms—for example, by insisting that major financial commitments be made to faith-based organizations. The awarding by USAID/Ghana of a major reproductive health contract to Catholic Relief Services, apparently in response to the intervention of senior embassy staff, is a case in point. In any event, the traditional firewall that has existed between USAID and the State Department over past decades seems to be eroding, and one can anticipate much closer alignments between U.S. foreign policy and foreign assistance if current trends continue.

Despite USAID's large financial outlays for population and reproductive health programs, there are growing concerns about how well this funding is being used and how much of it is actually reaching intended recipients. Over the past decade, USAID has acquired an unenviable reputation within the donor community for excessive internal bureaucratic process and inefficient delivery of project services. One sometimes hears comments to the effect that USAID has gone from being a "can-do" organization in its more exuberant and idealistic youth, especially in the population assistance arena, to a "can't do" operation that appears increasingly hamstrung by internal rules, regulations, legalisms, and political interference. Others have noted that USAID has lost much of its technical capacity and is now little more than a passthrough contracting operation increasingly out-of-touch with field realities, program implementation, and the activities of other donors. Despite several attempts to reengineer the agency in recent decades, there remains considerable doubt whether its current bureaucratic culture is well suited to interact productively with institutions in the developing world.

USAID contracts for products and services in a variety of specialized areas. In 2000, for example, the Office of Population and Reproductive Health contracted for technical services pertaining to contraceptive procurement, the provision of training for service providers and program managers, the expansion of new reproductive health services, policy research, and program evaluation. Cooperating agencies, USAID's primary vehicle for the delivery of foreign assistance, as insiders in the process of securing contracts, are adept at spotting and responding to such opportunities. However, a certain amount of uncertainty exists in the outcome of contract bidding, which the cooperating agencies attempt to minimize by dressing up their personnel rosters and sometimes engaging in transient mergers among themselves.

The question of how much USAID population assistance is diverted before it reaches its intended beneficiaries is not easy to quantify. Significant resources flow directly to cooperating agencies from core budgets in Washington. USAID also supports population and reproductive health activities through bilateral project support. There can be considerable backflow of bilateral funds from USAID country missions to USAID/Washington (as field support allocations) to be made available for existing central contracts or cooperative agreements. These disbursement mechanisms work to the benefit of the cooperating agencies, lessen management loads within missions, and help expedite the movement of funds that are often stymied in budgetary gridlock. But for the ultimate recipients, it is a mysterious shadow play. They must wonder why funds for activities that have been agreed to cannot be transferred to them in a more straightforward fashion.

The cooperating agencies that USAID has nurtured over the past 30 years provide nearly all of the technical support for its population and health programs. USAID rarely provides resources or takes requests for technical support from institutions outside this network, in contrast to the 1960s, when university-based professionals were far more likely to be involved in foreign assistance programs. Today academics may occasionally be involved as consultants, although the norms of academic and government cultures can be irritatingly out of harmony.

While cooperating agencies that "partner" with the Office of Population and Reproductive Health are remarkably responsive to USAID's requests for programmatic assistance, they do not necessarily represent the most appropriate expertise that might be available from institutions in the United States. They are at the ready and familiar with USAID's ways. Compared with universities, cooperating agencies are better organized and conditioned to meet agency requirements with a minimal amount of conflict over the scheduling of activities and the ends to be served. They also provide USAID with some of the "surge capacity" that the agency considers important in its workforce planning.[3]

USAID has a long history of decentralizing program design, contracting, and responsibilities for project management to field missions that are seen as being "closer" to the problems. This strategy is becoming more difficult to sustain. USAID's field missions now tend to be understaffed (especially in terms of relevant technical expertise) and preoccupied with internal managerial tasks.

Over the past decade USAID's workforce has been significantly downsized through across-the-board rather than targeted reductions. The result has been a 37 percent decline between 1992 and 2002 in the number of what are called "direct hires," regular full-time government employees who are responsible for program design and management (U.S. General Accounting Office 2003: 3). This has resulted in a growing reliance on personal service contractors (PSCs),[4] program fellows placed in field missions through the auspices of cooperating agencies (e.g., the Center for Educational Development and Population Affairs, or CEDPA, and the Population Leadership Program at the Public Health Institute), and foreign-service national (FSN) staff in many USAID field missions. In particular, the growing influence of cooperating-agency fellows and foreign-service nationals in the awarding of contracts is an especially troubling trend as it opens the door ever wider to potential conflicts of interest and violations of federal procurement regulations. Staff shortages in overseas missions also appear to have encouraged the practice of returning bilateral funds from field missions back to centrally funded projects administered from Washington. The U.S. General Accounting Office (2003) report commented on USAID's current human resource crisis as follows:

> As a result of the decreases in U.S. direct-hire Foreign Service staff levels, increasing program demands, and a mostly ad hoc approach to workforce planning, USAID now faces several human capacity vulnerabilities. For example, attrition of its more experienced foreign service officers, difficulty in filling overseas positions, and limited opportunities for training and mentoring have sometimes led to (1) the deployment of direct-hire staff who lack essential skills and experience and (2) the reliance on contractors to perform most overseas functions. In addition, USAID lacks a "surge capacity" to enable it to respond quickly to emerging crises and changing strategic priorities. As a result, according to USAID officials and a recent overseas staffing assessment, the agency is finding it increasingly difficult to manage the delivery of foreign assistance. (p. 3)

In addition to staffing shortfalls, there are concerns that direct-hire employees based overseas in USAID field missions do not always use their time to good effect. Some foreign-based USAID direct hires rarely interact with their host-country counterparts or venture far from their desks (and internal management loads) to interact with the field activities under their purview. It is reasonable to wonder whether the bureaucratic routines that entrap USAID mission staff might not be carried out just as well in Washington, and at considerably less cost to the U.S. taxpayer.

A less obvious way to reduce the administrative burden on understaffed and overworked field staff is to concentrate planning and administration in large "flagship" consortium projects that weld together several cooperating agencies. To the extent that this means less reliance on individual agencies, it has the potential to dilute the degree of specialization brought to bear on particular components of USAID's population and health portfolio. Internal capacities within individual cooperating agencies are becoming more heterogeneous with agencies now routinely bidding on a wide range of contractual offerings in the belief that they can undertake practically any task for which there is funding.

While this broadened focus may be helpful in securing resources for large bilateral contracts, one fears that it may result in a loss of institutional comparative advantage and technical specialization previously on offer. Ross and Stover (2003) make essentially the same point, observing that "the shift of some central funding to field support . . . has enlarged the compass of the Mission priorities and has made for greater variation in what CAs [cooperating agencies] can do, since Missions differ considerably in the objectives and in their willingness to fund centrally conceived programs. For individual CAs, this has caused greater heterogeneity in what they do" (p. 18). They point out (p. 18) that the prerequisite in some contracts requiring cooperating agencies to fund part of the total cost from non-U.S. government sources (cost-sharing provisions) can be another source of heterogeneity.

USAID invigilates the work of its contractors by requiring periodic monitoring and evaluation of project activities. This involves examining the extent to which various benchmarks and performance indicators have been met and conducting qualitative field assessments and quantitative surveys that are now standard components of many USAID projects. These exercises entail considerable investments of time and resources and have as much to do with fulfilling USAID's internal administrative reporting requirements as they do with project monitoring and evaluation. They often appear to exceed actual need.

An example of excessively invasive donor management can be seen in efforts to institute performance-based disbursement procedures, whereby donor financial outlays are tied to the achievement of short-term project benchmarks. Current practice suggests that performance-based disbursement has not proven expeditious as a project management tool or as a mechanism for promoting more productive collaboration between donor and host-country institutions.

A ten year assessment of the Innovations in Family Planning Services (IFPS) project in India concluded that performance-based disbursement, by tying expenditure to an "all or nothing formula" that required the tracking of 344 benchmarks, had actually frustrated the implementation of the project. The assessment noted that benchmarks were "too numerous, too detailed, and too intrusive," resulting in "corrosive effects on learning and transparency" and confused "evaluative," "fiduciary," and "partnership roles of various stakeholders," making it hard "to make midcourse corrections based on experience" (POPTECH 2003: 20–21). In the event, the IFPS project also found it impossible to track all 344 benchmarks in a timely and reliable manner. The assessment was particularly concerned that performance-based disbursement had stifled the ability of the project to innovate in the field, its main objective. Whereas performance-based disbursement may help push an implementation-focused project forward, it is not attuned to the nuances of a more deliberate, risk-taking innovation strategy (p. 21).

This assessment also noted that performance-based disbursement frustrated the twin goals of effective project management and financial accountability:

> Performance-based disbursement . . . is not able to adequately track expenditures through the use of generally accepted accounting principles. The complexity of the process mitigates the positive impact of the incentive and accountability benefits of the system because payments are not disbursed as the benchmarks are accomplished but are instead lumped into one disbursement from the Government of India each year. (p. 21)

In addition, performance-based disbursement required the government of India to prepay (forward-fund) budgets for specific activities under the IFPS project. Only once benchmarks were achieved could the government be reimbursed for its initial outlays, and this could take up to one year. This requirement did nothing to strengthen coherent budgeting within the public sector.

Another USAID flagship project entitled "Basic Support for Institutionalizing Child Survival (BASICS II)" was intended to improve infant and child health in selected countries. This $79 million procurement involved nine consortium partners. A recent evaluation of the project indicates that BASICS II ran aground on the rocks of results management (Pielemeier et al. 2003). The evaluation found that considerable staff time and resources had been invested in data-collection efforts (including baseline and endline surveys) to track performance indicators required for annual performance reviews and the awarding of incentive payments to contractors. These requirements posed serious problems for the project and contributed to its poor implementation record during the first three years of operation. The project had four directors in its first twenty-seven months of operation and an unusually high turnover of technical staff. With respect to its performance-based contract and results indicators, the evaluation states:

> Some of the indicators are vague and the targets embedded in them often appear to be arbitrary, unrealistic, and/or meaningless. They promote vertical rather than integrated child survival approaches and seem to be inflexible . . . Technical staff, in particular, had a very difficult time switching from an activities orientation to a results orientation. Quite a few technical staff left the project as a result . . . The performance contract probably increased the contentiousness (between USAID and BASICS II staff) of adjusting program objectives. (pp. 47–59)

It was also difficult to attribute BASICS II efforts to the achievement of specific indicators because funding and field activities were often leveraged across various organizations and multiple donors.

The evaluation notes that "frustration built within the project as technical officers preferred to move forward with a series of technical activities while project management sought to clearly delineate the sequence of activities that would lead to results" (p. 46). At the country level, this led to planning that was "complex, not useful, continual, and frustrating" (p. 46). While the evaluation found evidence of recent improvements in the project's efforts to manage for results and adhere to the strictures of annual performance reviews, it had to admit that BASICS II was still having trouble relating activities to results.

In summary, although difficulties experienced in two large projects can be no more than exemplary, one must conclude that USAID's recent experience with results frameworks and performance-based disbursement procedures has not been a roaring success. Relying on increasingly complex and intrusive project management systems to implement field activities may not offer a sensible way forward. Working to design and implement management systems based on greater simplicity and user-friendliness (both for donors and host-country institutions) offers more promise.

The Millennium Challenge Account (MCA)

An overview of U.S. bilateral foreign aid must mention the latest effort to get foreign assistance "right." The Millennium Challenge Account (MCA), a proposed venture of the Bush administration, was outlined in March 2002 by President Bush at a meeting of the Inter-American Development Bank. The MCA was introduced in order to roughly double the level of American foreign assistance and channel these additional resources to developing countries that stood the best chance of making good use of them. The increase was not, however, meant to be just a new pool of international aid for achieving the UN's Millennium Development Goals, but rather an addition to the foreign assistance apparatus of the U.S. government.

An analysis by InterAction, an alliance of some 160 international and humanitarian NGOs, of the MCA and its executing agency, the Millennium Challenge Corporation (MCC), expresses the concern that "the creation of new entities along side a diminished—but otherwise unreformed—USAID, is leading to increased fragmentation of resources and responsibilities, duplication within the Administration, confusion externally about who is in charge, and a loss of coherence in the field as multiple agencies pursue similar goals with little coordination" (InterAction 2003: 3). There has been little transparency in this important policy maneuver and an apparent lack of effort to learn from USAID's long experience in foreign assistance. It appears that the "existing mechanisms and authorities of the U.S. Agency for International Development would not be used in this new endeavor, a decision in keeping with other Presidential initiatives on HIV/AIDS and the Middle East Partnership" (p. 3).[5]

The U.S. Senate and the House have held hearings on the many complex issues involved in creating the MCC. Congress wants to know how the MCC will relate to other development agencies such as USAID; by what criteria will the beneficiary countries be selected; what level of corruption will be tolerated in those countries in deciding whether to work in them; what types of programs will the MCC support; to what extent will it involve recipient countries in designing and implementing them; who will oversee their operations; and how will results be measured? Finally, as this list of questions goes, but uppermost in the minds of those who must provide the funding, how much money will it cost and over what period? All of these questions, and others, are unresolved as of this writing, although the air is filled with speculation and cautionary advice.

Writing on the important question of which countries would be eligible to receive funding from the MCC, Carol Lancaster (2002), a former deputy administrator for international development at USAID, has expressed fears that "this exercise could easily become one of those lengthy, contentious, convoluted bureaucratic morasses . . . that end up so complicated that they are unworkable both technically and politically and embarrass all involved" (p. 7). She cautions that the new organization must run its own show and be able to say no to multiple political pressures or "it will lose control of its money much the way USAID has, and will become little more than a collection of special interests" (p. 7). Thus far her comments appear prescient but, to fall back on the device of journalists when asked to peer ahead into an opaque future, only time will tell. Given the present administration's predilection for dangling initiatives and draining public resources, this would seem to be the only reasonable answer.

Besides questions of organization and function, there are matters of strategy to consider. For example, will the MCC allocate funds in small projects (the foundation approach) or in large blocks to governments? What will be the relative influence of the departments of state and defense in its operation? Will its portfolio consist of MCA-generated activities or projects transferred from existing agencies such as USAID? Inasmuch as the MCC board could be made up of cabinet officers, this would seem to favor the latter approach, although the disadvantages of dispersed responsibility are well recognized.

Brian Atwood (2002), the former administrator of USAID, has expressed other concerns about the creation of the MCA:

> I hope sincerely that this program is helpful but I have some serious concerns. I worry that the reform standards that govern the selection process will come across as paternalistic and that these conditions will increase resentment and achieve little new reform. I worry that a small corporation will be incapable of expending such large sums in an effective way. I worry that MCA funds will go to only the countries that have achieved significant development progress. Meanwhile, the Agency for International Development will be relegated to spending its development assistance on the more difficult countries where results will be more difficult to achieve. (p. 1)

Even if the MCC manages to avoid the fragmentation of its efforts that implementation through existing agencies might produce, and even if it can achieve a country focus consistent with its global goals, questions remain about the fate of bypassed agencies and, more fundamentally, whether the time is right for launching a new foreign aid agency rather than fixing existing ones, which are, most assuredly, candidates for reform.

Clemens and Radelet (2003) also raise questions about absorptive capacity within recipient countries, the amount of time the U.S. government "should be prepared to continue to fund MCA countries, and how recipient countries might exit from MCA funding over time—presumably due to success or failure" (p. 17). They discourage belief in "a brief, big-bang Marshall Plan for developing countries in which the MCA provides a large amount of funding for a short period of time in hopes of igniting rapid development [which is] probably wishful thinking" (p. 17).

In some ways the MCA is already having an effect on population assistance operations. Apparently stung by criticisms of its manpower planning by the General Accounting Office, USAID administrator Andrew Natsios established a workforce group to develop an overseas allocation "template" to rationalize staffing deployments of USAID direct-hire employees. The workforce group identified 20 variables they considered relevant to the deployment of direct hires. The key variable was program size in dollar terms—possibly a backward-looking consideration that could lock in past policy and program failures. The ranking of countries according to their allotment of direct hires would also be based on the Millennium Challenge Account (MCA) eligibility criteria (good governance, investing in social development, and promoting economic freedom). This is a truly revolutionary notion that may compromise USAID's ability to work in countries where it is most needed.

The MCA/MCC premise that foreign assistance money has the best chance of being used effectively in countries with enlightened governance has strong appeal. Natsios even believes that some countries may decide to clean up their acts in order to qualify for MCA funds (Gedda 2004: 1). It seems likely, however, that this view of governance fails to appreciate how varied and deeply rooted are the political, economic, and social practices that, synoptically, define the quality of governance. And that is likely to be MCAs' greatest vulnerability.

There is also concern that countries selected by the MCC to receive MCA funding may not be those in greatest need of assistance. Sixteen countries were initially selected to receive MCA support; Armenia, Benin, Bolivia, Cape Verde, Georgia, Ghana, Honduras, Lesotho, Madagascar, Mali, Mongolia, Mozambique, Nicaragua, Senegal, Sri Lanka, and Vanuatu. While these countries are no doubt deserving of assistance, it is hard to see how the United States could stake a claim to world leadership in international development by confining itself to this subset of countries while ignoring the many larger, more significant ones on the cusp of chaos.

The fears and reservations of Lancaster, Atwood, and others may not be misplaced. Since the MCC was established in 2002 with the goal of identifying countries that would be eligible for assistance in combating poverty, hunger, disease, illiteracy, environmental degradation, and discrimination against women, it has managed to provide funding to only two countries—Madagascar and Honduras. Two more—Nicaragua and Cape Verde—are currently finalizing funding proposals. Given the extent and urgency of global poverty, the MCC obviously cannot be credited as a bold and effective program just yet.

It is not that there are not many countries that could qualify for assistance even under the restrictive criteria for eligibility established by the MCC and could put it to good use. In an editorial commenting on the unimpressive performance of the Corporation and its odd selection of programs to be funded in the few countries in which it is now working, the *New York Times* (A Timely Departure, June 19, 2005) calls for a fresh start with less time spent "in assembling a staff of neophytes who narrowly defined strategies for growth to fit their ideological bent" (p. 11). In Madagascar, a country "where many villages do not have running water, clinics, and schools," the $108 million allocated by the MCC is supporting "land titling, bank reforms, and agribusiness centers"—all worthwhile, but eccentrically wide of the mark judged by current priorities.

Other Bilateral Donors

In 2006, the five largest bilateral contributors to international population and reproductive health programs were the United States, the United Kingdom, the Netherlands, the European Union, and Japan (UNFPA 2008). However, a strikingly different ranking is derived when population assistance is measured as a percentage of gross national income. In this accounting, Norway, Sweden, and the Netherlands were the three most generous contributors. The United States ranked ninth and Japan fifteenth in 2006, mediocre showings that tend to undermine claims to leadership in the field. While many donor countries have increased their population assistance between 1998 and 2006, this increase has been largely for HIV/AIDS rather than for family planning and other reproductive health activities.

Much of the population funding provided by European donors, Canada and Japan is channeled through multilateral agencies such as UNFPA. The Netherlands, Japan, Norway and Sweden have been UNFPA's most generous supporters in recent years. Sweden and Norway once maintained large bilateral population programs, but their support is now committed largely through multilateral organizations. Besides the United States, countries that still have prominent bilateral programs in reproductive health are the United Kingdom, Germany, and Japan.

Bilateral government contributions comprise the major source of funding for the IPPF, the largest NGO supporting family planning and reproductive health services in the developing world. Unfortunately, IPPF funding has deteriorated badly, due largely to the cutoff of American support in 2002. To make matters worse, other major contributors, such as Japan and Denmark, have been reducing their support in recent years (IPPF 2003: 19).

Many bilateral development programs have embraced the attainment of the UN's Millennium Development Goals and new poverty-reduction strategies championed by the World Bank. These are incorporated into poverty-reduction strategy papers or plans. The mechanisms for reducing poverty are still largely untested, but a preliminary assessment of health-sector needs in a sample of poverty-reduction strategy papers concludes that assistance agencies often pay considerable attention to setting goals and targets, but offer little analysis of how health conditions can be financed and organized to best serve the poor (Dodd and Hinshelwood, n.d.).

In addition, with the notable exceptions of the United States and Japan, many countries are now committing sizable portions of their overseas development assistance to SWAps that encourage "reform" of health services. These funding mechanisms generally channel assistance to governments rather than NGOs (their civil society partners) and attempt to address a wide array of system-wide health issues. The International Development Committee of the British House of Commons (2003) commented on this change of direction in Britain's development assistance by noting that "with the introduction of the MDGs [Millennium Development Goals], DFID [Department for International Development] has increasingly shifted away from its historical support for bilateral programs and toward supporting SWAps, providing general budget support and contributing to multilateral programs" (p. 26).

As noted previously, it is not clear what priority governments will give to population and reproductive health assistance within these new assistance frameworks. To date, there has been disturbingly little contact between health-sector reformers and reproductive health advocates and service providers in many developing countries. For example, in Uganda, Mayhew (2002) notes that "weak leadership and lack of involvement of sexual and reproductive health advocates in the design of the SWAp led to sexual and reproductive health being left out of the SWAp targets and resource allocations altogether . . . (p. 222).

Of particular concern is the fate of reproductive health within the Millennium Development Goals and the possibility that funding for HIV/AIDS may swamp other reproductive health needs. The fact that some bilateral agencies (e.g., DFID and the Swedish International Development Agency) are now lumping their HIV/AIDS and reproductive health funding together in their annual budget reporting to the Netherlands Interdisciplinary Demographic Institute will make it more difficult to monitor trends in individual components of population assistance. The future role of NGOs and the need to balance recipient countries' ownership of programs with donor countries' policies and priorities are other emerging worries within the newly ascendant world of Millennium Development Goals, poverty-reduction strategy papers, and SWAps. (A detailed review of bilateral population assistance programs can be found in Ethelston et al. 2004.)

The Reemergence of Private Philanthropy

In the 1950s and 1960s, several East Coast foundations played pivotal roles in calling attention to population issues, funding biomedical research on contraception and reproductive physiology, and supporting early family planning service provision efforts. The Rockefeller and Ford Foundations were the most prominent of these organizations, but the Mellon Foundation plus several other smaller philanthropies also provided early support to population activities.

By the 1980s, interest in population issues began to fade at many of the larger, "old money" foundations on the East Coast. The Ford Foundation was the first major foundation to head off in new directions, first jettisoning its highly respected and long-standing program of support for research on population and contraceptive technology in favor of women's empowerment and reproductive health advocacy, and later abandoning the field altogether. The Rockefeller Foundation's interest in population and reproductive health was slower to close its doors, but by the beginning of the current decade its support had all but disappeared save for an important program on microbicide research to combat HIV/AIDS. The Mellon Foundation has also ended its population program, which provided much-needed support for advanced training in the population sciences.

While most of the East Coast foundations have been changing directions or withdrawing from the field, several West Coast foundations have expanded their activities and, in dollar terms at least, are more than filling the void. Drawing upon significant new endowments generated by the success of the information-technology industry, the Gates, Packard, and Hewlett Foundations have become the dominant private-sector organizations supporting international population and reproductive health activities. The United Nations Foundation, the MacArthur Foundation, and the Wellcome Trust (based in the United Kingdom) have also become important contributors to international population activities.

Although the resource levels of the new foundations are impressive, it is less clear to what extent this considerable wealth is being directed to the most pressing population and reproductive health needs in the developing world. Here we offer some tentative impressions.

The Gates Foundation currently deploys much of its funding for global health to the control of infectious diseases, childhood immunization, maternal health, vaccine and microbicide research, HIV/AIDS, tuberculosis, and malaria programs, and to other global health initiatives. The foundation's interest in family planning and reproductive health is unclear, although the senior Bill Gates, after listening to a presentation of research on health topics at John Hopkins University (many of them only tangentially related to reproductive health) took the floor to point out that the foundation's broad interest in population and family planning seemed to be receiving scant attention. Several prominent public health schools have received grants for training foreign students in population and reproductive health. But early project support for family planning over the period from 1997 to 2000 seems to have given way to other initiatives since then (e.g., cervical cancer detection and treatment and syphilis control). It may be instructive to note that family planning and the interplay between high fertility and infant and maternal mortality receive little mention on the Gates Foundation website. The effect of population dynamics on development outcomes also seems to be downplayed, whether deliberately or otherwise we cannot say.

Health-sector programming at the Gates Foundation appears to be guided largely by a disease-specific (targeted) medical interventionist model dependent on the application of new diagnostic and treatment technologies. This approach may be most effective in countries with strong health infrastructures and advanced systems for confronting public health problems. Typifying this approach is a recently announced grant to the newly created foundation for the National Institutes of Health to further medical research and the application of new interventions for HIV/AIDS, malaria, and other infectious diseases. This reliance on medical science and technology tends to de-emphasize behavioral and epidemiological dimensions of disease in developing countries—for example, linkages between nutrition, water quality, sanitation, housing, and the environment, which often drive the multi-causal dynamics of morbidity and mortality in the compromised health settings of many developing countries.

This is a much larger issue than merely the philanthropic style or donor philosophy of the Gates Foundation. It reflects the presumptions of developed country donors who have experienced the success of technological solutions to health problems under conditions of advanced governmental and public health infrastructures that are often the sine qua non for successful technical intervention. Analyses of significant and sustained historical declines in mortality where it has occurred have shown the overwhelming importance of social change and economic prosperity in providing the necessary underlying conditions for improved survivorship.

A recent critique of the Gates Foundation's targeted goals for improving global health concludes that "the Gates Foundation has turned to a narrowly conceived understanding of health as the product of technical interventions divorced from economic, social, and political contexts" (Birn 2005: 2). The author notes that such factors as education, housing, sanitation, the distribution of income, workplace and environmental protection, social security, the coverage of medical services, and racial, gender, and class tolerance have been shown to be important in promoting long-term improvements in health outcomes (p. 4). It is of course not practical for a private foundation to simultaneously account for all these factors in its health-sector programming. But that is not the point.

What is at issue is the likely success of technical interventions, and thus the commitment of resources, absent knowledge of their interactions with social factors, which in given contexts are defining for possible health outcomes. Birn quotes Rudolph Virchow, the father of cellular pathology and social medicine to the effect that "the improvement of medicine may eventually prolong human life, but the improvement of social conditions can achieve this result more rapidly and more successfully" (cited in Birn 2005: 5). The challenge for an organization such as Gates, whose resources exceed those of the WHO, is to work both sides of the street and search out the conditions under which given technical interventions have an optimal chance for success.

The Packard Foundation is giving attention to the provision of reproductive health services (including a major emphasis on post-abortion care), the mobilization of resources for population and reproductive health activities, advocacy projects promoting women's reproductive and human rights, and the training of future leaders in population and health program management.

Packard initially channeled its international assistance primarily to NGOs working in seven priority countries (Ethiopia, India, Myanmar, Nigeria, Pakistan, the Philippines, and Sudan). Recently, Myanmar and Sudan were dropped from this list. The criteria employed for selecting the seven countries are not clear, although the international donor community has certainly neglected Myanmar and Sudan—probably for good reason, given their extremely compromised administrative, governance, and security environments. Packard has also been generous in supporting donor country NGOs undertaking ICPD advocacy and communication activities (e.g., Population Action International (PAI) in the United States, the Australian Reproductive Health Alliance, Action Canada for Population and Development (ACPD), the German Foundation for World Population (DSW), and the New Zealand Family Planning Association).

Packard has recruited much of its professional leadership in reproductive health from USAID or affiliated cooperating agencies. These connections may have subtly influenced the organization's administrative culture and programmatic priorities. This may not be entirely a bad thing, since many in USAID, given the chance, would gladly forsake its procedural bureaucratic culture and strike out in new directions. Unfortunately, there have been substantial cutbacks in Packard funding between 2000 and 2003 due to contractions in the foundation's endowment, which is tied to the rapidly descending value of Hewlett–Packard stock. It is unclear, therefore, what its future course might be. It appears doubtful that it can resume its broad eclectic program.

The Hewlett Foundation is the oldest foundation on the West Coast that has an active international population assistance program. In past years, Hewlett has provided support mainly to U.S.-based organizations and traditionally preferred to fund organizations that combine research, policy development, and service delivery. In addition, Hewlett assistance was typically targeted to established organizations with extensive knowledge of developing-country conditions, which allowed grants to provide "flexible general operating support rather than project-level support" (Hewlett Foundation 2003).

Hewlett has been notable for focusing on unmet programmatic needs in family planning and reproductive health and to some extent resisting the temptation to dilute the effectiveness of its assistance by addressing too many competing elements of the ICPD agenda. Hewlett decided not to provide major funding for HIV/AIDS since other West Coast foundations (mainly Gates) were covering this area. Hewlett emphasized four program components: resource mobilization for family planning and reproductive health programs;

improving access to information and services; supporting the development of new reproductive health technology; and training demographers, social scientists, and health professionals (Hewlett Foundation 2003). Over the past decade, Hewlett continued to emphasize unfinished business in family planning at the risk of being out of step with certain donor fashions of the moment.

The Hewlett Foundation has also been instrumental in funding university-based population studies centers in the United States and abroad that have been important incubators for junior professionals. Hewlett's role has become more critical as the Mellon and Rockefeller foundations close down their population programs and what's left of the Ford Foundation's international programs drift off into other areas.

Hewlett's senior leadership in population and reproductive health is now undergoing its first major change in more than a decade. The 2004 Strategic Plan identifies three "program guidelines" that will inform Hewlett's future programming: improving access to family planning and reproductive health care; ensuring adequate funding and evidence-based policies for family planning and reproductive health; and promoting family planning and reproductive health in the United States (Seims et al. 2004). Hewlett also takes the position that its future funding will be directed to insuring that HIV/AIDS programs recognize the importance of family planning and reproductive health in their operations (Seims et al. 2004: 10–12).

Early indications are that there will be some retrenchment in Hewlett's long-standing support of academic programs at U.S. universities and that it will have a strong interest in institution building in sub-Saharan Africa and South Asia—along with its support for family planning and reproductive health activities in the state of California. The Strategic Plan is quite ambitious and suggests the foundation may aspire to promote population assistance by assuming a tutelage responsibility toward donors such as the World Bank and the field of economic development generally.

To carry this program forward, the foundation will engage institutions in the Untied States and United Kingdom to assist with improving the research and training capacity of selected African and South Asian institutions. The countries in which Hewlett funds will be committed are unclear, except that preference will be given to countries below particular national income thresholds.

Training and institution building, however much they are needed, are expensive and time intensive activities for the sponsor. The costly material side of institution building might more appropriately be left to large public donors. And it does strike us as a missed opportunity to turn one's back on other parts of the world, in particular important countries such as China and Vietnam where private foundations may have opportunities not available to USAID and other aid organizations. Their role could be especially important in the area of training, professional exchanges, and institutional strengthening.

The United Nations Foundation (UNF), funded in large measure from resources provided by Ted Turner, the American media entrepreneur, channels most of its resources to UN development programs. Since its inception in 1999, the foundation has contributed to UN efforts in four main areas: children's health; women and population; the environment; and peace, security, and human rights. Its population activities aim to "reduce population growth and encourage development through providing the information, services, and opportunities that individuals and couples need to determine freely the number, spacing and timing of their children" (United Nations Foundation 2003). The programs support the implementation of action plans developed at the 1994 ICPD in Cairo and the 1995 Fourth World Conference on Women. Special emphasis is given to the provision of programs for adolescents and upgrading the quality of reproductive health services in the developing world.

The MacArthur Foundation supports rights initiatives and education on sexuality and reproduction through its Fund for Leadership Development (MacArthur Foundation 2003). MacArthur concentrates its grants in activities designed to promote reproductive health (particularly among young adults), strengthen sexual and reproductive rights, and reduce maternal mortality and morbidity. Its international support is currently focused on three priority countries—India, Mexico, and Nigeria; it also gave emphasis to Brazil prior to 2003. Columbia University's Mailman School of Public Health and the International Women's Health Coalition are two of MacArthur's largest grant recipients.

The Wellcome Trust of the United Kingdom supports biomedical research and training in both developed and developing countries. Its international programs provide resources for basic biomedical research on major diseases in the developing world, research on the health consequences of population growth, and the development of research capacity and collaborative research on tropical diseases in both developing countries and in the United Kingdom (Wellcome Trust 2003).

The advent of these foundations has engendered hope for productive intellectual policy ferment and an increase in badly needed resources. Compared to the East Coast foundations of yesteryear, the new philanthropies have been more determined to establish their own philanthropic identities. Gates is proceeding by its own lights; Packard and Hewlett are sources of hope but future funding, program directions and resolve are hard to read. With the greater proliferation of issues to be addressed today, greater diversity in approach may be an appropriate strategy compared to the time when a coordinated assault on high fertility seemed to call for close collaboration among foundations.

CHAPTER SEVEN
WHERE DO WE GO FROM HERE?

Population growth ranked among the greatest sources of anxiety about the future 50 years ago. What has happened? Has it been replaced by other, bigger worries? Have we taken care of it? Has it taken care of itself? The answer to these questions is an unqualified "yes—but." Nevertheless, the comforting view that rapid population growth is no longer a problem has gained wide currency.

The principal reason for this moderation of concern may be that birth rates are down. However, since death rates have also declined, population growth rates have not fallen to the same extent—a demographic truism, but something that in the heat of debate is sometimes overlooked. The demographic goal of the past, replacement fertility, has been reached and surpassed in developed countries. It appears to be in view for some developing countries. The job is done, many would say. Time to take on new challenges. Put our money elsewhere. Get on with new matters. Or refocus the effort by transferring technology, and program know-how to less-developed countries that need it and may be able to use it. The ultimate goal would be to put these countries in charge of their own population and reproductive health programs with declining dependence on international assistance.

Where Matters Stand Today

Population funding centered on family planning and reproductive health has been on the losing end of international development assistance since the mid-nineties. There are a number of factors that may account for why this is so. It is worth reviewing them.

- Population growth has lost some of its presumed causal prominence. Many of the problems foreseen 50 or more years ago as stemming from rapid population growth (crowding, environmental degradation, natural resource shortages, civil conflict, and dampened economic growth) are now understood, as they were then by careful scholars, to have multiple causes. While population growth may appear among those causes, its salience has been diluted.

- Economists generally agree that "population still matters," but so do many other factors that affect economic growth, such as the quality of governance; the health, education, and work ethic of the labor force; and social and economic policy. Moreover, demographic change is no longer seen wholly in negative terms. As population growth rates moderate, changing age compositions may present opportunities for economic growth by reducing the burden of dependency and increasing the proportion of population of working age. This creates a "window of opportunity" for development. Of course, if the window is nailed shut by ineffective, corrupt governance or by policy failures that leave countries ill equipped to take advantage of the opportunity, this "demographic gift" will remain unwrapped beyond its useful sell date (see, e.g., Mason 2002 and Bloom, Canning, and Sevilla 2003). Furthermore, some of the major demographic challenges that lie ahead—providing for the health needs of adolescents, accommodating aging populations, devising fair immigration policies, dealing with exploding cities (which are all to some degree consequences of past population growth)—are already with us and require more direct, faster-acting approaches than the slow indirect process of reducing the rate of population growth.

- Population policy has become increasingly politicized. Antiabortion politics and a conservative commitment to the dismantling of social policies and programs for ideological reasons became the order of the day in the United States during the first eight years of the new millennium. The United States reversed direction on international reproductive health programming every chance it got.

- At the other end of the political spectrum, there has been the introduction of a so-called new paradigm that intermingles family planning and reproductive health services with a broad assortment of sexuality, empowerment, and human rights measures directed primarily toward women, giving little attention to their separate priorities. This development, a product of the 1994 International Conference on Population and Development (ICPD), uncomfortably stretches inadequate budgets over a broad range of commitments and has resulted in confusion at the level of program design and implementation.

- Concern has shifted from reducing population growth to reducing poverty and attaining the Millennium Development Goals. Major international donors are revamping their policy agendas to confront issues of poverty, inequality of income, and specific correlates of poverty, such as poor education, malnutrition, and disease. However, demographic, family planning and broader reproductive health concerns were conspicuously absent from the first release of the Millennium Development Goals. The reasons for this omission are not clear, but the drafters of the goals may have viewed the contentiousness that has characterized the population field in recent years as a political liability, something better not to confront directly.

- The allocation of health-sector resources in relation to disease-adjusted life-year equivalents, an initiative spearheaded by the World Bank, may have deflected attention away from reproductive health since childbearing is not typically viewed as a disease requiring curative interventions. This development, along with the designation of essential services packages for primary health-care and curative care, may have unwittingly demoted interest in reproductive health.

- Many donors appear to be discouraged by the lack of success of interventionist policies in less developed countries owing to problems associated with weak governance and limited institutional capacity. This "donor fatigue," if that is really what it is, has diminished their enthusiasm for interventionist programs, including efforts to improve reproductive health and reduce population growth.

• The issue of population seemingly has been overwhelmed by larger global concerns: the war on terrorism, economic stagnation, inequities stemming from the process of globalization, setbacks resulting from the HIV/AIDS epidemic, global warming, and even the prospect of a "clash of civilizations."[1]

The past decade has been a destabilizing time for supporters of international population assistance. Western feminists and advocacy-oriented nongovernmental organizations (NGOs) have harshly criticized the legitimacy of pre-Cairo family planning programs. Goldberg's view that "America's international commitment to birth control was intended to fight communism, not to liberate women" is a commonly held characterization. While criticisms of early birth control efforts are not wholly unjustified, they also tend to project unfair characterizations of much pre-Cairo family planning effort and unfairly denigrate the dedication and commitment of early family planning pioneers.

An illustration of this genre can be found in Connelly (2008) who purports to view the past through the unclouded lens of a professional historian. His reading, very much in league with the feminist catechisms that dominated debate at Cairo, is that post-war family planning programs were little more than efforts to extinguish individual choice on matters involving procreation and to extend coercive controls dating from the age of imperialism and the Nazi domination of Europe. He notes that the "fatal misconception" of "population control" was "to think that one could know other people's interests better than they knew it themselves" (Connelly 2008, 378), a statement that only begins to make sense if one accepts the premise that pre-Cairo family planning programs were universally driven by the determination to deny women a say in the number of children they wanted to have. In fact, early family planning programs were nearly always grounded in voluntarism and motivated by the intention of providing women with the means to control the number and spacing of their children, a hugely empowering act in itself.[2]

More recently, the policy revolution at the core of the ICPD Programme of Action has itself come under serious attack by conservative forces, primarily in the United States, that regard calls for enhanced reproductive health and women's rights as covers for the legalization of abortion and antifamily cultural subversion. In effect, one can make the case that international family planning has been caught in a pincer movement over the past decade. First, the ICPD Programme of Action undermined the legitimacy of much pre-1994 family planning effort. Later, antiabortion activism and a resurgent political conservatism, along with calls to refocus development efforts on poverty alleviation, have seriously threatened funding for broadened reproductive health agendas and the Programme of Action itself.

Some commentators have maintained that there is still broad consensus on international population policy, it has merely changed from a focus on demographic rationales and fertility reduction to a sexual and reproductive heath and rights (SRHR) orientation. History will be the best judge of this, but our view is that there is no real consensus on international population policy at the present time (although fiercelyheld consensus abounds within various factional camps). Debate and policy divides have become increasingly counter-productive, to the point that resources for family planning and reproductive health programs have seriously faltered.

Even with the arrival of the Obama Administration in Washington, the future of international population assistance remains uncertain. President Obama rolled back the Mexicio City Policy (the global gag rule) and reinstated US funding for UNFPA during his first days in office. However, even with the promise of a more supportive political environment in Washington, currently anticipated funding levels are not keeping up with projected needs in family planning and reproductive health.[3] The current program environment is made more difficult by broad policy agendas that encompass sexuality, reproductive health, women's empowerment, human rights, and cultural transformations that lack focus and broad appeal among donors, and offer little clear guidance with respect to programmatic priorities, implementation strategies, and the measurement of results in resource-scarce environments.

In addition, the global HIV/AIDS epidemic appears to be redirecting funding away from these program areas—although the financial response to the HIV/AIDS crisis is still inadequate. As

Stephen Lewis noted recently, it appears unlikely that donors will provide the needed $30 billion for HIV/AIDS prevention and treatment programs by 2010. In addition, WHO's failure to raise sufficient funding to treat 3 million AIDS patients by 2005 with anti-retroviral drugs (WHO's 3 by 5 campaign) and substantial funding shortfalls at the Global Fund to Fight HIV/AIDS, Malaria, and Tuberculosis do not bode well for efforts to contain the HIV/AIDS epidemic (see Global Health Council 2005: 11, 26 and Lewis 2005:154–162).

There are some hopeful auguries, however. The effort to define the policy goals of the new millennium is a needed exercise, and stringent circumstances can call forth more clear-headed thinking about program priorities. So far, the outlook is pregnant with promise, but uncertain as to the outcome. Perhaps the most encouraging sign is the renewed commitment to the area of population and reproductive health by several large private philanthropic organizations. Support from these foundations comes in the form of grants and thus avoids the contractual straightjacketing and micromanagement familiar to recipients of much government funding.

Given the uncertain environment for international population assistance at present, what options might be proposed for meeting future population and reproductive health needs in the developing world? Views on this vary widely among professionals whose training and experience entitle them to a hearing. At one extreme are pessimists who argue that the field has not succeeded in promoting positive change, but instead worked itself into such a state of dysfunctionality that the rational course is to declare defeat and go home. At the other extreme are those who advise, putting a better face on things, declaring victory and going home.

When listening to the pessimists' war stories from the trenches of program implementation it is hard not to sympathize with their conclusions. They ascribe the "population industry's" embrace of the new Cairo paradigm or "consensus" on population policy to its desire to survive now that fertility rates have fallen in many countries. The pessimists claim that old-style family planning has lost its salience in the realm of policy. Less nihilistic and immediate in its effect, but leading eventually to a similar end, is the argument that many of the most successful family planning programs will, by mid-century, have died of their own success, a proposition entertained by Caldwell, Phillips, and Barkat-e-Khuda (2002).[4] This is actually an unremarkable conclusion and merely provides an upper bound to the time that may be needed in developing countries to make family planning and reproductive health care sustainable components of functional health systems. We accept the terms of this broad outlook. A 50-year time horizon gives most sensible recommendations time to work.

But before closing the book on family planning, let us stop and consider where we are. In a comprehensive summing up of the challenges still outstanding in this field, Ross and Stover (2003: 19) calculate that 114 million women in the developing world (excluding those in China) are still in need of contraception. If Russia and the former republics of the Soviet Union are included, 123 million women are in need of contraception (pp. 20–21). These figures would be considerably higher still if traditional contraceptive methods were not defined as met need.[5]

Moreover, potential future demand for contraception will increase as populations grow and as desired family size continues to decrease. The number will rise also as more effective or acceptable methods become available. As Ross and Stover state, "very large subgroups of women and couples in the developing world lack access to the contraception that would protect them from pregnancies they do not want . . . [and] this attests to the continuing gap between need and program response, as well as to the continuing justification for donor support of the programs"[6] (p. 21).

Goals of Future International Population Assistance

Over the past decade the international community (primarily under UN auspices) has invested considerable time and treasure convening large international conferences on development issues that attempt to forge and solidify new consensuses on policy and programmatic action. The comprehensive programs of action generated by these gatherings have generally been unrealistic in terms of programmatic reach, financial commitment, and the administrative capacity of many recipient countries to implement. As McIntosh and Finkle

(1995) state, "these large global meetings produce an unwieldy, excessively comprehensive, and indigestible set of recommendations that bind no one" (p. 252). The result can also place considerable pressure on governments to be responsive. Such pressure can risk compromising initiatives that governments might otherwise undertake to address their own needs and priorities.

The 1994 ICPD considerably broadened the population and reproductive health agenda. Governments are now expected to integrate family planning services with additional reproductive health interventions such as the diagnosis and treatment of sexually transmitted diseases (STDs) and the provision of postabortion care (the basic services approach); strengthen programs that enhance the status of women (e.g., promoting new opportunities for women in education and microenterprise); improve human and reproductive rights (e.g., by reducing genital cutting and violence against women); develop program services tailored for adolescents; promote greater "male involvement" in reproductive health programs; enhance the enjoyment of human sexuality; and engender cultural transformations. Besides being broad in conception, the Programme of Action does not prioritize these goals or specify achievement outcomes.

These agendas also appear to be increasingly out of touch with emerging programmatic needs in reproductive health. They provide little guidance with respect to coping with the HIV/AIDS epidemic, responding to the crisis posed by degrading health delivery systems in much of sub-Saharan Africa, dealing with problems resulting from the rush to decentralize and integrate health services, and repositioning development assistance in relation to poverty-alleviation goals. Just maintaining, not to mention upgrading, access to quality health care presents a huge and growing challenge in the developing world.

Investments in human and institutional capacities required to promote effective service delivery, as well as providing for the procurement, distribution, and dispensing of essential commodities and supplies (e.g., contraceptives, vitamin A, iron supplementation tablets, oral rehydration solution, and antiretroviral drugs for HIV/AIDS) will lay claim to an ever-growing share of international assistance. Given current funding prospects, it seems doubtful whether

sufficient resources will be forthcoming to meet these service requirements and simultaneously address even more ambitious agendas.

There has been insufficient consideration of the extent to which
developing countries have been able to respond to the Cairo
Program—beyond the rhetorical reaffirmations declared at gatherings
such as the ICPD + 5 Special Session of the UN General Assembly
held in New York in 1999. The few reviews of country-level experience that do exist suggest faltering implementation of the Programme
of Action in individual programs. Mayhew (2002) places much of the
blame on developed country policies in noting that "donors have been
slow to change to ways of providing support that would promote provision of the integrated and expanded reproductive health services
envisioned at ICPD," owing in part to continuing adherence to
"donor-accountability requirements" (pp. 222–223). Some observers
have expressed fear that a close reexamination of difficulties entailed
in implementing the ICPD agenda might be undesirable in that it
could encourage a rollback of the entire Cairo paradigm.

There has also been little systematic analysis of the budgetary and
technical requirements needed to scale-up new reproductive health
services within existing national health care systems or achieve more
integrated service delivery structures. Gillespie (2004) notes that constraints imposed by field realities can pose serious difficulties in implementing new program innovations and delivery systems. For example,
USAID's efforts during the 1990s to integrate family planning and
STD diagnoses and treatment programs proved administratively
cumbersome and financially infeasible, and led some to conclude that
such efforts were "unimpressive" and even "deleterious" (p. 36).

An insightful critique of the problems faced in implementing
the ICPD Programme of Action has been provided by Lush and
Campbell (2001). While acknowledging that the Cairo paradigm
has succeeded in drawing attention to a fuller range of reproductive
health issues facing the women of poor countries, they note that the
search for affordable and effective interventions was much less successful. They attribute this shortcoming to the failure to bridge the
gulf between rhetoric and on-the-ground reality. This may have been
partly due to the weak representation at Cairo of technical experts
and seasoned public health professionals that left matters of policy

"vulnerable to the whims of less informed more ideological groups" (p. 191). Combined with the overriding need to achieve consensus on a set of grand and empirically vague recommendations and faced with divergent views coming from several quarters, the Cairo conference ultimately lost sight of "feasibility."

The rapid expansion of programmatic attention and resources in combating the global HIV/AIDS epidemic has also had the effect of directing donor attention and funds away from family planning and reproductive health. This is an unfortunate development because there are natural program synergies between reproductive health and HIV/AIDS care—for example, in communication and education efforts; stemming maternal-to-child transmission of HIV; antenatal care; services for youth; and research on new anti-HIV formulations such as microbicides that also prevent pregnancy. If used properly, condoms can also be an effective means of preventing the transmission of HIV/AIDS.

To date, there has been little formal integration of reproductive health and HIV/AIDS programs at the policy level within the donor community. In fact, as Sinding (2005) notes, the Global Fund to Fight AIDS, Tuberculosis, and Malaria and the World Health Organization (WHO) have actually reinforced the divide between sexual and reproductive health and HIV/AIDS activities.

> The establishment of a Global Fund to Fight AIDS, Tuberculosis and Malaria as separate and distinct from sexual and reproductive health has deepened the gulf, as has the World Health Organization's decision to move responsibility for the fight against HIV/AIDS from the sexual and reproductive health unit to the unit on communicable and infectious diseases. Given that 70 percent or more of new HIV infections are sexually transmitted, this separation of HIV/AIDS control efforts from its natural ally, the field of family planning and reproductive health, is self-defeating. (p. 141)

Although considerable integration has occurred at the field level in response to the shortage of service providers and health facilities, more effective HIV/AIDS education and prevention programs could have been incorporated into existing reproductive health services sooner than was generally the case (especially when HIV/AIDS infections started crossing over from small high-risk groups to the general population). It must also be acknowledged that the main impediment in combating the HIV/AIDS crisis until recently has been the lack of affordable and effective treatment options. The growing competition for resources between organizations (primarily NGOs) that undertake advocacy activities and those that actually provide services to women requires striking the right balance between these two activities. For example, a substantial number of NGOs funded by USAID through the Innovations in Family Planning Services Project in India are community-based advocacy organizations promoting, inter alia, sexual and reproductive rights for women, but they are often not medically staffed or equipped to provide services. Sujatha Rao (2003), the joint secretary of the Indian Department of Family Welfare within the Ministry and Health and Family Welfare, has underscored this point:

> Unfortunately, NGOs are not quickly making the transition from mere advocacy to service delivery. It is very important that NGO capacity be strengthened for them to become more professional. After all, health is not just talk—it must have clinical, medical, and service content. (p. 4)

It is of course important to reaffirm the importance of advocacy and educational activities for better informing women about sexuality and reproduction as well as reforming outmoded practices that can impede the accessibility and use of reproductive health care. Our concern here is one of balance and priority setting.

Future Program Strategies in Family Planning and Reproductive Health

A major feature of many health-sector reforms has been the integration of health services through the delivery of essential packages of clinic-based services. Vertically structured family planning and reproductive health programs face challenges from those who argue that health services combining primary care with more specialized services and unified management can save money and provide higher-quality care. However, there is little operational research that clearly points to service integration as the best or only option for providing reproductive health care, despite the obvious conceptual attraction of the notion.

The WHO and many developing countries continue to champion traditional vertical programs for the management of such diseases as tuberculosis, malaria, and HIV/AIDS. In fact, new vertical program designs seemingly abound. The Global Fund to Fight AIDS, Malaria, and Tuberculosis, the International AIDS Vaccine Initiative, STOP TB, and Rollback Malaria are recent examples of new vertical program initiatives. Why family planning and reproductive health programs should be integrated (often with weak primary heath care systems) when vertical approaches are often preferred for other health interventions is puzzling. The lack of consistency in donor policies may in fact be frustrating efforts to establish integrated service delivery systems. Lush comments that "when national reproductive health managers are committed to separate programs to retain donor support, tensions are created between the goals of decentralized, locally accountable, integrated health service delivery and the reality of vertical technical and financial inputs for particular reproductive health activities" (Lush 2002: 73).

Our brief is that decisions on program strategy should be made on pragmatic grounds, on what approach appears appropriate to the circumstances. For example, in many situations it would be advantageous to integrate reproductive health services with other components of the health care system (e.g., infant and child health services, nutrition support, prenatal and postpartum maternal care). Integrating reproductive health services with HIV/AIDS care (especially in providing information to women about behavioral risks and preventive measures) also has obvious merit. But there are settings where, at a given time and under particular conditions, integration may prove to be a mere will-o-the-wisp. Rearranging institutional furniture around is bound to meet resistance. Sometimes it is better to buy new furniture.

Many developing countries, particularly in sub-Saharan Africa, still do not have the necessary health infrastructure in place for providing high-quality family planning and reproductive health care. As a recent evaluation of USAID's reproductive health programming noted, the agency is not giving sufficient priority to long-term investments in the essentials of service delivery.

In many countries around the world, most particularly in Sub-Saharan Africa, the basic building blocks of effective FP/RH service delivery are still not in place. Planning capacity is weak and delivery systems are severely strained by personnel shortages, insufficient skills, weak logistics systems, shortages of key equipment and supplies (including contraceptives), poor supervisory and monitoring systems and financial crises. Such problems often are further compounded by high HIV incidence and prevalence, and by the departure of trained personnel to the private sector, often in Europe or North America. (Foster et al. 2003: 71)

The range of relevant specialized assistance geared to upgrading reproductive health-service delivery systems is extensive and varies considerably from country to country. Strengthening human resources and infrastructure capacity in order to improve the accessibility and utilization of services heads the list. The agenda also should include reenergizing services that have fallen into a state of relative neglect or suffered from faltering commitment. Among these is the revival of the earlier emphasis on postpartum services; securing funding for voluntary surgical sterilization; and providing safe abortion services (where it is legal) and adequate postabortion care. In addition, the tendency among postabortion care programs to exclude family planning is especially troubling. As Gillespie (2004) notes, "it is especially deplorable that women subjected to an unsafe and often life-threatening abortion are not given the information and services they need to avoid having to subject themselves to the procedure again" (p. 37).

The HIV/AIDS crisis has placed new demands on service delivery structures and the need to rationalize costs. At the very least consideration should be given to the benefits that might result from an integration of reproductive health and HIV/AIDS services. Among the benefits that could result are reductions in the extent of mother-to-child transmission of the disease. For example, a recent study in

14 developing countries found that the number of infections averted among infants rose from 39,000 with the use of antiretroviral drugs alone to 71,000 when combined with family planning methods (USAID 2003b: 1). Given such findings it probably makes little sense to wall these services off from each other in separate vertical delivery systems. While relevant data are not abundant, it seems likely that integrated services could also be more cost effective.

As important as anything else is the recent tendency among donors to "phase out" support for contraceptive commodities, essential drugs, and logistical services. The hope is that developing countries will be able on their own to procure necessary supplies. This has sometimes been a forlorn hope. For example, when USAID announced that it was withdrawing commodity support in the Philippines, it failed to announce a plan to ensure provision of supplies through alternative mechanisms (other than handing much of the responsibility to the German foreign aid program). Although recommendations have been made to USAID on how to handle commodity phase-outs (Bowers and Hemmer 2002), it is not clear to what extent these have been heeded.

This constitutes a very full programmatic agenda and, of course, additional program elements can well be envisioned. A commendable effort to prioritize reproductive health interventions that partly reflects the scope of the ICPD Programme of Action is provided by Tsui, Wasserheit, and Haaga (1997). New service elements responsive to needs in human sexuality, infection-free sexual activity and reproduction, contraception, pregnancy and childbearing, and program design and implementation are proposed. While better focused programmatically than the ICPD Programme of Action, the Tsui et al. agenda is still probably beyond the reach of most resource-poor countries unless substantially larger budgets can be secured, new program interventions phased in gradually, and health delivery systems substantially upgraded.

While broadened agendas in sexuality, reproductive health, human rights, and women's empowerment have been vigorously advocated in recent years, less attention has been given to building professional and technical competency in family planning and reproductive health services in developing countries. Past investments in health-service delivery (especially investments in long-term medical and public health training) are rapidly eroding in many developing locales, especially in sub-Saharan Africa. Low salaries and poor working conditions for health professionals are making it more difficult to recruit and retain service providers, particularly in remote rural settings. The migration of health workers seeking better salaries and career prospects is reducing their availability in areas of greatest need. The HIV/AIDS epidemic is also taking its toll. Tawfik and Kinoti (2003: 1) conclude that about 20 percent of the African health workforce could eventually be lost to the HIV/AIDS epidemic.

Several private foundations in the United States have recognized the need for building professional capacity in the population and health sciences. This has led to the development of "leadership training" programs that focus primarily on imparting advocacy and managerial skills. It remains to be seen whether such efforts provide a useful alternative to more traditional, longer-term professional training. It is also unclear whether leadership skills can be effectively transferred in formal pedagogical settings. Learning the essentials of public speaking, systems of managerial control, and the workings of PowerPoint are poor substitutes for the hard slog of acquiring in-depth knowledge in medicine, public health, and the behavioral sciences, traditionally a prerequisite for achieving leadership in international health.

Some donors are still supporting short-term in-country training for service providers (e.g., nurses and midwives), but these activities are generally not sufficient to meet country needs. In addition, the value of much short-term training (both preservice and in-service) has not been well documented. It is generally assumed that such efforts improve service quality, but how effective and long-lasting the results have been is open to question. For example a recent assessment of the impact of traditional birth attendant (TBA) training on reducing maternal mortality, has pointed to disappointing results (Koblinsky, Campbell, and Heichelheim 1999).

Deficiencies and imbalances in the functionality of health care systems also deserve greater attention. Concerns have tended to focus on the supply of health workers and the quality of the work they perform. Equally important, but often overlooked by donors, is the distribution of health workers within countries and between regions, the provision of adequate salaries and benefits, and other conditions of work that motivate health workers to provide quality care.

There have been some promising initiatives in the training area. For example, the Gates Foundation is funding intermediate-term educational opportunities in the population and health sciences at Johns Hopkins University, Columbia University, and the University of Montreal. The American International Health Alliance Partnership supports collaborative exchanges between health providers in the United States and the countries of Eastern Europe and Eurasia, although often at considerable expense. Opportunities for acquiring professional training (through either formal instruction or project-based mentoring activities) need to be greatly expanded.

In addition to building the professional capacity of country programs, the issue of financial sustainability requires much greater attention. Since the international community appears unwilling to provide its share of the projected resources necessary for human resource capacity development and basic reproductive health services, developing countries will have to place greater reliance on cost-recovery mechanisms to fund these programs. They will need to use graduated ability-to-pay criteria when providing essential reproductive health services to both reduce health care subsidies and ensure that resources are efficiently allocated.

This won't be easy since it remains the case that many of the world's poorest countries cannot generate significant domestic resources to fund their programs themselves:

> Many countries, especially those in sub-Saharan Africa, are simply unable to generate the necessary resources to finance their own national population programs. Case studies confirm that, to a large extent, developing countries are dependent on the international donor community to finance population activities. (UNFPA 2002b: 43)

Although many women in the developing world may prefer private health providers, the vast majority of clients rely upon public facilities and will continue to do so for the foreseeable future. Finding the proper balance between public- and private-sector instrumentalities in any country will always be a delicate matter. At present there is justified concern that public-sector services have been allowed to degrade in the rush to "partner" with NGOs and embrace private-sector (for-profit) solutions to health care delivery.

Developing countries that have been most successful in achieving functional pluralism in their health care delivery systems (Bangladesh and Thailand come to mind) have developed consultative arrangements between public-and private-sector program administrators and service providers, which coordinate such issues as the allocation of service areas, the specification of basic services to be offered, and the management of care (including systems of client referral and follow-up). Such collaboration allows each sector to learn from the other. In many settings, experience with program innovations tends to run from NGOs to the public sector, a tendency that underlines the importance of having a strong NGO presence. If, however, partnering consists of little more than a struggle for resources and programmatic domination, few benefits will accrue.

Assuming that adequate funding is forthcoming to address program needs, there remains the even more challenging issue of how resources can best be deployed to ensure program success in widely varying social and environmental settings. The term "evidence-based" has become popular as a concept for assessing the effectiveness of health project designs and outcomes. On first hearing the term one's initial reaction is "of course, let's dispense with pet ideas and demand some real evidence of what works." If done properly, this mode of analysis involves the consideration of the ecological setting, the social adaptations to that setting, and the way programmatic interventions are likely to be regarded in a particular population.

To illustrate this approach, Phillips et al. (2003) analyze the social organization of two diverse rural areas in Bangladesh (Matlab) and Ghana (Navrongo) in an effort to evaluate the appropriateness of various program strategies. Bangladesh society, they find, is diffusely organized, in part because pervasive environmental uncertainties narrow the range and reliability of social obligations to family members. Social organization at the local level is fragmented and socially turbulent. As a result, people take refuge in patron–client relations rather than in community-based action and individuals attempt to maximize their personal gain. In spite of pervasive poverty and other common disadvantages, there is no readily mobilized constituency for grassroots protest or organization. A long history of central domination stretching back at least to Mogul times has created the expectation that change, if it comes, will be from the top down, not as a result of grassroots collective action. Bureaucracy is highly formalized, discouraging "bottom–up" communication.

By contrast, colonial rulers in West Africa allowed local organizations the autonomy to run their affairs apart from those that touched on such matters as resource extraction, over which the central government retained control. In Ghana, strong lineage ties and subordination of individuals to collective decision making shape much village life. The touchstone for local decisions is consensus rather than executive order. Even village headmen avoid making arbitrary decisions, remaining detached from debates until a consensus has formed and then pronouncing the "opinion of the people." Ghanaian social structure thus encourages active community participation.

Their analysis leads them to expect a collaborative relationship between local action and higher authority in Ghana in matters such as health policy. Thus, when local groups consider program options, they are already in touch with "cognizant" government agencies. The famous Navrongo project in Ghana, whose designers explored ways to institute primary health programs, is a collaboration with the Ministry of Health to which it reported. Not only did this arrangement provide a head start on the perennial problem of "scaling up," but it fostered in the government a sense of ownership in the project, a result that is hard to achieve when the government is left out as an initial stakeholder. On the other hand, in Bangladesh the government has delivered health services to clients' homes, utilizing a corps of government health workers. NGOs, which in Bangladesh are appealing as a way to circumvent government inefficiency, may have a lesser role in Ghana.

Understanding the two contrasting situations suggests that program decentralization may not work very well in Bangladesh, but may be more appropriate for Ghana, at least in those parts of Ghana that present social profiles similar to Navrongo. Whereas in Bangladesh the government has delivered health services to clients' homes, in a more socially cohesive situation, such as exists in Ghana, it may be possible to dispense with corps of government health workers and devise ways of using functioning, locally organized institutions to do the same job.

What all this means in broad compass is that general discussions of evidence-based program efforts are moot without detailed specifications of the social situations in which they are rooted. It is hard to imagine a future international conference that would attempt to lay out an agenda and develop a plan of action of broad applicability without paying serious attention to the implementation requirements of evidence-based systems.

Future Donor Response in Family Planning and Reproductive Health

Much remains to be done in family planning and reproductive health before the work begun 50 years ago is completed. The population field needs new ideas, refurbished institutions, enhanced human resources, and strategically placed new funding. Donor countries will need to remain engaged in this effort if additional gains in global reproductive health are to be secured. However, the manner in which donor countries shape their future efforts will be critical in ensuring future programmatic success.

It is natural for donor countries to have preferences on how their resources are allocated. To maintain the flow of foreign aid, recipient countries often have little choice but to adhere to programmatic prescriptions handed down from the donor community. But as Shiffman and Wu (2003) argue, if democracy, managerial transparency, and sustainability are to be attained, developing countries need to have greater say in setting their health agendas and priorities.

If the ideas of democracy and representation are to be taken seriously, it matters not just whether resource-poor nations have the power to shape their health agendas. It matters also who within these nations has such power. Which parties are consulted, and who is bypassed in the process? Are legitimate democratic and participatory mechanisms used? Or are agendas set by small groups of officials at the pinnacles of health bureaucracies, international organizations, donor consortiums, pharmaceutical ventures and transnational advocacy networks? (p. 2)

The multilateral development agencies of the United Nations are probably best positioned to nurture collaborative and productive compacts between the international community and developing countries. However, the UN's major development agencies are grossly underfunded, often poorly managed, and not always appropriately staffed. Despite these limitations, some UN agencies [e.g., United Nations Children's Fund (UNICEF) and the World Food Program] have compiled admirable records over the years – particularly agencies with well focused agendas and delimited program directions. This legacy needs to be built upon rather than denigrated, as has been the fashion within the corridors of power in Washington in recent times.

So long as the United States remains a principal contributor in this area, it is likely that bilateral assistance will remain the dominant mechanism for supporting population programs. As with multilateral aid, however, future bilateral assistance should afford developing countries maximum opportunity to design and implement their own population and reproductive health programs. This will entail greater investments in training, research, and technology transfers in order to build sustainable institutions and professional capacity in these countries. Much development assistance as is now provided often leaves little behind once projects end.

Bilateral donors would be well advised to review and modify their administrative requirements, which tend to add unproductive complexity to the delivery of their assistance. The growing tendency of some donors to assume greater responsibility for managing projects, a tendency that usually stems from legal and budgetary rules and regulations, sends a signal that host-country institutions cannot be trusted to manage donors' funds. While this is certainly sometimes the case, there should be limits on the invasiveness of donor administrative requirements. If the management of bilateral assistance becomes too demanding and untrusting, then even the best of donor intentions are tarnished by suspicion and resentment.

Private foundations have been crucial sources of financial and technical support for international population and reproductive health activities for the past 50 years. They have provided intellectual leadership for the population field and support for program innovations and new technologies. What directions will emerge from the new foundations cannot be fully apprehended at this juncture. If they simply take their cues from the operational cultures and programmatic priorities of long-established donors, they will have missed an important opportunity to redefine the field and move it in new directions.

Foundations with open slates can address important issues in population assistance that await clarification. Private funding is especially useful for trying out new programmatic strategies that may entail risk, to see what works and how successful innovations can be scaled-up. Private philanthropies can also be very effective in promoting professional technical leadership, for example, by funding collaborative research, supporting long-term technical training, and developing institutional capacity at universities and institutes in the developing world.[7] They can undertake assessments of various approaches to human resource development and health system strengthening.

Over the past three decades, the three largest organizations supporting population and reproductive health programs have been the United Nations Population Fund (UNFPA), the World Bank, and USAID. The ability of these three organizations to remain productively deployed will go a long way to determining the future of international population assistance. Each of these organizations is currently facing serious challenges in implementing effective country programs and generating adequate resources.

United Nations Population Fund (UNFPA)

The most immediate threat to population and reproductive health activities within the UN system is the lack of resources. UNFPA budgets are well below what they should be to ensure that essential components of reproductive health services—commodities, provider training, program monitoring and evaluation—are adequately funded. UNFPA has no chance of meeting the high expectations articulated at its founding in 1967 without continued strong international support. Generous donors such as the Netherlands, Denmark, and Sweden should not be expected to continue funding much of UNFPA's annual operating budget. Among wealthier nations, the United States, Australia, and France have been some of the least generous supporters of UNFPA. It is reasonable to expect that increasingly prosperous middle-income countries, such as Brazil, China, Thailand, and India, could begin making meaningful contributions to UNFPA in future years.

To merit increased support, UNFPA will need to delimit its core agenda more clearly and direct its resources to needs with the greatest priorities. In recent years it has spread its limited resources across too many program areas. In rethinking where it is going as an organization, UNFPA should examine whether large outlays for expensive promotional and consensus-building activities may be compromising its country program budgets.

UNFPA has a top-heavy personnel structure. Regular promotions and limited staff turnover have resulted in heavy salary and benefit obligations, to say nothing of the consequent sluggishness in its professional life. Future recruitment efforts should aim to provide a well-rounded professional staff with expertise across the full range of population and reproductive health specializations that fall under its purview. In recent years, UNFPA's recruitment appears to have favored individuals with backgrounds in advocacy, gender, and human rights over core public health and medical specializations that are central to its mission.

The World Bank

Resource constraints and personnel policies are lesser issues for the World Bank. The World Bank has shown a growing appetite for promoting health-sector reform and using conditionalities attached to loan agreements as a means of achieving its aims. These efforts have not always enjoyed the unqualified support of host-country officials or been adequately cognizant of local circumstances and requirements. In addition, as has been demonstrated in Bangladesh, the World Bank has at times given insufficient attention to monitoring and evaluating the impact of its program activities, and has been slow to consider mid-course corrections when evidence of dysfunctionality emerges. Irrespective of specific program focus, the World Bank clearly needs more technical staff with operational program experience (particularly in field missions) to track the implementation of country programs.

It is still unclear whether the broad-scale health-sector reforms enacted as part of the World Bank's sector-wide assistance programs (SWAps) have greatly improved the efficiency of health systems or the quality of service delivery. In their review of health-sector reform and the sector-wide initiatives undertaken during the 1990s, Hardee and Smith (2000: 25) conclude that "the evidence . . . shows few current examples of successful reform that have had a favorable effect on reproductive health programs," although Zambia and other sub-Saharan countries participating in the Bamako Initiative were reportedly making some headway. Picazo, Huddart, and Duale (2003) comment on the complexities often encountered when implementing sector-wide initiatives, particularly the more time-intensive consultations required between donors and host-country officials:

> These approaches are process-intensive (planning, deliberation, and negotiation), widely consultative and collaborative (all stakeholders, at all levels), highly technical (essential packages of care under given resource envelopes), and policy-oriented (requiring the presence of very senior personnel). They therefore require an inordinate amount of government staff time because government officials are expected to drive the process. Initial hopes that sector investment programs and SWAps may lessen the amount of time and transactions between donors and the government appear to be too optimistic; in fact, they may require more government staff time and more skillful and experienced government managers. (p. 22)

Less not more complexity in the way the Bank interacts with developing country institutions is desirable. SWAps do not necessarily promote this goal. "One-size-fits-all" approaches to health-sector reform that make little allowance for local circumstances tend to undermine program ownership and harmonious donor–recipient country relations. The World Bank might fruitfully pay greater heed to such concerns in its future health-sector initiatives.

Where the World Bank is heading with respect to funding international population activities is still unclear. Most of the Bank's resources are currently being allocated for HIV/AIDS and other infectious diseases. A discussion paper issued in 2007 signaled that the Bank accorded high priority to family planning and reproductive health programs as a means of promoting women's health and combating poverty (World Bank 2007). The report concluded that "global attention and resources for population issues have been declining, and an urgent response is now required on the part of the Bank, as well as from other development partners, to reposition family planning within the ICPD agenda" (World Bank 2007:vii). However, the most recent figures on population assistance funding reported by UNFPA and NIDI (2008) show that budget allocations for family planning and reproductive health from multinational development banks have continued to decline.

United States Agency for International Development (USAID)

Currently great uncertainty exists about the future of the world's largest bilateral donor, USAID. In addition to its onerous internal management procedures and shortage of human resources, USAID is facing growing threats to its autonomy vis-à-vis other federal agencies and to its central position as the U.S. government's principal agency for official development assistance. The Millennium Challenge Corporation and other federal agencies (most notably the Department of Defense) have the potential to marginalize the central role USAID has played in development assistance since 1961. In our opinion, this would be a serious setback for America's efforts to promote social and economic advance in the developing world. Despite its current preoccupation with bureaucratic process, which is due in part to excessive congressional oversight, USAID still constitutes the largest concentration of professional competency and experience in international development within the federal government.

That said, the challenge of making USAID more effective in what it does is daunting. Immediate first steps should be to significantly upgrade the number and quality of USAID direct-hire staff, in part by recruiting more personnel with relevant professional competencies rather than generalists with managerial backgrounds; to rebuild USAID's field missions by deploying more seasoned technical staff with knowledge of the countries (or regions) to which they will be sent; to streamline internal management systems so that USAID staff have more time to interact with the projects and countries under their purview; and to direct a much greater share of available resources to intended beneficiaries rather than to U.S.-based intermediaries.

Some argue that the system of cooperating agencies that USAID has nurtured over the years helps to ensure that as little money as possible reaches the countries that need it, thus delaying the day when recipient countries take on greater responsibility for implementing their own programs. The agency should also consider developing new mechanisms to allow American aid and expertise to participate in SWAps and other reform initiatives being championed by the World Bank, the European Union, and other bilateral donors.

These and other remedial initiatives have been recommended before, but efforts to address them have come up short. USAID's many reengineering exercises under both Democratic and Republican administrations have done little more than create additional bureaucratic confusion and complexity in the way USAID conducts its affairs. Getting the agency back on track as a "can-do" operation that can interact productively with developing- country governments and institutions should be a major priority for U.S. foreign operations.

This task is all the more urgent given the demands that are now being made on the Department of State to process large new resource allocations for HIV/AIDS programs—in particular, money that has been authorized for President Bush's Emergency Plan for AIDS Relief (PEPFAR). A report by the U.S. Government's General Accounting Office (2003) warns that USAID's staff shortages (especially the lack of contract officers based in field missions), problems of administrative coordination with host-country governments and other donors,[8] and the constraints imposed by U.S. policy prescriptions (e.g, the prohibition against needle exchange programs for intravenous drug users) are compromising the effectiveness of the Agency's HIV/AIDS response (2003).

The transition from the Bush to Obama Administrations presents a fresh opportunity to reexamine the objectives of US foreign assistance; the modes of delivering foreign assistance funding and technical support (including how to enhance the effectiveness of USAID as the US Government's lead international development entity); how to more effectively engage host country governments and institutions; how to participate more productively in multilateral development agencies (especially those of the UN); and how to collaborate more closely with other bilateral aid programs. These are daunting challenges that need to be carefully considered by America's new administration.

Two thoughtful efforts to initiate debate on these issues can be found in Levine (2008) and Herring and Radelet (2008). Their prescriptions for change in US priorities include achieving better balance in funding allocations for health programs (e.g., additional resources for reproductive and child health and infectious diseases other than HIV/AIDS); allocating more resources for HIV prevention efforts relative to spending on treatment; promoting more effective professional exchanges for clinical and public health training, research, and practices; and strengthening funding and technical support to multilateral development institutions.

Putting Population Back on the Table

In this review we have not dwelled on larger implications of population dynamics. Our aim, instead, has been to consider where matters stand with respect to the policies and programs that were initially concerned with the provision of family planning services and were later expanded to include reproductive health. That has been the central core of population assistance over the past half-century.

Though family planning programs were making good headway in earlier decades (particularly during the decade of the 1980s), it is never amiss to take stock and reassess where things now are headed. Despite our sense that the ICPD Programme of Action was overly optimistic about the reception it would receive in developing countries and the eagerness of donors to get behind it, the field was put on notice that some things had to change. Never again will family planning and reproductive health services be casual or indifferent to issues of quality, or deny governments and their partnering agencies the opportunity to have a major say in the design and implementation of programs. Women's needs, as they define them, will be respected and neither age, marital status, nor restrictive cultural practices should remain barriers to accessing services having to do with sexuality and reproduction. We totally concur with Goldberg's observation that "the search for human commonality among vastly diverse people is tricky and elusive, but it is callous to surrender to relativism when so many women are clearly suffering" (Goldberg 2009:9). If these accomplishments were not all attributable to Cairo, they were vigorously underscored on that occasion.

But we believe demographic issues still matter as well. One major concern is that the decline of fertility in some developing countries appears to have stalled at levels ranging between three and four births per woman (e.g., Bangladesh, Kenya, and the Philippines). With mortality rates generally tending downward (except in high HIV/AIDS prevalence countries), fertility at these levels will result in significantly more population growth than is usually anticipated. The "birth dearth" that Ben Wattenberg of the American Enterprise Institute calls "the biggest story of our time" is confined so far, largely to advanced countries.[9] Fertility rates for countries with suspected fertility stalls may resume their downward trend. If that does happen, family planning programs may not be the chief cause, but they will hasten the process, make it more efficient, and reduce dependence on abortion.

Concern is also growing about recent reversals in contraceptive use in countries such as Kenya and Indonesia. Sara Seims, a veteran family planning and reproductive health professional who spent much of early career in Africa, recently noted that access to contraception in many African countries is worse now than in the 1970s. She notes that "in the last year I have visited clinics in major capitals, including places like Johannesburgh and Nairobi, and they don't have the full array of methods . . . if the situation is dire in Nairobi, what on earth is it like in Kisumu and Mombassa and these other towns that are growing so rapidly" (cited in Goldberg 2009:233). In addition, the 2007 Demographic and Health Survey from Indonesia reports stagnating or falling levels of family planning use in several regions of the country between 2002 and 2007, most notably in the urban centers of Jakarta and Jogjakarta (Statistics Indonesia 2008: 77). During this same period, family planning use fell among women with less education, contraceptive choice became more restricted, and levels of unsafe abortion remained high.

Such laurels as have been won in reproductive health are not yet grounds for complacency. Human reproduction is still a hazardous affair. Maternal mortality remains unacceptably high in many countries, as does infant mortality. Progress in the prevention of the major childhood diseases still presents a full slate of challenges. Reproductive health programs will need to become more effective in combating HIV/AIDS, preventing its transmission from mother to child, and providing more affordable care for people living with AIDS. These activities should be linked to larger efforts to defeat this scourge and to support its victims. Ways must also be found for reproductive health to establish its bona fides and shake the perverse perception that it is the code language for abortion. The termination of pregnancy should not be exiled beyond the pale of legitimate medical practice.

Reproductive health, shorn of some of Cairo's overreach and offering an essential array of services, has a consistent, understandable core mission, one that we believe will make sense to donors. There is no lack of suggestions on how to implement such a reproductive health agenda. This review has touched on some of them: community participation and decentralization, the removal of demographic targets, program "ownership," health-sector reform and sector-wide approaches, the involvement of NGOs, client centeredness, and human resource capacity development. Persuasive and plausible as these measures sound, there is no guarantee that they will work, even when brought into play simultaneously.

It is especially unlikely that anything will work as advertised when donors take too great an interest in changing individual behavior and institutions. It must become gospel that what works depends on social, economic, and political context and that donors should be handmaidens, not handlers. By extension, donors and Western interests should tread warily in the area of human and reproductive rights, making sure not to define them in their own ethnocentric image. Casting development policy in terms of rights for which, it is claimed, there is "an international obligation that must be fulfilled" (Nelson and Dorsey 2003: 2014) is an interesting idea, but, may not convince policy makers through moral suasion or lead to concerted action.

It is our belief that international population assistance has become increasingly unfocused, lacking in sensibly articulated priorities, and overly broad in conception. At the same time, important linkages between population dynamics and development outcomes have been largely set aside, apparently in an unwarranted zeal to remove demographic imperatives as justification for program action. While there is obviously merit in not tying program operations exclusively to the attainment of demographic objectives, the field has also become less vital to development and thus less capable of generating resources. However, overlooking the importance of demographic change (including the distribution, composition, and mobility of populations) in relation to such concerns as food and agriculture, education, employment, the generation of human capital, natural resource management, and environmental protection runs the risk of weakening governmental support for population reproductive health programs.

For the field to attain the desirable goal of providing ready access to high-quality reproductive health services for women and men around the world, those working in it need to give greater priority to the deficiencies of service-delivery systems. This entails not only introducing greater empathy between providers and clients, but must also include the specification of service-delivery standards; preservice and in-service training to meet those standards; the development of management systems that reward good performance; making available "best practice" technologies for ensuring good clinical outcomes; upgrading physical facilities; and ensuring that basic commodities and essential drugs are widely available and affordable.

These basic tasks constitute a full agenda. To suggest, as we have, that the entire ICPD Programme of Action may be beyond the ability of donors and recipients to implement does not constitute "resistance to change," a predilection for paradigm "rollback," or unease stemming from "the challenge to authority and tradition posed by women's empowerment" (as suggested by George Brown 2002: xii). Rather, it is a pragmatic response to competing programmatic needs, inadequate resources, and insufficient absorptive capacities in recipient countries.

Future global needs in reproductive health are truly daunting, especially given the rapid spread of HIV/AIDS that is already placing severe strain not just on development resources, but on the health delivery systems of developing countries stricken by the epidemic. The international health community has never faced greater challenges and potential threats (e.g., from an avian or swine flu pandemic), ones that are compounded by insufficient donor resources, weak political resolve, and misplaced certitude on how best to proceed.

Some changes in policy could help in this regard. Reassessing program interventions with a view to better prioritizing service needs might help constrain the growing demand for resources. Weaning some developing countries from high dependency on donor support, especially those increasingly able to make greater financial contributions themselves, would also help. Working to improve the financial sustainability of health systems through more effective cost recovery mechanisms (both in the public and private sector) should be given much greater attention.

More discipline on the part of donors relating to expenditures for various forms of international cheerleading might also make it possible to redirect funds to more critical ends. A stringent pruning of hypertrophied bureaucratic demands for proof of progress could be expected to release additional resources for more productive purposes. And while we have noted that overseas donor missions are often understaffed, it can be argued persuasively (particularly with respect to USAID) that staffing, which is more appropriately attuned to the technical requirements of program design and implementation, might enhance the utilization of resources and, as a bonus, improve the quality of interaction with host-country governments and institutions. There is much more that might be done along such lines, given well-directed policy, good management, and administrative courage.

By far the biggest hurdle to be surmounted is set by the United States. Prior to the election of President Barack Obama, America's total funding for population assistance had eroded since the mid-nineties. What it will be in the years ahead is somewhat imponderable given the advent of the Millennium Challenge Corporation, the upsurge in HIV/AIDS spending, and the still uncertain political support for population assistance. Overriding everything else in the United States is the present and future financial stringencies resulting from the global economic recession that began in 2007, heavy military expenditures, the legacy of revenue depleting tax policy, and urgent domestic spending. With a badly neglected physical infrastructure, insistent demands for a universally accessible health-care system on a par with other developed countries, an educational system that comes up short, and the lack of adequate provision for the future of social security, the outlook for increased funding for international health and social programs appears unpromising. It may not be possible, simultaneously, to pursue the goals of empire and social responsibility—domestic and foreign.

Finally, even if resources should miraculously increase to levels appropriate to meet reproductive health and HIV/AIDS needs now in view, there is every chance that we will misread some of the most basic challenges before us in this century. Population growth will continue to overwhelm hope for better lives in many parts of the developing world. This is particularly true for most countries in Africa, where high fertility and rapid population growth persist despite the ravages caused by the HIV/AIDS epidemic.

Contemporary international policy debates seldom reflect the fact that several billion future claimants on the world's shrinking bounty will be joining us in the none-too-distant future. Many national governments somehow remain immune to the distraction of current international policy preoccupations. They persist with the old-fashioned task of reducing birth rates, not in the belief that this is all they should do, but never doubting that it is something they must try to do. It would be the height of folly to weaken their commitment to this goal by advocating policies that may be more appropriate in other contexts—or to suggest that fertility declines that have occurred in some places will come for others as dependably as the monsoon rains.

APPENDIX A

AN OVERVIEW OF GLOBAL
DEMOGRAPHIC CONDITIONS

(Tables and text updated with latest United Nations estimates)

Although much has been accomplished in the years since rapid population growth and its consequences came front and center in official and public notice, the "problem of population" is still very much with us. As can be seen in Table A.1, the world's population grew from 2.5 billion in 1950 to 6.5 billion by 2005 (and is projected to reach nearly 7 billion by 2010). Most of the increase occurred in the less developed countries of the world.

As Table A.2 shows, the average annual rate of world population growth fell from a high of 2.02 percent in 1965–70 to 1.26 percent in 2000–05. In the less developed regions of the world, average annual rates of population growth for the same period fell from 2.48 percent in 1965–70 to 1.43

Table A.1 Trends in total population, 1950–2010 (population in millions)

Year	More developed regions	Less developed regions	Least developed countries	Total population (cols 2 + 3)
1950	812	1,717	200	2,529
1955	863	1,901	222	2,763
1960	915	2,109	247	3,023
1965	966	2,366	278	3,337
1970	1,007	2,678	315	3,686
1975	1,047	3,014	357	4,061
1980	1,082	3,356	406	4,438
1985	1,113	3,733	461	4,846
1990	1,147	4,143	525	5,290
1995	1,175	4,538	599	5,713
2000	1,195	4,920	677	6,115
2005	1,216	5,296	762	6,512
2010	1,237	5,671	855	6,909

Note: Figures may not sum to totals shown because of rounding.

Source: United Nations Population Division (2009). UN medium estimation series.

Table A.2 Trends in the rate of annual population growth, 1950–2010

Period	More developed regions	Less developed regions	Least developed countries	Total population growth (cols 2 + 3)
1950–55	1.21	2.03	2.01	1.77
1955–60	1.17	2.08	2.19	1.80
1960–65	1.09	2.30	2.33	1.94
1965–70	0.85	2.48	2.51	2.02
1970–75	0.77	2.37	2.54	1.94
1975–80	0.66	2.15	2.54	1.77
1980–85	0.58	2.13	2.55	1.76
1985–90	0.60	2.09	2.59	1.75
1990–95	0.47	1.82	2.65	1.54
1995–2000	0.34	1.62	2.44	1.36
2000–05	0.36	1.47	2.36	1.26
2005–10	0.34	1.37	2.30	1.18

Source: United Nations Population Division (2009). UN medium estimation series.

percent by 2000–05. Much of that decline can be attributed to fertility declines in China, Southeast Asia, and Latin America. In the least developed countries of the world, which are concentrated in sub-Saharan Africa and South Asia, population growth rates have remained high. According to UN estimates, the annual rate of population growth for 2000–05 was 2.36 percent in the world's least developed countries (a doubling time of just 29 years). Changes in the rate of population growth were typically driven by initial reductions in mortality (principally infant and child mortality), followed by dramatic and historically unprecedented reductions in fertility.

The infant mortality rate, the number of infant deaths per 1,000 births, has fallen substantially throughout the developing world over the past half-century; but disparities in infant mortality levels between more developed and less developed countries are still very pronounced (Table A.3). By the period 2000–05, only 7 infants died per 1,000 births in more developed regions, compared with 89 infants per 1,000 births in the least developed countries. Boys are at greater risk of death than girls in the first year of life in all regions. The UN estimates that under five child mortality is lower for girls in least developed countries, but nearly the same as boys in more advantaged regions as of 2000–05 (United Nations Population Division 2009), but this pattern may not typify all least developed countries.

Improvements in infant mortality and child mortality have been largely responsible for substantial gains in life expectancy over the past half-century.

Table A.3 Infant mortality rates (IMRs) by sex, 1950–2010 (infant deaths per 1,000 live births)

Period	More developed regions			Less developed regions			Least developed countries			Global IMR (cols 2 + 3)		
	M	F	M + F	M	F	M + F	M	F	M + F	M	F	M + F
1950–55	65	53	59	186	161	174	204	184	194	163	163	152
1955–60	47	38	43	168	147	158	189	171	180	189	127	136
1960–65	37	29	33	139	125	132	176	158	167	122	109	116
1965–70	30	22	26	117	108	113	163	146	155	105	96	100
1970–75	25	18	21	106	98	102	153	136	145	95	86	91
1975–80	22	15	18	97	89	93	144	128	136	87	79	83
1980–85	17	12	15	85	78	82	132	117	124	77	70	74
1985–90	14	11	13	74	69	72	122	108	115	67	63	65
1990–95	12	9	10	69	65	67	114	101	108	63	59	61
1995–2000	9	8	8	64	61	62	106	94	100	58	56	57
2000–05	8	7	7	58	56	57	95	84	89	53	51	52
2005–10	7	6	6	53	51	52	88	77	82	48	46	47

Source: United Nations Population Division (2009). UN medium estimation series.

Table A.4 Life expectancy at birth by sex, 1950–2010

Period	More developed regions			Less developed regions			Least developed countries			Global IMR (cols 2 + 3)		
	M	F	M + F	M	F	M + F	M	F	M + F	M	F	M + F
1950–55	63.4	68.4	66.0	40.3	41.8	41.0	35.8	37.1	36.4	45.2	48.0	46.6
1955–60	65.5	70.9	68.3	43.4	45.0	44.2	37.9	39.3	38.6	48.1	50.9	49.5
1960–65	66.7	72.7	69.8	46.9	48.2	47.5	39.8	41.4	40.6	51.0	53.7	52.4
1965–70	67.2	73.7	70.5	51.5	53.0	52.2	41.7	43.6	42.7	54.6	57.6	56.1
1970–75	67.7	74.7	71.3	54.0	55.8	54.9	43.3	45.4	44.4	56.6	59.8	58.2
1975–80	68.4	75.7	72.1	56.1	58.3	57.2	44.8	47.0	45.9	58.3	62.0	60.2
1980–85	69.1	76.5	72.9	57.7	60.3	59.0	46.9	49.2	48.0	59.7	63.7	61.7
1985–90	70.3	77.4	74.0	59.2	62.0	60.6	48.4	50.9	49.6	61.2	65.2	63.2
1990–95	70.3	77.9	74.1	60.2	63.3	61.7	49.1	51.7	50.4	61.9	66.2	64.0
1995–2000	71.3	78.6	75.0	61.5	64.8	63.1	50.8	53.4	52.1	63.0	67.4	65.2
2000–05	72.2	79.5	75.8	62.8	66.1	64.4	52.8	55.3	54.0	64.2	68.6	66.4
2005–10	73.6	80.5	77.1	63.9	67.4	65.6	54.7	57.2	55.9	65.4	69.8	67.6

Source: United Nations Population Division (2009). UN medium estimation series.

As is shown in Table A.4, life expectancy rose from 46.6 years in 1950–55 to 66.4 years by 2000–05. Women live longer than men in developed, less developed, and least developed countries, although their relative longevity lessens considerably in poorer environments. With the growing spread of

HIV/AIDS and other infectious diseases, however, it is unclear whether these improvements can be sustained, particularly in the least developed countries of the world. In fact, life expectancy in Africa began to decline around 1995.

The total fertility rate—that is, the average number of children born to women during their reproductive life spans—fell from an average of 4.9 births per woman in 1950–55 to 2.7 in 2000–05 (Table A.5). This substantial reduction occurred primarily in less developed countries, although fertility remained quite high in the least developed countries of the world (close to 5 births per woman) by the start of the twenty-first century.

By making modern contraceptive services available to women in less developed countries, family planning programs were instrumental in producing this reproductive slowdown. Undeniably, fertility rates might have declined without access to the organized delivery of modern contraceptive services. It has happened before, for example, among the Bushmen of the Kalahari Desert, the Magyars of Hungary, the Greeks after World War II, and Americans during the Great Depression. These were, each in different ways, populations facing sharp limits on their ability to care for excess offspring. But these historic examples, interesting as they are, are no more an argument against the efficacy of modern family planning programs than croup kettles are against antibiotics.

Table A.5 Total fertility rates (TFRs), 1950–2010 (average number of births per woman over the reproductive life span)

Period	More developed regions	Less developed regions	Least developed countries	Global TFR (cols 2 + 3)
1950–55	2.82	6.00	6.62	4.92
1955–60	2.78	5.80	6.65	4.81
1960–65	2.67	5.94	6.73	4.91
1965–70	2.37	5.81	6.76	4.78
1970–75	2.17	5.18	6.74	4.32
1975–80	1.94	4.53	6.61	3.83
1980–85	1.86	4.19	6.43	3.61
1985–90	1.82	3.89	6.06	3.43
1990–95	1.67	3.43	5.64	3.08
1995–2000	1.56	3.10	5.21	2.82
2000–05	1.58	2.89	4.78	2.67
2005–10	1.64	2.73	4.39	2.56

Source: United Nations Population Division (2009). UN medium estimation series.

With the advent of enhanced child survival, women of the developing world now must raise more children than they might have anticipated under earlier mortality regimes. This is a main source of "unwanted births" or "unwanted children"—two elusive and unstable concepts. Whatever they are called, more of them now survive to adulthood, swelling the claimants for jobs. To find a livelihood many desert their rural communities, where strong normative traditions trump most other considerations related to family size. Not surprisingly, early family planning programs spent much effort on "motivating clients" and on attempts to establish a "two-child norm." These efforts, often naively conducted, eventually gave way to more realistic programs that recognized the need for well-organized, dependable, and considerately delivered services, although it was not always clear why some couples accepted the services on offer whereas others did not.

Despite the success of family planning in many developing countries, population growth remains a prominent feature of the contemporary social and economic landscape in many less developed regions of the world. It has remained stubbornly high, in part because declines in fertility have been offset by reductions in mortality. The age structures of many developing-country populations, which reflect past high fertility, ensure that the momentum of population growth will continue well into the future.

Recent UN projections underscore the magnitude of future population growth. According to the UN's "medium variant" projection, the world's population can be anticipated to rise from 6.5 billion in 2005 to 9.1 billion by 2050. This projection assumes that fertility estimates are valid and that current rates will continue to fall rapidly. There is still some uncertainty about actual levels and trends of fertility and mortality in some developing countries, most notably in India.[1]

The United Nations assumes that a global population-replacement level of 2.1–2.2 births per woman will be reached by 2025–30. It also assumes that all regions of the developing world except Africa will have reached replacement fertility by 2050 (with Asia and Latin America actually falling slightly below 2.1 births per woman). If these assumptions turn out to be overly optimistic, the world's population could be considerably larger by 2050. For example, if global fertility rates were to plateau at current levels for the next 50 years, by 2050 the world's population could reach 11.0 billion (or nearly double its size in 2000).

Underlying this future population growth are continued advances in life expectancy. No country fails to benefit in this regard, according to the UN projections. Nonetheless, there is a high degree of uncertainty in these estimates. The effects of wars, famine, disease, civil disorder, and the possibility of declining effectiveness in our pharmacopoeia cannot be confidently foreseen. This is especially true in the case of the HIV/AIDS epidemic.

UN projections made in 2004 estimate that 344.5 million excess deaths may result from HIV/AIDS by 2050 in the 60 countries most affected by the epidemic as of 2000 (United Nations Population Division 2004a: 17). Much of this mortality will be concentrated in Africa (266.2 million excess deaths by 2050). Unfortunately, past experience in projecting the spread of HIV/AIDS does not instill great confidence in accounting for the future course of the disease. It is probably fair to say that early projections tended to underestimate growth in the rate of HIV/AIDS transmission in sub-Saharan Africa and overstated the rate of spread in some Southeast Asian countries (e.g., Indonesia, the Philippines, and Thailand).

Despite this high degree of uncertainty, the medium UN forecast calls for continued overall population growth accompanied by massive redistributions of people to cities and alien lands. This outlook is in line with historic trends in which short run spikes in mortality due to war, famine, disease, and other calamities have been compensated by the continued reproductive output of the populations so affected.

Although the UN projections incorporate assumptions about the spread of HIV/AIDS, they show little apparent effect on future gains in life expectancy. The United Nations assumes that behavioral change within subpopulations most subject to the risk of infection will greatly slow HIV/AIDS transmission rates after 2010. The projections even assume that the spread of HIV/AIDS will not greatly inhibit future gains in life expectancy in Africa. Given what we know now about the rapid spread of HIV/AIDS in sub-Saharan Africa and the potential for huge epidemics in China and India, these assumptions may prove too hopeful.

More remarkably, it should be noted that there is currently much controversy surrounding actual levels of HIV seroprevalence in much of the developing world. Estimates produced by UNAIDS to monitor and project the epidemic are based largely on surveys of pregnant urban women who attend antenatal clinics. As James Chin (2007) and others have argued, these surveys are not capable of generating valid measures of HIV seroprevalance in general populations or provide good baselines for projection work. Population-based surveys conducted by the Demographic and Health Surveys (DHS) Project at Macro International have often found lower rates of HIV seroprevalance than typically reported by UNAIDS. For example, in Rwanda, UNAIDS was reporting a national HIV positive rate of 13 percent while DHS found just a 3 percent rate and in Zambia national estimates diverged by 21.5 percent (UNAIDS) and 15.6 (DHS) (Timberg

2006:1–2). The largest overstatement of HIV cases appears to have occurred in India, which raises considerable uncertainty about the true size of the global HIV/AIDS epidemic.

This view of future demographic events is at odds with the prospect of a universal "shrinking of populations" encountered in some popular accounts. Through a disingenuous mixing of trends from developed and underdeveloped countries, this version of demographic reality leaves the impression that schemes to stimulate fertility will be the major preoccupation of future population policy. These journalistic sorties into the future ignore the real possibility that recent declines in the fertility of underdeveloped countries have been overstated. In the absence of credible vital registration systems, fertility rates for many countries are based on survey data. Diagnostic measures have shown that births and deaths can be missed in these surveys. Techniques currently employed in estimating fertility rates from survey birth histories can underestimate current fertility by omitting births (particularly among children who have died) and overstating the ages of children. The fertility rates generated from survey data for some developing countries (e.g., India and Pakistan) sometimes strain credulity and appear inconsistent with estimates derived from sample registration and census age distributions (see Kantner and He 2001).

Most of the projected gains in population over the coming 50 years, regardless of how much there will be, will occur in developing countries. The coming shifts in the balance of population among the major areas of the world will be momentous, although it is unclear what they portend for relations among countries. The pattern for the 100-year period from 1950 to 2050 is projected to look something like that shown in Table A.6. The percentage of the world's population living in less developed regions is expected to rise from 80.4 to 86.1 percent between 2000 and 2050. The percentage living in the least developed countries will nearly double, rising from 11.1 percent in 2000 to 18.3 percent in 2050.

Table A.6   Total and percentage distribution of world population, 1950–2050

Region	Total population (millions)			Percentage distribution		
	1950	2000	2050	1950	2000	2050
More developed	812	1,194	1,275	32.1	19.5	13.9
Less developed	1,717	4,920	7,874	67.9	80.4	86.1
Least developed	200	677	1,672	7.9	11.1	18.3
World total	2,529	6,115	9,149			

Source: United Nations Population Division (2009). UN medium variant projection.

Table A.7 Total and percentage distribution of world and regional populations, 1950–2050

	Total population (millions)			Percentage distribution		
Region	1950	2000	2050	1950	2000	2050
Africa	227	819	1,998	9.0	13.4	21.8
Asia	1,403	3,698	5,231	55.5	60.5	57.2
Europe	547	726	691	21.6	11.9	7.6
Latin America	167	521	729	6.6	8.5	8.0
North America	172	319	448	6.8	5.2	4.9
Oceania	13	31	51	0.5	0.5	0.5
World total	2,529	6,115	9,149	100.0	100.0	100.0

Source: United Nations Population Division (2009). UN medium variant projection.

Africa and Asia together will make up 79.0 percent of the world's population by 2050 (Table A.7). Europe and North America are projected to decline from 17.1 percent in 2000 to 12.5 percent. What this may entail is impossible to say with any certainty. That it is portentous is beyond doubt. Most of the new arrivals in the less developed countries will need to be accommodated where they are rooted unless the developed world is ready to welcome new immigrants in far greater numbers.

Many developed countries (principally Japan and those in Europe) are now experiencing negative rates of population growth. China too has drastically reduced its rate of growth. But more than declining growth is in prospect for these countries. Europe and Japan can anticipate severe labor shortages as the result of their aging populations and have yet to develop ways to accept and accommodate the large number of immigrants they will need to staff their economies. The US and Canadian populations continue to grow, thanks to immigration, but neither country has devised long-term policies to deal with ongoing gains in population size or changes in their ethnic compositions.

In the developing world, the main concern of this book, the situation is much more daunting. Most developing counties still have very youthful populations. For example, as of 2000, the percentage of the population under age 15 was 30.2 in Indonesia, 34.1 in India, 37.5 in Bangladesh, 41.3 in Pakistan, and 45.3 in Nigeria. The task of educating these large youth cohorts and generating jobs for them a decade or so hence looms large. By contrast, in countries that have completed the transition from high to low fertility, only 18.3 percent of the population, on average, is under 15 years of age.

Table A.8 Levels and trends in urban population, 1950–2030

Region	Total urban population (millions)			Percentage of urban population		
	1950	2000	2030	1950	2000	2030
Africa	32	296	739	14.7	37.2	41.0
Asia	243	1,380	2,645	17.4	37.5	50.7
Europe	287	534	552	52.4	73.4	87.3
Latin America	70	392	598	41.9	75.4	77.9
North America	109	245	344	63.9	77.4	76.8
Oceania	8	23	32	61.6	74.1	69.5
World total	750	2,866	4,896	29.8	47.2	54.9

Source: United Nations Population Division 2003. UN medium variant projection.

The world will also be far more urbanized by the middle of the twenty-first century. UN projections anticipate that more than half of the world's population will be living in urban areas by mid-century (Table A.8). Europe, North America, and Latin America will be the most highly urbanized regions. More than three-quarters of all people residing in these regions will be urban-based. By 2015, many cities in the developing world will have more than 20 million inhabitants (United Nations Population Division 2003)—for example, Dhaka (22.8 million), Mumbai (22.6 million), Sao Paulo (21.2 million), Delhi (20.9 million), and Mexico City (20.4 million). Such rapid urban growth will pose serious challenges to governments attempting to cope with the growing demand for social services and infrastructure investment in urban settings.

NOTES

1 Introduction

1. And what should be the proper business of foreign assistance? Ideally it should emerge out of an attempt to define a vision of global society—one that would benefit both giver and receiver. A recent attempt to identify areas where assistance would be mutually helpful (Allin, Gordon, and O'Hanlon 2003) fails to provide a logically closed theory of the objectives of foreign assistance but does offer an ad hoc list that touches the major bases. The list includes humanitarian intervention against genocidal violence, cooperation against global warming and other environmental scourges, free trade, large investments to combat HIV/AIDS, and family planning.

2. For simplicity, we use the term reproductive health to include family planning and other basic reproductive health interventions (e.g., the diagnosis and treatment of sexually transmitted diseases, postabortion care, and adolescent services) that enhance maternal and child health. Broader definitions of reproductive health that embrace "a state of complete physical, mental and social well-being . . . in all matters relating to the reproductive system and to its functions and processes" (Caro et al. 2003: 5) strike us as operationally vague and programmatically unworkable.

2 The Early Years of International Population Assistance: The Striving for Consensus

1. Sanger's belief in the importance of scientific research, not always biological research, dates back at least to 1928, when she was instrumental in organizing the founding meeting of the International Union for the Scientific Study of Population (IUSSP), a session that, although invited to do so, she declined to address for fear her presence would somehow detract from the scientific aura conferred on the meeting. Ironically the first president of the IUSSP, Raymond Pearl, elected at that meeting,

appears to have been chosen more for his eminence as a scientist than as someone with even a sanitized interest in voluntary birth control. At the time and until his painful conversion in the face of new statistical evidence, Pearl viewed population dynamics through the lens of a biological mechanism whereby population growth would be slowed, as with the fruit fly, by diminished fecundity brought about by crowding and the insalubrious nature of modern life.

2. Margaret Sanger had her differences with the leaders of the family planning movement in America who followed her. She found their decision to pursue the struggle through legislation and legalistic strategies too lacking in revolutionary verve and regarded the term "family planning" as flaccid and a concession to the prissiness that found "birth control" a bit too brass-knuckled.

3. An attempt to conceptualize and model the intermediate factors involved in health, inspired in part by the popularity of Bongaarts' work, generated some momentary expectations, but failed to catch on primarily because of the greater complexity of the disease process and the diffuseness of the end state—health. Some have suggested the need for a Bongaarts-like model for family planning and reproductive health. There are many diagrammatic representations of the factors involved, but thus far nothing of general applicability with well-grounded mathematical interconnections.

4. This account of USAID and the Ravenholt era draws on the work of Donaldson (1987), Sinding (2001), and various documents available from ravenrt@oz.net and www.ravenholt.com.

3   The Emergence of New Priorities for International Population Assistance: The Years of Growing Policy and Program Discord

1. Population Council presidents Frank Notestein and Bernard Berelson acknowledged that family planning programs alone would not be sufficient to reduce high rates of fertility. However, they disagreed with Rockefeller's attempt to recast the mission of the Population Council. As Harkavy notes, "they parted company with Rockefeller's speech writers on the question of whether alleviation of poverty and improvement of women's health, education, and status were the proper business of a population agency, or whether it should stick to its population knitting and leave these broader issues to the development assistance community"—which as

Berelson pointed out represented 98% of total overseas development at that time (Harkavy 1995: 186).

2. After much debate, the U.S. Commission on Population and the American Future (1970–72), chaired by John D. Rockefeller III, enunciated a position that sought to soften the hard demographic edges of population policy. Rejecting the goal of achieving zero population growth as inappropriate for the United States (and by implication for developing countries as well), the Commission called for a more flexible policy in which population policy would focus on reducing levels of unwanted fertility. This approach encouraged women to have the number of children they wanted rather than pressing for a population growth target. This was a welcome shift in policy since it put women rather than distant policy makers squarely in the picture—a shift in direction that was not unfamiliar to the UN Expert Committee preparing for the 1974 Bucharest conference. It had its limitations however. If pursued in Africa today, according to data from surveys that measure the extent of unwanted fertility, fertility would average around five rather than six births per woman (Charles Westoff, personal communication).

3. Berelson was among the scholars in the 1970s who were intrigued by the idea of development and behavioral thresholds as these might be identified by various social and economic indicators. It was thus a short step from that to the conception of social settings as the categorical framework within which to analyze the effects of program effort.

4. This view is not universally accorded. Hartman (1987: 109) calls it a "time of retrenchment" and well it might have seemed to one energized by the high hopes aroused at Bucharest for the primacy of development initiatives. But in our view family planning and MCH programs became more effective in meeting the needs of clients during the 1980s when compared to previous decades.

5. If population growth had positive as well as negative consequences and if in the long run the former tended to outweigh the latter, this could, indeed, become "the best of all *possible* worlds," as Voltaire's Dr. Pangloss promised.

6. An influential statement of this argument is developed in detail in Simon's (1981) book *The Ultimate Resource*.

7. Revisionist theory and analysis was pursued at the macroeconomic level. Also creating an academic buzz in those years was the microeconomic theory of fertility, which, treating the household analogously to a business firm, attempted to develop a production function for the household,

the main output being children with their varying utilities. A thorough review of this application of consumer-demand theory (Robinson 1997) concludes that in the end it did little to enhance one's understanding of fertility or population policy directed toward influencing it.

8. Caldwell notes that "a major aspect of the decline" in Asian fertility has been the success among governments there in persuading couples "that they will be better off with smaller families. Hardly anyone at Cairo . . . dared to mention this" (Caldwell 1996: 72).

9. The SRHR label is now being used to describe resource flows for international population assistance (see, e.g., Claeys and Wuyts 2004). However, the presumably matching budget figures compiled by the Netherlands Interdisciplinary Demographic Institute and reported by UNFPA for international population assistance do not include costs of sexuality initiatives, women's empowerment programs, or human and reproductive rights advocacy. They refer simply to allocations for family planning, other reproductive health interventions (such as maternity care, postabortion services, and adolescent programs), STD/HIV/AIDS, and research. Using the SRHR label to describe levels of donor or recipient country resources that refer only to population and reproductive health activities is misleading.

4 The New Millennium: The Ascendancy of Antiabortion Politics and Millennium Development Goals

1. At the heart of the moral argument against abortion and contraception is the sanctified conception of the family as the guarantor of social stability. The validity of this idealized view of social structure is rarely contested, yet in wide sociological perspective it is undeniable that although "kinship affords mutual aid to its members, it harbors many malignancies in its relation to the larger social universe. It fosters parochialism which not infrequently proves the source of internecine conflict. Nepotistic commitments trade competence for loyalty, enlightenment for tradition, and humanity for ethnocentrism. Kinship is the enemy of civility. The demise of one is essential to the rise of the other . . ." (Hawley 1998).

2. The term refers to a grizzly procedure involving the collapsing of the brain case of a partially delivered birth and the evacuation of the cranial contents so that delivery can be completed. For many the nature of this

uncommon procedure is less at issue than the wisdom of legislating medical decisions and ignoring the mother's health in the decision.

3. In its first court test, partial birth abortion was declared unconstitutional by a federal judge on the grounds that it violates a woman's right to choice in the matter of abortion.

4. Asserting the claim that life begins at conception and opposing any procedure that interferes with the fulfillment of that process effectively closes the possibility of women escaping from an unwanted pregnancy afforded by the morning-after-pill or emergency contraception if the pill's mechanism of action involves death of a fertilized ovum or implantation. If, as some research suggests, the mechanism is one that disrupts the timing of events so that egg and sperm never get acquainted, then escape from unwanted pregnancy should be available. A further objection often made to emergency contraception is that it provides an escape from irresponsible reproduction.

5. Much of the empirical rationale for the MDGs is presented by Jeffery Sach in his book *The End of Poverty: Economic Possibilities for Our Time* (Sachs 2005). A subsequent release in 2008, *Common Wealth: Economics for a Crowded Planet*, more directly focused on population size, growth, and distribution as factors influencing development outcomes and the attainment of the MDGs. These were neglected issues in the thinking that led to the original MDG formulation.

5 International Population Assistance since Cairo: Trends in Policy and Program Action

1. As noted by UNFPA (2003a: 6–7) and by Claeys and Wuyts (2004: 3), it is becoming increasingly difficult to track levels and trends in international population assistance. With the transition from family planning to reproductive health programming, the range of services incorporated as part of international population assistance has expanded considerably, most notably between 1995 and 1996. The infusion of new funding for HIV/AIDS is also causing confusion because some countries (e.g., Sweden and the United Kingdom) include these figures under reproductive health whereas others (e.g., the United States and Japan) do not. Calls to integrate reproductive health care with other health services (e.g., primary health care and MCH care) and sector-wide assistance programs (SWAps), in which donor funding is aggregated into large resource pools to be

allocated by host governments, are also confounding efforts to measure reproductive health spending. Finally, the estimate of private-sector contributions from recipient countries is a rough approximation, which casts considerable uncertainty on the true level of support for international population activities.

2. The effectiveness of providing family planning services through domiciliary delivery was demonstrated through years of field trials undertaken in the Matlab Maternal and Child Health Service Program at the International Centre for Diarrheal Disease Research, Bangladesh. For accounts of this work, see Arends-Kuenning (2001); Cleland, Phillips, and Amin (1994); Phillips et al. (1993); Simmons et al. (1988). Dixon-Mueller (1993) states that female outreach workers in Bangladesh "have served as effective change agents in altering the 'calculus of choice' that binds women and men to patriarchal attitudes and practices" (p. 233).

3. This decision was taken prior to any considered operational field-testing of how such programmatic change should be implemented. The operations research funded by USAID at the Extension Project of the International Centre for Diarrheal Disease Research, Bangladesh, after 1998 served more to justify programmatic transformations that were already being enacted than to provide guidance on how best to proceed with the newly revised program.

4. Nevertheless, the authors state that in NGO service areas "many [women] now are actively seeking out and successfully using clinical methods, which are available on a more reliable basis and are supported by higher quality services" (Schuler, Bates, and Islam 2001: 196). They also claim that women prefer to visit clinics and accept longer-acting clinical methods (such as IUDs, injectable contraceptives, and sterilization), which are generally unavailable through less formal channels. Nevertheless, the authors state that in NGO service areas "many [women] now are actively seeking out and successfully using clinical methods, which are available on a more reliable basis and are supported by higher quality services" (Schuler, Bates, and Islam 2001: 196). However, recently released national data on contraceptive use from the 2004 Bangladesh Demographic and Health Survey suggests that clinical methods have become less popular among the majority of Bangladeshi women over the past decade. The 2004 Demographic and Health Survey reports that the percentage of currently married women using non-clinical methods (pills and condoms) rose from 20.4% in 1993–94 to 30.4% in 2004 while clinical methods (IUDs, implants, and sterilization) fell from

11.4% to 7.2% over the same period (NIPORT 2005: 67). The use of injectables, which are provided through clinics, fieldworker domiciliary delivery, and pharmacies, has risen from 4.5% to 9.7% of currently married women between 1993–94 and 2004.

5. Whatever this popular and somewhat amorphous term means, it clearly refers to entities and movements that are not part of the apparatus of government in a direct way. NGOs are a constituent and increasingly visible part of civil society.

6. A subset of NGOs is sometimes referred to as grass roots organizations (GROs). Annis (1987: 139) observes that GROs are generally intertwined with government and that their character is determined by state policy.

7. The summary report mentions several, including the training of health workers, development of reproductive/health camps, filling assistant nurse midwife positions, upgrading of health centers, providing tetanus toxoid immunization for pregnant women, expansion of social marketing activity, extension of family planning and rural health outreach services of NGOs, and development of a communication strategy for health and family planning in Uttar Pradesh.

6 An Overview of Major Donor Organizations Currently Providing International Population Assistance

1. Perhaps as the result of a bit of retributive justice exercised through UNFPA's recruitment policy, the U.S. policy toward the UNFPA has the unfortunate effect of denying fuller participation of American professionals in UNFPA affairs. For most openings at the professional level, it is now tacitly understood that Americans need not apply.

2. Even this view, which at the time verged on the platitudinous, was challenged a decade later by a World Bank economist (Pritchett 1994) who argued that the main goal of population policy aimed at reducing fertility should be to change the desired number of offspring. He asserted that Family Planning Programs have no independent power to do this and that a policy to lower fertility was fruitless unless couples were motivated to have fewer children. This line of argument totally ignores the role of domestic political support in promoting the desire for smaller families and the demand for contraception. An instructive case study of the bureaucratic and political management skills of the Indonesian National Family Planning Coordinating Board (BKKBN) during the Suharto era is provided by Shiffman (2004). It is doubtful whether Indonesian

fertility would have fallen so rapidly over the past two decades without the strikingly proactive political mobilization campaigns of BKKBN, both within the country's central bureaucratic structure and at district and subdistrict levels.

3. The chief advantage to USAID of procuring commodities and services through cooperating-agency mechanisms is that it evades hobbling procurement restrictions that have typified federal procurement procedures since the days of the Marshall Plan. This is a significant factor in the proliferation of agencies. The down side of this arrangement is that it tends to extract a sense of project ownership from developing countries and to bypass their local institutions. It places the cooperating agencies in an intermediate position between the recipient country and the funds officially appropriated for the programs and projects in which they are participants.

4. PSCs often do not qualify for post-differentials in pay, housing support, or educational and family home leave benefits provided to USAID's direct-hire staff. PSCs also must usually cover their health insurance costs and are not entitled to retirement benefits other than social security. In addition, their salaries are typically not in line with those provided to direct hires.

5. An additional indication of the growing bypassing of USAID is the fact that the much heralded Bush initiative for HIV/AIDS prevention and care will be handled by a coordinator at the State Department who will fund and manage activities "above and beyond those of USAID and the UN Global Fund on HIV/AIDS" (InterAction 2003: 6). The Office of Management and Budget and the Pentagon are also encroaching further on areas formerly entrusted to USAID, as are the departments of Treasury, Health and Human Services, Labor, Energy, and Environmental Protection.

7   Where Do We Go from Here?

1   Speidel et al., (2007:4) note that population issues are now less readily considered by environmentalists than in earlier decades. Since the publication of Paul Erlich's *The Population Bomb* forty years ago, "population seems to have largely dropped off the environmental movement's agenda due to at least three factors: uncertainty and controversy around population and related issues, such as family planning, abortion, and reproductive health; the political dominance of a largely anti-environmental

White House and Congress within the United States; and a shifting of priorities within the US movement due to difficult fights over a broad variety of immediate threats to the environment."

2 Connelly contends that "population controllers preferred to deal with the high fertility of poor and uneducated people with increasingly blunt instruments" and that "if the 'dumb millions' did not plan their families in ways experts found intelligible, contraception had to be dumbed-down". (Connelly 2008:375). He contends that women were routinely coerced into using contraception through financial payments, were threatened with contraceptive agents broadcast through the air and water, were denied maternity leave, housing, and health care if found not to be practicing family planning, or were "simply dragged" to abortion and sterilization clinics. He likens family planning efforts to "experiments involving tens of millions" who were teated "as if they were bacteria in a petri dish" (Connelly 2008:375). While there is no question that family planning programs were occasionally guilty of overstepping the line and engaging in abusive practices, it is historically inaccurate to portray these events as the norm or in any way synonymous with the views of most family planning advocates and practitioners. This "impoverished sense of the past" undercuts much of what Connelly subsequently has to say about prescriptive population policy and his hoped-for reconciliation of the pro-life and pro-choice movements.

3 A recent assessment of future US funding requirements for international family planning programs calls for an increase from $457 million in FY 2008 to $1.205 billion in FY 2010, and a further rise to $1.562 billion by 2014 (Speidel et al., 2008:1).

4 It is worth noting that there may be some inconsistency in Caldwell's positions. On the one hand he concludes that family planning can't be credited with much of the fertility decline in Bangladesh but then claims that the success of international family planning programs in reducing global fertility suggests that these programs are no longer needed.

5 These needs are so apparent that one brave commentator has argued that unmet need should be the unifying force that unites all factions of the population debate—pro-life advocates, defenders of family planning programs, and women's health and rights advocates alike (Halfon: 2007). This sensible notion has not yet taken root.

6. The logistical implications of supplying the contraceptives needed to meet this anticipated demand over the next 15 years are staggering. For example, Ross and Stover (2003) calculate that 14.2 billion pill cycles will be needed to meet projected demand between 2000 and 2015.

Cumulative commodity requirements for other methods are equally daunting; e.g., 1.6 billion injectables, 214 million IUDs, and 105.5 billion condoms will be needed over the same period (p. 22). These projections "pose serious problems for donor priorities, as commodity supplies must compete with other budget items" (p. 22). One can argue with the precise values of their estimates, but the underlying dynamics are unquestionable. Also not to be questioned is the fact that donor contributions for contraceptive resupply have not kept pace with inflation, placing the security of many logistics systems in jeopardy. Ross and Stover conclude that "the glass, besides being only half full, may lose some water unless innovative steps are taken and [a] sense of urgency sharpens" (p. 23).

7. For example, the relatively new field of microbicide development in the United States currently involves ten nonprofit research organizations and twelve funding agencies from both the public and private sectors (INFO Reports 2005: 13). The activities of these organizations cover research and development issues of marketing and feasibility, clinical trials, and the funding of research. Microbicide research has been directed largely to HIV prevention, but most of the formulations that have reached Phase III clinical trials have the potential for pregnancy prevention and the avoidance of sexually transmitted diseases. Vaginal gels that combine several drugs may also prove more effective than single compounds acting alone.

8. For example, the pressure placed on recipient countries to implement abstinence prevention programs has met with considerable skepticism and ridicule. In addition, the U.S. government's insistence that the procurement of antiretroviral drugs with U.S. funds be limited to those in conformity with American patents and approved by the U.S. Food and Drug Administration has complicated U.S. efforts to provide constructive support for HIV/AIDS programs.

9. Wattenberg relies for his reading of fertility on recent population projections produced by the United Nations Population Division. They assume that most developing countries outside sub-Saharan Africa will reach or fall below replacement fertility within the next 25 years. Given current evidence of stalls in fertility decline in some developing countries and lingering doubts about the validity of recent fertility estimates from Demographic and Health Surveys in other countries (e.g., in India), there are reasonable grounds for being skeptical about the optimistic assumptions underlying the UN's latest population forecasts—not to mention Wattenberg's rosy view of future demographic dynamics in the developing world.

Appendix A An Overview of Global Demographic Conditions

1. The 1997–98 National Family Health Survey reported that India's national total fertility rate had declined to 2.8 births per woman, whereas the Sample Registration System (SRS) reported a figure around 0.5 births higher for the same time period. There is also some uncertainty about the reliability of SRS fertility data. For example, fertility estimates derived by reverse-surviving the age distribution from the 1991 Indian census suggest that SRS fertility rates for 1988–91 may be a little low or, at best, at the lower bound of a plausible range.

BIBLIOGRAPHY

Advisory Committee on Health Research (ACHR). 1996. *The Daly and Setting Priorities for Health.* Geneva: World Health Organization, Chapter 4.

Allin, Dana H., Philip H. Gordon, and Michael E. O'Hanlon. 2003. "The Democratic Party and foreign policy," *World Policy Journal* (Spring): 7–16.

Annis, Sheldon. 1987. "Can small-scale development be a large-scale policy? The case of Latin America," in *Development Alternatives: The Challenge for NGOs,* ed. Anne Gordon Drabek, *World Development* 5 (Supplement): 129–34.

Arends-Kuenning, Mary. 2001. "How do family planning workers' visits affect women's contraceptive behavior in Bangladesh?" *Demography* 38(4): 481–96.

Atwood, J. Brian. 2002. "Is there a future in foreign assistance?" speech presented at the Minnesota International Center, Minneapolis, December 3.

Bairagi, Radheshyam. 2001. "Demographic transition in Bangladesh: what happened here in the 20th century and what is next," Dhaka: International Centre for Diarrhoeal Disease Research, Bangladesh (ICDDR, B): 1–19.

Basu, Alaka. 1997. "The 'politicization' of fertility to achieve non-demographic objectives," *Population Studies* 51(1): 5–18.

———. 2000. "Gender in population research: confusing implications for health policy," *Population Studies* 7(6): 19–28.

———. 2005. "The Millennium Development Goals minus reproductive health: an unfortunate, but not disastrous, omission," *Studies in Family Planning* 36(2): 132–35.

Bellagio Study Group on Child Survival. 2003. "Knowledge into action for child survival," *Lancet* 362: 323–27.

Berelson, Bernard. 1974. "An evaluation of the effects of population control programs," *Studies in Family Planning* 5(1): 1–12.

Berman, Peter, et al. 1997. "The influence of maternal labor force participation on spending for child health: results from four villages in Haryana State, India," *Health Transition Review* 7(2): 187–204.

Bernstein, Stan. 2005. "The changing discourse on population and development: toward a new political demography," *Studies in Family Planning* 36(2): 128–32.

Bhatia, Jagdish and John Cleland. 2001. "The contribution of reproductive ill-health to the overall burden of perceived illness in South Indian women," *Bulletin of the World Health Organization* 79: 1065–69.

Birn, Anne-Emanuelle. 2005. "Gates's grandest challenge: transcending technology as public health ideology," *Viewpoint*, published online by *Lancet*, http://image.thelancet.com.extras/04art6429web.pdf.

Bloom, David E., David Canning, and Jaypee Sevilla. 2003. *The Demographic Dividend: A New Perspective on the Economic Consequences of Population Change*. Santa Monica, California: RAND Corporation.

Bongaarts, John. 2001. *The End of the Fertility Transition in the Developed World*, working paper no. 152. New York: The Population Council.

———. 2002. *The End of the Fertility Transition in the Developing World*, working paper no. 161. New York: The Population Council.

———. 2003. *Completing the Fertility Transition in the Developing World: The Role of Educational Differences and Fertility Preferences*, working paper no. 177. New York: The Population Council.

Bossert, Thomas, Joel Beauvais, and Diane Bowser. 2000. *Decentralization of Health Systems: Preliminary Review of Four Country Case Studies*. Washington, DC: Partnerships for Health Reform Project, Abt Associates.

Bowers, Gerard and Carl Hemmer. 2002. *Planning and Managing Contraceptive Phaseout: Applying Lessons Learned*. Washington, DC: POPTECH Project, LTG Associates.

Brown, George F. 2002. "Foreword," in *Responding to Cairo: Case Studies of Changing Practice in Reproductive Health and Family Planning*, eds. Nicole Haberland and Diana Measham. New York: The Population Council, pp. xi–xiv.

Brown, Lester. 2004. "China's shrinking grain harvest," *agWorld Wide—Correspondent*, www.agriculture.com/default.sph/agnotebook.class? NNC-Co.

Brown, Lester, Gary Gardner, and Brian Halweil. 2000. *Beyond Malthus: 19 Dimensions of the Population Challenge*. London: Earthscan Publishers.

Bruce, Judith. 1990. "Fundamental elements of the quality of care: a simple framework," *Studies in Family Planning* 21(2): 61–91.

Bruce, Judith and Anrudh Jain. 1995. *The Progress of Nations*. New York: UNICEF, www.unicef.org/pon95/famiooo2.html.

Bryce, Jennifer, et al. 2003. "Reducing child mortality: can public health deliver?" *Lancet* 362: 159–84.

Buchanan, Patrick. 2002. *The Death of the West: How Dying Populations and Immigrant Invasions Imperil Our Country and Civilization*. New York: St. Martins Press.

Bulatao, Rodolfo A. 1998. *The Value of Family Planning Programs in Developing Countries*. Santa Monica, California: RAND Corporation.

Caldwell, John C. 1996. "The International Conference on Population and Development, Cairo, 1994: Is its Plan of Action important, desirable and feasible?" *Health Transition Review* 6: 71–122.

Caldwell, John C., J. Phillips, and Barkat-e-Khuda. 2002. "Introduction: the future of family planning programs," *Studies in Family Planning* 33(1): 1–10.

Caldwell, John C., et al. 1999. "The Bangladesh fertility decline: an interpretation," *Population and Development Review* 25(1): 67–84.

Caro, Deborah, et al. 2003. *A Manual for Integrating Gender into Reproductive Health and HIV Programs: From Commitment to Action*. Washington, DC: International Gender Working Group of the USAID Bureau for Global Health.

Catley-Carlson, Margaret. 1998. "Foreword," in *Do Population Policies Matter? Fertility and Policies in Egypt, India, Kenya, and Mexico*, ed. Anrudh Jain. New York: The Population Council, pp. ix–xiv.

Centers for Disease Control (CDC), USAID, and Measure DHS+. 2003. *Reproductive, Maternal, and Child Health in Eastern Europe and Eurasia: A Comparative Report*. Washington, DC: Department of Health and Human Services.

Chambers, Robert. 1996. "The primacy of the personal," in *Beyond the Magic Bullet: NGO Performance and Accountability*, eds. Michael Edwards and David Hulme. West Hartford, Connecticut: Kumarian Press, pp. 207–18.

Chemonics International. 2002. *Final Assessment Report: USAID/Philippines Support to Local Governments for Family Planning and Health*. Manila: Chemonics and USAID Office of Population and Health.

Chin, James. 2007. *The AIDS Pandemic: The Collision of Epidemiology and Political Correctness*. Oxford and Seattle: Radcliff Publishers.

Claeys, Vicky and Eef Wuyts. 2004. *Official Development Assistance Levels and Spending for Sexual and Reproductive Health and Rights since the ICPD*, background paper for the session Global Population and Development Trends: The European View at the UNECE European Population Forum 2004—Population Challenges and Policy Response, Geneva, Switzerland. Brussels: IPPF European Network.

Claxton, Philander. 1965. "Action memorandum," available from Population Council Archives, Rockefeller Estate, Pocantico Hills, New York.

Cleland, John. 1996. "ICPD and the feminization of population and development issues," *Health Transition Review* 6(1): 107–10.

Cleland, John and Georgia Kaufmann. 1998. "Education, fertility and child survival: unraveling the links," in *The Methods and Uses of Anthropological Demography*, eds. Alaka Basu and Peter Aaby. Oxford: Clarendon Press, pp. 128–52.

Cleland, John, George Bicego, and Greg Fegan. 1991. "Socio-economic inequalities in childhood mortality: the 1970s compared with the 1980s," *Health Transition Review* 2(1): 1–18.

Cleland, John, James F. Phillips, and Sajeda Amin. 1994. *The Determinants of Reproductive Health in Bangladesh*. Washington, DC: The World Bank.

Cleland, John, et al. 2006. "Family planning: the unfinished agenda," The Lancet.Com Article DOI:10:1016/S0140-6736(06)69480-4: 1–32.

Clemens, Michael and Steven Radelet. 2003. *The Millennium Challenge Account: How Much is Too Much and How Long is Long Enough?* Washington, DC: Center for Global Development.

Coale, Ansley and E. Hoover. 1958. *Population Growth and Economic Development in Low Income Countries: A Case Study for India's Prospects*. Princeton, New Jersey: Princeton University Press.

Cohen, Joel. 1995. *How Many People Can the Earth Support?* New York: W.W. Norton.

Collins, Charles. 1994. *Management and Organization of Developing Health Systems*. Oxford: Oxford University Press.

Collins, Charles and A. Green. 1994. "Decentralization and primary health care: some negative implications in developing countries," *International Journal of Health Services* 24(3): 459–76.

Connelly, Matthew. 2008. *Fatal Misconception: The Struggle to Control World Population*. Cambridge, Massachusetts: The Belknap Press of Harvard University.

Cross, Harry, Karen Hardee, and John Ross. 2002. *Completing the Demographic Transition in Developing Countries*, policy occasional paper no. 8. Washington, DC: The Futures Group International.

Cross, Harry, Karen Hardee, and Norine Jewell (eds.). 2000. *Reforming Operational Policies: A Pathway to Improving Reproductive Health Programs*, The Policy Project. Washington, DC: The Futures Group International.

Cross, John C. 1997. "Development NGOs, the state and neo-liberalism: competition, partnership or co-conspiracy," *Informal Cyberspace* www.openair.org/cross: 1–12.

Crossette, Barbara. 2003a. "Sixteen wise people and the future of the UN," *UN Wire*, December 1. Washington, DC: United Nations Foundation.

———. 2003b. "UNICEF in the crosshairs," *UN Wire*, September 2. Washington, DC: United Nations Foundation.

———. 2004. "Reproductive health and the Millennium Development Goals: the missing link," Commissioned by the Population Program of the William and Flora Hewlett Foundation, December.

Das Gupta, Monica. 1987. "Selective discrimination against female children in rural Punjab, India," *Population and Development Review* 13(1): 77–100.

Dasgupta, Jashodhara and Gita Sen. 1998. "From contraceptive targets to reproductive health: India's family planning program after Cairo," in *Confounding the Critics: Cairo, Five Years On—Executive Summary*, Health, Empowerment, Rights, and Accountability (HERA), The National Forum of Women and Population Policy, and the Feminist Millennium, Cocoyoc, Mexico, November 15–18. New York: International Women's Health Coalition.

DaVanzo, Julie and David M. Adamson. 1998. *Family Planning in Developing Countries, An Unfinished Success Story*, Population Matters Issue Paper. Santa Monica, California: RAND Corporation.

Davis, Kingsley and Judith Blake. 1956. "Social structure and fertility: an analytic framework," *Economic Development and Cultural Change* 4(3): 211–35.

Demeny, Paul. 2003. *Population Policy: A Concise Summary*, working paper no. 173. New York: The Population Council.

Dixon-Mueller, Ruth. 1993. *Population Policy and Women's Rights: Transforming Reproductive Choice*. Westport, Connecticut: Praeger.

Dixon-Mueller, Ruth and Adrienne Germain. 1992. "Stalking the elusive 'unmet need' for family planning," *Studies in Family Planning* 23(5): 330–35.

———. 2000. "Reproductive health and the demographic imagination," in *Women's Empowerment and Demographic Processes: Moving Beyond Cairo*, eds. Harriet B. Presser and Gita Sen. New York: Oxford University Press, pp. 69–94.

Dodd, Rebecca and Emily Hinshelwood. No date. *Poverty Reduction Strategy Papers—Their Significance for Health*. Geneva: World Health Organization.

Donabedian, Avedis. 1980. *The Criteria and Standards of Quality*. Ann Arbor, Michigan: Health Administration Press.

———. 1988. "The quality of care: how it can be assessed," *Journal of the American Medical Association* 260(12): 1743–48.

Donaldson, Peter. 1987. "The origins and implementation of America's international population policy," paper prepared for delivery at the Annual Meeting of the Population Association of America, Chicago, April 30–May 2.

Dunlop, Joan, Rachel Kyte, and Mia MacDonald. No date. *Women Redrawing the Map: The World after the Beijing and Cairo Conferences.* New York: International Women's Health Coalition.

Eager, Paige W. 2004. *Global Population Policy: From Population Control to Reproductive Rights.* Aldershot, England: Ashgate Publishing Limited.

The Economist. 2000. "Sins of the secular missionaries," January 27, pp. 130–32.

———. 2003a. "Bangladesh NGOs: Being well-meaning is no protection: when humanitarianism gets caught up with politics," March 15, p. 39.

———. 2003b. "Indonesia: autonomy or anarchy: devolution isn't working as planned?" February 13, pp. 38–39.

Edwards, Michael and David Holmes. 1994. "NGOs and development: performance and accountability in the 'new world order,'" background paper for SCF/IDPM Workshop on NGOs and Development, Manchester, England, June 27–29.

Edwards, Michael and David Hulme. 1996. *Beyond the Magic Bullet: NGO Performance and Accountability.* West Hartford, Connecticut: Kumarian Press.

Ehrlich, Paul. 1968 (reprint in 1997). *The Population Bomb: Population Control or Race to Oblivion.* Cutchogue, New York: Buccaneer Books, Inc.

Engleman, Robert, et al. 2000. *People in the Balance: Population and Natural Resources at the Turn of the Millennium.* Washington, DC: Population Action International.

Enke, Stephen. 1960, "The economics of government payments to limit population," *Economic Development and Cultural Change* 8(4): 339–48.

Ethelston, Sally, et al. 2004. *Progress and Promises: Trends in International Assistance for Reproductive Health and Population.* Washington, DC: Population Action International.

Family Care International. 1998a. *Implementation of ICPD Commitments on Women's Reproductive & Sexual Health: A Report on Four African Countries.* New York.

———. 1998b. *Implementation of ICPD Commitments on Women's Reproductive & Sexual Health: A South Asia Report.* New York.

Finkle, Jason and Alison McIntosh. 1994. *The New Politics of Population: Conflict in Family Planning.* New York: Oxford University Press.

———. 1996. "Cairo revisited: some thoughts on the implications of the ICPD," *Health Transition Review* 6: 110–13.

Food and Agriculture Organization of the United Nations (FAO). 2003. *The State of Food Insecurity in the World: Monitoring Progress towards the World Food Summit and Millennium Development Goals.* Rome.

Foster, Pamela, et al. 2003. *Evaluation of the Training in Reproductive Health Project.* Washington, DC: POPTECH Project.

Gates Foundation. 2003. *Global Health: Reducing Global Health Inequities.* Seattle, Washington: www.gatesfoundation.org/GlobalHealth/.

Gedda, George. 2004. "US to begin new approach on foreign aid: program favors countries with just rulers," *Associated Press,* AOL News Service, January 3.

Germain, Adrienne. 1993. *Are We Speaking the Same Language? Women's Health Advocates and Scientists Talk about Contraceptive Technology.* New York: International Women's Health Coalition.

———. 1997. "Addressing the demographic imperative through health, empowerment, and rights: ICPD implementation in Bangladesh," *Health Transition Review* 7(Supplement 4): 33–36.

———. 2000. "Population and reproductive health: where do we go next?" *American Journal of Public Health* 90(12): 1844–47.

———. 2005. *Making Progress: An International Agenda to Secure and Advance Sexual and Reproductive Rights and Health.* Speech given to the workshop "HIV/AIDS and Reproductive Health: Everybody's Business" convened by the Ministry of Foreign Affairs, the Netherlands, October 25.

Germain, Adrienne, Sia Nowrojee, and Hnin Hnin Pyne. 1994. "Setting a new agenda: sexual and reproductive health and rights," in *Population Policies Reconsidered: Health, Empowerment, and Rights,* eds. Gita Sen, Adrienne Germain, and Lincoln C. Chen. Cambridge, Massachusetts: Harvard School of Public Health, pp. 27–46.

Gillespie, Duff G. 2004. "Whatever happened to family planning and, for that matter, reproductive health," *International Family Planning Perspectives* 30(1): 34–38.

Gilson, Lucy and A. Mills. 1995. "Health sector reforms in Sub-Saharan Africa: lessons of the last 10 years," *Health Policy* 32: 215–43.

Global Health Council. 2004. *Banking on Reproductive Health: The World Bank's Support for Population, the Cairo Agenda, and the Millennium Development Goals.* Washington, DC: Global Health Council.

———. 2005. "Money money everywhere". *Global AIDSLink* November/December: 11, 25.

Goldberg, Michelle. 2009. *The Means of Reproduction: Sex, Power, and the Future of the World.* New York: The Penguin Press.

Government of the People's Republic of Bangladesh. 1997. *Health and Population Sector Strategy.* Dhaka: Ministry of Health and Family Welfare.

Green, Andrew. 1999. *An Introduction to Health Planning in Developing Countries* (2nd ed.). Oxford: Oxford University Press.

Green, Cynthia. 1996. *Profiles of UN Organizations Working in Population.* Washington, DC: Population Action International.

Greenhalgh, Susan. 1995. "Anthropology theorizes reproduction: integrating practice, political economic, and feminist perspectives," in *Situating Fertility: Anthropology and Demographic Inquiry*, ed. Susan Greenhalgh. Cambridge: Cambridge University Press, pp. 3–28.

———. 1996. "The social construction of population science: an intellectual, institutional, and political history of twentieth century demography," *Comparative Studies in Society and History* 38(1): 26–66.

———. 2003. "Science, modernity and the making of China's one-child policy," *Population and Development Review* 29(2): 163–96.

Haberland, Nicole and Diana Measham (eds.). 2002a. *Responding to Cairo: Case Studies of Changing Practices in Reproductive Health and Family Planning.* New York: The Population Council.

Haberland, Nicole, et al. 2002b. "Pitfalls and possibilities: managing RTIs in family planning and general reproductive health services," in *Responding to Cairo: Case Studies of Changing Practice in Reproductive Health and Family Planning*, eds. Nicole Haberland and Diane Measham. New York: The Population Council, pp. 292–317.

Halfon, Saul. 2007. *The Cairo Consensus: Demographic Surveys, Women's Empowerment, and regime Change in Population Policy.* Lanham, Maryland: Lexington Press.

Hardee, Karen and Janet Smith. 2000. *Implementing Reproductive Health Services in an Era of Health Sector Reform*, The Policy Project. Washington, DC: The Futures Group International.

Hardee, Karen, et al. 1998a. *Post-Cairo Reproductive Health Policies and Programs: A Comparative Study of Eight Countries*, Policy Project occasional paper no. 2. Washington, DC: The Futures Group International.

———. 1998b. "What have we learned from studying changes in service delivery practices?" *International Family Planning Perspectives* 24(2): 84–90.

Harkavy, Oscar. 1995. *Curbing Population Growth: An Insider's Perspective on the Population Movement.* New York: Plenum Press.

Hartman, Betsy. 1987. *Reproductive Rights and Women: The Global Politics of Population Control and Contraceptive Choice*. New York: Harper and Row.

Hashemi, Syed. 1996. "NGO accountability in Bangladesh: beneficiaries, donors, and the state," in *Beyond the Magic Bullet: NGO Performance and Accountability*, eds. Michael Edwards and David Hulme. West Hartford, Connecticut: Kumarian Press, pp. 103–11.

Hawley, Amos. 1998. "Confession of a sometime ecologist, mostly human," epilogue in *Continuities in Sociological Human Ecology*, eds. Michael Mecklin and Dudley Poston. New York: Plenum Press, pp. 11–26.

Hempel, Margaret. 1996. "Reproductive health and rights: origins and challenges to the ICPD," *Health Transition Review* 6: 70–83.

Herring, Sheila and Steve Radelet. 2008. "Modernizing foreign assistance for the 21st century: An agenda for the next US president., in Nancy Birdsall, ed., *The White House and the World: A Global Development Agenda for the Next US President*. Washington, DC: Center for Global Development, pp. 273–298.

Hewlett Foundation. 2003. *Program Descriptions: Population*. Menlo Park, California: www.hewlett.org/Programs/Population/.

Hobcraft, John. 2000. "Female empowerment and child well-being," in *Women's Empowerment and Demographic Processes: Moving Beyond Cairo*, eds. Harriett Presser and Gita Sen. Oxford: Oxford University Press, pp. 159–85.

Hoben, Allan. 1989. "USAID: organizational and institutional issues and effectiveness," in *International Development: The United States and the Third World in the 1990s*, eds. Robert Berg and David Gordon. Boulder, Colorado: Lynne Rienner Publishers, pp. 253–78.

Hodgson, Dennis. 1998. "Orthodoxy and revisionism in American demography," *Population and Development Review* 14(4): 541–69.

Hodgson, Dennis and Susan Cotts Watkins. 1997. "Feminists and neo-Malthusians: past and present alliances," *Population and Development Review* 23(3): 469–523.

Ibrahim, Saad E. and Barbara Ibrahim. 1998. "Egypt's population policy: the long march of state and civil society," in *Do Population Policies Matter? Fertility and Politics in Egypt, India, Kenya, and Mexico*, ed. Anrudh Jain. New York: The Population Council, pp. 19–52.

INFO Reports, 2005. Microbicides: New Potential for Protection, January, Issue number 3.

InterAction. 2002. *The Millennium Challenge Account: A New Vision for Development—A Policy Paper from Interaction*. Washington, DC.

InterAction. 2003. *Emerging Trends: An InterAction Policy Paper*. Washington, DC.

International Planned Parenthood Federation (IPPF). 2003. *Financial Statements 2002*. London.

International Women's Health Coalition. 1997. *A Women's Lens on Foreign Policy: A Symposium*. New York: iwhc.org.

————. 2003a. *Bush's Other War: The Assault on Women's Sexual and Reproductive Health and Rights*. New York: iwhc.org.

————. 2003b. *The 108th Congress: More Bad News for Women*. New York: iwhc.org.

Itano, Nicole. 2003. "Africa's family planning drought," *Christian Science Monitor*, November 5, www.csmonitor.com/2003/1105/p07s02-woaf.html.

Jacobson, Jodi. 2001. "Transforming family planning programs: towards a framework for advancing the reproductive rights agenda," in *Reproductive Health, Gender, and Human Rights: A Dialogue*, eds. Elaine Murphy and Karen Ringheim. Washington, DC: Program for Appropriate Technologies in Health (PATH), pp. 53–65.

Jahan, Rounaq. 2003. "Restructuring the health system: experiences of advocates for gender equity in Bangladesh," *Reproductive Health Matters* 11(21): 183–91.

Jain, Anrudh. 1998. "The future of population policies," in *Do Population Policies Matter? Fertility and Politics in Egypt, India, Kenya, and Mexico*, ed. Anrudh Jain. New York: The Population Council, pp. 193–202.

Jain, Anrudh, et al. 2002. "Family planning field workers in the Philippines," in *Responding to Cairo: Case Studies of Changing Practice in Reproductive Health and Family Planning*, eds. Nicole Haberland and Diana Measham. New York: The Population Council, pp. 99–113.

Johnston, Timothy and Susan Stout. 1999. *Investing in Health: Development Effectiveness in the Health, Nutrition, and Population Sector*. Washington, DC: Operations Evaluation Department, The World Bank.

Kantner, Andrew and Shi-Jen He. 2001. "Levels and trends in fertility and mortality in South Asia," in *Fertility Transition in South Asia*, eds. Zeba Sathar and James Phillips. New York: Oxford University Press, pp. 23–50.

Kaplan, Robert D. 2000. *The Coming Anarchy: Shattering the Dreams of the Post Cold War*. New York: Random House.

Kaufman, Carol. 1997. *Reproductive Control in South Africa*, Policy Research Division working paper no. 97. New York: The Population Council.

Kelley, Allen C. 2001. "The population debate in historical perspective: revisionism revised," in *Population Does Matter: Demography Growth, and Poverty in the Developing World*, eds. Nancy Birsdsall, Allen C. Kelley, and Steven Sinding. New York: Oxford University Press, pp. 24–54.

Kennedy, Paul. 1993. *Preparing for the Twenty-First Century*. New York: Harper Collins.

Knodel, John and Gavin W. Jones. 1996. "Post-Cairo population policy: does promoting girls' education miss the mark?" *Population and Development Review* 22(4): 683–702.

Koblinshy, Marge, O. Campbell, and J. Heichelheim. 1999. "Organizing delivery care: what works for safe motherhood?" *Bulletin of the World Health Organization* 77(5): 399–406.

Koenig, Michael A. and M.E. Khan (eds.). 1999. *Improving Quality of Care in India's Family Welfare Programme: The Challenge Ahead*. New York: The Population Council.

Kolehmainen-Aitken, Riita-Liisa (ed.). 1999. *Myths and Realities about Decentralization of Health Systems*. Boston: Management Sciences for Health.

Kols, Adrienne. 2003. "A rights-based approach to reproductive health," *Outlook* 20(4): 1–8.

Kristof, Nicholas. 2003a. "The secret war on condoms," *The New York Times*, January 10, p. 23.

———. 2003b. "The war against women," editorial, *The New York Times*, January 12, section 4, p. 14.

La Croix, Sumner, Andrew Mason, and Shigeyuki Abe. 2003. *Population and Globalization*. Asia-Pacifc Population and Policy, no. 64. Honolulu: East-West Center.

Lakshminarayanan, Rama. 2003. "Decentralization and its implications for reproductive health: the Philippines experience," *Reproductive Health Matters* 11(21): 96–107.

Lancaster, Carol. 1999. *Aid to Africa: So Much to Do, So Little Done*. Chicago: The University of Chicago Press.

———. 2002. *The Devil is in the Details: From the Millennium Challenge Account to the Millennium Challenge Corporation*. Washington, DC: Center for Global Development.

Leete, Richard and I. Alam (eds.). 1993. *The Revolution in Asian Fertility: Dimensions, Causes, and Implications*. Oxford: Clarendon Press.

Levine, Ruth. 2008. "Healthy foreign policy: Bringing coherence to the global health agenda", in Nancy Birdsall, ed., *The White House and the*

World: A Global Development Agenda for the Next US President. Washington, DC: Center for Global Development, pp. 43–61.

Lewis, Stephen. 2005. *Race Against Time.* CBC Massey Lecture Series. Toronto: House of Anansi Press.

Litvack, Jennie, J. Ahmed, and R. Bird. 1998. *Rethinking Decentralization in Developing Countries.* Washington, DC: The World Bank.

Luke, Nancy and Susan Watkins. 2002. "Reactions of developing-country elites to international population policy," *Population and Development Review* 28(4): 707–33.

Lush, Louisana. 2002. "Integration: an overview of policy developments," *International Family Planning Perspectives* 28(2): 71–76.

Lush, Louisiana and Oona Campbell. 2001. "International cooperation for reproductive health: too much ideology?" in *International Co-Operation in Health*, eds. Martin McKee, Paul Garner, and Robin Stott. London: Oxford University Press, pp. 175–96.

Lush, Louisiana, et al. 1999. "Defining 'integration': myth and ideology," *Bulletin of the World Health Organization* 77(9): 771–77.

Lush, Louisiana, et al. 2003. "The role of MCH and family planning services in HIV/STD control: is 'integration' the answer?" *African Journal of Reproductive Health* 5(3): 29–49.

MacArthur Foundation. 2003. *The General Program: Large Institutional Grants.* Chicago: www.macfound.org/gen/large_grants.htm.

Macro International. 2003. *DHS Surveys: Statistical Compiler.* Calverton, Maryland: ORC/Macro, www.measuredhs.com.

Maren, Michael. 1997. *The Road to Hell: The Ravaging Effects of Foreign Aid and International Charity.* New York: The Free Press.

Mason, Andrew. 2002. *Population Change and Economic Development in East Asia: Challenges Met, Opportunities Seized.* Stanford, California: Stanford University Press.

Mason, Karen O. 1996. "Population programs and human rights," in *The Impact of Population Growth on Well-Being in Developing Countries*, eds. Dennis Ahlburg, Allen C. Kelley, and Karen O. Mason. Berlin: Springer, pp. 299–335.

———. 2003. "Measuring empowerment: a social demographer's view," paper prepared for the Workshop on Measuring Empowerment: Cross-Disciplinary Perspectives, The World Bank, Washington, DC, February 4–5.

Mason, Karen O. and Herbert Smith. 2003. "Women's empowerment and social context: results from five Asian countries," unpublished paper drafted at the Rockefeller Foundation's Bellagio Study and Conference Center.

Mauldin, W. Parker and Bernard Berelson. 1978. "Conditions of fertility decline in developing countries, 1965–75," *Studies in Family Planning* 9(5): 89–148.

Mavalankar, Dileep. 1996. *Quality of Family Planning Programs: A Review of Public and Private Sector*. New Delhi: The Population Council.

Mayhew, Susannah. 2002. "Donor dealings: the impact of international donor aid on sexual and reproductive health: viewpoint," *International Family Planning Perspectives* 28(4): 220–24.

Mayhew, Susannah, et al. 2000. "Integrating component services of reproductive health: the problem of implementation" *Studies in Family Planning* 31(2): 151–67.

McIntosh, Alison and Jason Finkle. 1995. "The Cairo Conference on Population and Development," *Population and Development Review* 21(2): 223–60.

Meadows, Donella, et al. 1972. *A Report for the Club of Rome's Project on the Predicament of Mankind*. New York: Universe Books.

Mitra, S.N., Nawab Ali, Shahidal Islam, Anne R. Cross, and Tulshi Saha. 1994. *Bangladesh Demographic and Health Survey, 1993–94*. Calverton, Maryland: National Institute of Population Research and Training (NIPORT), Mitra and Associates, and Macro International Inc.

Murthy, Nirmala, et al. 2002. "Dismantling India's contraceptive target system: an overview of three case studies," in *Responding to Cairo: Case Studies of Changing Practice in Reproductive Health and Family Planning*, eds. Nicole Haberland and Diane Measham. New York: The Population Council, pp. 25–57.

Narayana, Gadde and John Kantner. 1992. *Doing the Needful: The Dilemma of India's Population Policy*. Boulder, Colorado: Westview Press.

Narayana, Gadde and Naveen Sangwan. 2000. "Implementation of the community needs assessment approach in India," in *Review of Implementation of Community Needs Assessment Approach for Family Welfare in India*. Washington DC: Policy Project II and the Futures Group International, pp. 1–18.

National Institute of Population Research and Training (NIPORT), Mitra and Associates, and ORC Macro. 2005. *Bangladesh Demographic and Health Survey 2004*. Dhaka: Bangladesh and Calverton, Maryland: National Institute of Population Research and Training, Mitra and Associates, and ORC Macro.

Nelson, Paul and Ellen Dorsey. 2003. "At the nexus of human rights and development: new methods and strategies of global NGOs," *World Development* 31(12): 2013–26.

Ness, Gayle and Meghan Gholay. 1997. *Population and Strategies for National Sustainable Development.* London: Earthscan Publishers.

New York Times, editorial. 2005. "A timely departure," Sunday, June 19, p. 11.

Nixon, Richard. 1969. *President Nixon's Special Message on Population.* Washington, DC: The White House.

Notestein, Frank W. 1944. "Problems of policy in relation to areas of heavy population pressure," in *Proceedings of the Round Table on Population Problems, Twenty-Second Annual Conference of the Milbank Memorial Fund, New York, April 12–13, 1944.* Reprinted in *Milbank Memorial Fund Quarterly* (10): 138–59.

Office of the Registrar General and Census Commissioner. 2009. *Census of India, Provisional Population Totals, Chapter 3.* New Delhi, India: GOI internet site http://censusindia.gov.in/Data_Products/Library/Provisional_Population_Total_link/PDF_Links/chapter3.pdf.

Organization for Economic Cooperation and Development (OECD). 2002. *International Development Statistics.* ISBN 92-64-09859-3. Paris.

———. 2004. *Net Official Development Assistance.* Paris: OECD Statistical Data Base, oecd.org/dataoecd/3/2/22460411.pdf.

———. 2009. *Net Official Development Assistance.* Paris: OECD Statistical Data Base oecd.org/dataoecd/48/34/42459170.pdf

Packard Foundation. 2003. *Population Program Funding History in 2003.* Los Altos, California: www.packard.org/index.cgi?page-pop-fund.

Perin, Inez and Amir Attaran. 2003. "Trading ideology for dialogue: an opportunity to fix international aid for health?" *Lancet* 361: 1216–19.

[Philippines] National Statistical Office, Department of Health, and Macro International. 1999. *Philippines National Demographic and Health Survey, 1998.* Manila and Washington, DC.

Phillips, James F. and Mian Bazle Hossain. 2003. "The impact of household delivery of family planning services on women's status in Bangladesh," *International Family Planning Perspectives* 29(3): 138–45.

Phillips, James, et al. 1993. "Worker–client exchanges and contraceptive use in rural Bangladesh," *Studies in Family Planning* 24: 329–42.

Phillips, James, et al. 2003. *Evidence-Based Development of Health and Family Planning Programs in Bangladesh and Ghana*, working paper no. 175. New York: The Population Council.

Phillips, Michael and Matt Moffett. 2005. "Leading the news: Brazil refuses US AIDS funds due to antiprostitution pledge," *Wall Street Journal*, May 2.

Picazo, Oscar, J. Huddart, and S. Duale. 2003. *The Health Sector Human Resource Crisis in Africa: An Issues Paper*. Washington, DC: USAID, Bureau for Africa, Office of Sustainable Development, AED and the SARA Project.

Pielemeier, John, et al. 2003. *Assessment of the Basic Support for Institutionalizing Child Survival (Basics II) Project*. Washington, DC: POPTECH Project.

Piotrow, Phyllis. 1973. *World Population Crisis: US Response*. New York: Praeger.

Policy Project II and the Futures Group International. 1999. *Making Things Happen: Decentralized Planning in RCH in Uttar Pradesh, India*. Washington, DC: The Futures Group International.

POPTECH. 2003. "Assessment of the innovations in Family Planning Services Project: summary report," submitted to USAID/Washington, DC, April.

Population Action International. 1996. *The United Nations and Population Assistance*. Washington, DC.

———. 2001. *Meeting the Challenge: Contraceptive Projections and the Donor Gap*. Washington, DC.

———. 2002. *Trends in US Assistance*. Washington: Population Action International, www.populationaction.org/sitemap.htm.

Population Research Institute. 2001. *UNFPA, China and Coercive Family Planning*. Front Royal, Virginia: pop.org/main.cfm?EID=312.

Potts, Malcolm. 1997. "Sex and the birth rate," *Population and Development Review* 23(1): 1–39.

Preker, Alexander, Richard Feachem, and David De Ferranti. 1997. *Past Performance and Future Strategy for the World Bank in the Health, Nutrition, and Population Sector*. Washington, DC: Health, Nutrition, and Population Division, Human Development Department, World Bank.

Pritchett, Lant. 1994. "Desired fertility and the impact of population policies," *Population and Development Review* 20(1): 1–55.

Program for Appropriate Technologies in Health (PATH). 2003. "A rights-based approach to reproductive health," *Outlook* 20(4): 1–8.

Prud'homme, Remy. 1994. *On the Dangers of Decentralization*, Policy Research working paper no. 1252. Washington, DC: The World Bank.

Putnam, Robert D. 2001. *Bowling Alone: The Collapse and Revival of American Community*. New York: Simon and Schuster.

RamaRao, Saumya and Raji Mohanam. 2003. "The quality of family planning programs: concepts, measurement, interventions, and effects," *Studies in Family Planning* 34(4): 227–48.

RAND Corporation. 2000. *How Americans View World Issues: A Survey of World Population Issues*, Population Matters Series. Santa Monica, California.

Rao, Sujatha. 2003. *Keynote Address*. Conference on global agendas, local realities: implications of health sector reforms on women's access to reproductive health services in India, New Delhi, India, March 7, pp. 1–5.

Ravenholt, Reimert T. 1969. "AID's family planning strategy," *Science* 163: 124–25.

———. 1977. "The power of availability," in *Village and Household Availability of Contraceptives*, eds. J.S. Gardner, M.T. Mertaugh, M. Micklin, and G.W. Duncan. Seattle: Battle Human Affairs Research Center and available at ravenholt.com, pp. 1–4.

Ravenholt, Reimert T. No date. *Taking Contraceptives to the World's Poor: Creation of USAID's Population/Family Planning Program, 1965–80*. Seattle: www.ravenholt.com.

Robinson, Warren. 1997. "The economic theory of fertility over three decades," *Population Studies* 51: 63–74.

Robinson, Warren and Fatma H. El-Zanaty. 2005. *The Demographic Revolution in Modern Egypt*. Lanham, Maryland: Lexington Books.

Rogow, Debbie and Susan Wood, 2002. "ReproSalud: feminism meets USAID in Peru," in *Responding to Cairo: Case Studies of Changing Practice in Reproductive Health and Family Planning*, eds. Nicole Haberland and Diana Measham. New York: The Population Council, pp. 376–94.

Ross, John. 1999. *Review of Implementation of Community Needs Assessment Approach for Family Welfare in India*. Washington, DC: The Futures Group International.

Ross, John and John Stover. 2003. *Trends and Issues Affecting Service Delivery over the Next Decade*. Washington, DC: The Futures Group International.

Ross, John and W. Parker Mauldin. 1997. *Measuring the Strength of Family Planning Programs*. Washington, DC: The Futures Group International and The Population Council.

Ross, John and William Winfrey. 2002. "Unmet need for contraception in the developing world and the former Soviet Union: an updated estimate," *International Family Planning Perspectives* 28(3): 138–43.

Royal Commission on Macroeconomics and Health. 2000. "Investing in health for economic development," paper presented by Jeffrey D. Sachs to

Ms. Gro Harlem Brundtland, director general, World Health Organization, Geneva.

Sachs, Jeffrey. 2005. "The development challenge," *Foreign Affairs* 84(2): 78–90.

———. 2005. *The End of Poverty: Economic Possibilities for Our Time.* New York: The Penguin Press.

———. 2008. *Common Wealth: Economics for a Crowded Plant.* New York: The Penguin Press.

Sadik, Nafis. 1998. "Population growth and global stability," in *Population and Global Security,* ed. Nicholas Polunin. Cambridge: Cambridge University Press, pp. 1–15.

Salaman, Lester. 1993. *The Global Associational Revolution: The Rise of the Third Sector on the World Scene,* occasional bulletin 15. Baltimore, Maryland: Institute of Policy Studies, Johns Hopkins University.

Schuler, Sidney, Lisa Bates, and Md. Khairul Islam. 2001. "The persistence of a service delivery 'culture': findings from a qualitative study in Bangladesh," *International Family Planning Perspectives* 27(4): 194–200.

Schuler, Sidney, Md. Khairul Islam, and Lisa Bates. 2000a. *From Home to the Clinic: The Next Chapter in Bangladesh's Family Planning Success Story—Rural Sites.* Washington, DC: John Snow International and The Policy Project.

———. 2000b. *From Home to the Clinic: The Next Chapter in Bangladesh's Family Planning Success Story—Urban Sites.* Washington, DC: John Snow International and The Policy Project.

Schultz, T. Paul. 1992. "Assessing family planning cost effectiveness: applicability of individual demand–program supply framework," in *Family Planning Programs and Fertility,* eds. James Phillips and John Ross. New York: Oxford University Press, pp. 78–105.

Segal, Sheldon. 2003. *Under the Banyan Tree: A Population Scientist's Odyssey.* New York: Oxford University Press.

Seims, Sara, Nicole Gray, Tamara Fox, Vignetta Charles, Karen Andrews, and Kim Brehm. 2004. *Population Program Strategic Plan.* Menlo Park, California: The William and Flora Hewlett Foundation.

Seltzer, Judith R. 2002. *The Origins and Evolution of Family Planning Programs in Developing Countries.* Population Matters: A RAND Program of Policy-Relevant Research Communication. Santa Monica, California: RAND Corporation.

Sen, Gita, Adrienne Germain, and Lincoln C. Chen (eds.). 1994. *Population Policies Reconsidered: Health, Empowerment, and Rights.* Boston: Harvard

Center for Population and Development Studies, Harvard School of Public Health; and the International Women's Health Coalition.

Shelton, Jim. 2001. "The provider perspective: human after all," *International Family Planning Perspectives* 27(3): 152–61.

Shiffman, Jeremy. 2004. "Political management in the Indonesian family planning program," *International Family Planning Perspectives* 30(1): 27–33.

Shiffman, Jeremy and Yonghong Wu. 2003. "Norms in tension: democracy and efficiency in Bangladeshi health and population sector reform," *Social Science and Medicine* 5696: 1547–57.

Simmons, Ruth, et al. 1988. "Beyond supply: the importance of female family planning workers in rural Bangladesh," *Studies in Family Planning* 19(1): 29–38.

Simon, Julian. 1981. *The Ultimate Resource*. Princeton, New Jersey: Princeton University Press.

Sinding, Steven. 1996. "UN fund for population activities," remarks presented at the ODC Congressional Staff Forum Roundtable on Reform of UN Specialized Agencies, Washington, DC, April 9, pp. 1–3.

———. 2000. "The great population debates: how relevant are they for the 21st century?" *American Journal of Public Health* 90(12): 1841–47.

———. 2001. "Learning by doing: testing the supply-side hypothesis at USAID," paper prepared for IUSSP Seminar on the Production and Dissemination of Population Knowledge, Brown University, Providence, Rhode Island, March 20–25.

———. 2005. "Keeping sexual and reproductive health at the forefront of global efforts to reduce poverty," *Studies in Family Planning* 36(2): 140–43.

Sinding, Steven and Med Bouzidi. 2002. "Partnerships and resources: towards Cairo +10: achievements, unfinished business, and new challenges," in *Fifth Asian and Pacific Population Conference: Selected Papers*. Asian Population Studies Series, no. 158. Bangkok: Economic and Social Commission for Asia and the Pacific, pp. 323–41.

Singh, Jyoti S. (ed.). 1998. *Creating a New Consensus on Population*. London: Earthscan Publications.

Singh, Susheela, et al. 2004. "Adding it up: the benefits of investing in sexual and reproductive health care," report prepared for the Alan Guttmacher Institute and UNFPA.

Sivakami, M. 1996. "Female work participation and child health: an investigation in Tamil Nadu, India," *Health Transition Review* 7(1): 21–32.

Sobhan, Rehman. 1993. *Bangladesh: Problems of Governance*, report prepared under the auspices of the Centre for Policy Research, New Delhi. New Delhi: Konark Publishers.

Speidel, J. Joseoh, Deborah Weiss, Sally Ethelston, and Sarah Gilbert. 2007. *Family Planning and Reproductive Health: the Link to Environmental Preservation.* San Francisco: Bixby Center for Reproductive Health Research and Policy, University of California, San Francisco.

Speidel, J. Joseph, Steven Sinding, Duff Gillespie, Elizabeth McGuire, and Margaret Neuse. 2009. *Making the Case for International Population Assistance.* Baltimore, Maryland: Gates Institute, Bloomberg School of Public Health, Johns Hopkins University.

Stamper, B. Maxwell. 1977. *Population and Planning in Developing Nations: A Review of Sixty Development Plans from the 1970s.* New York: The Population Council.

Statistics Indonesia (Badan Pusat Statistik-BPS) and Macro International. 2008. *Indonesia: Demographic and Health Survey 2007.* Calverton, Maryland: BPS and macro International.

Stevenson, Richard. 1997. "A chief banker for nations at the bottom of the heap," *The New York Times*, September 14, p. 1.

Stout, Susan, et al. 1997. *Evaluating Health Projects: Lessons from the Literature*, discussion paper no. 356. Washington, DC: The World Bank.

Sylva, Douglas. 2003. *The United Nations Children's Fund: Women or Children First?* working paper no. 3. New York: Catholic Family and Human Rights Institute.

Symonds, Richard and Michael Carder. 1973. *The UN and the Population Question, 1945–1970.* New York: McGraw-Hill.

Tantchou, Justine and Ellen Wilson. 2000. *Post-Cairo Reproductive Health Policies and Programs: A Study of Five Francophone African Countries.* Washington, DC: The Futures Group International.

Tawfik, Linda and Stephen Kinoti. 2003. *The Impact of HIV/AIDS on the Health Sector in Sub-Saharan Africa: The Issue of Human Resources.* Washington, DC: USAID/SARA Project, and the Academy for Educational Development.

Tendler, Judith. 1997. *Good Government in the Tropics.* Baltimore: Johns Hopkins University Press.

Timberg, Craig. 2006. "How AIDS in Africa was overstated: reliance on data from urban prenatal clinics skewed early projections," The Washington Post.Com, April 6, 2006, pp. 1–2.

Toner, Robin. 2003. "Foes of abortion ready major bills for new Congress," *New York Times*, January 2, p. 1.

Tsui, Amy, Judith Wasserheit, and John Haaga (eds.). 1997. *Reproductive Health in Developing Countries: Expanding Dimensions, Building Solutions.* Washington, DC: National Academy Press.

UNAIDSa (Joint United Nations Program on HIV/AIDS) and the World Health Organization. 2002. *AIDS Epidemic Update.* Geneva.

———. 2003a. *Report on the State of HIV/AIDS Financing (Revised/Updated March 2003).* Geneva.

———. 2003b. *AIDS Epidemic Update.* Geneva.

United Kingdom (U.K.) House of Commons, International Development Committee. 2003. *Departmental Report: International Development Committee: 2002–03 Session.* London: Department for International Development, Parliament of the United Kingdom.

United Kingdom (U.K.) Select Committee on International Development. 2003. *International Development—Eighth Report.* London: House of Commons, Parliament of the United Kingdom.

United Nations. 1994. *International Conference on Population and Development: Summary of the Programme of Action.* New York: ECOSOC development website, un.org/ecosocdev/genino/population/icpd.htm.

———. 1995. *Report of the International Conference on Population and Development, Cairo, 5–13 September 1994.* UN publication A/CONFF.171/13/Rev.1. New York.

———. 1999a. *Proposals for Key Actions for Further Implementation of the Programme of Action of the International Conference on Population and Development.* E/CN.9/1999/PC/4. New York: Commission on Population and Development, Economic and Social Council.

———. 1999b. *Review and Appraisal of the Progress Made in Achieving the Goals and Objectives of the Programme of Action of the International Conference on Population and Development.* New York: United Nations Population Fund.

———. 1999c. *Twenty-First Special Session of the General Assembly for an Overall Review and Appraisal of the Implementation of the Programme of Action of the International Conference on Population and Development.* Report of the secretary general. A/54/442. New York.

———. 2000. *Levels and Trends of Contraceptive Use As Assessed in 1998.* New York: United Nations Population Division.

———. 2001a. *Millennium Development Goals for the 21st Century.* New York: United Nations, www.un.org/millenniumgoals.

———. 2001b. *Road Map towards the Implementation of the United Nations Millennium Declaration: Report of the Secretary General.* Fifty-sixth session of the General Assembly, follow-up to the outcome of the Millennium Summit. A/56/326. New York.

———. 2002. *The Flow of Financial Resources for Assisting in the Implementation of the Programme of Action of the International Conference on Population and Development.* E/CN.9/2002/4. New York: Economic and Social Council, Commission on Population and Development, thirty-fifth session.

United Nations Economic and Social Council. 2004. *The Flow of Financial Resources for Assisting in the Implementation of the Programme of Action of the International Conference on Population and Development: A Ten-Year Review Report of the Secretary General.* Commission on Population and Development, thirty-seventh session, New York, March 22–26.

———. 2005. *The Flow of Financial Resources for Assisting in the Implementation of the Programme of Action of the International Conference on Population and Development: Report of the Secretary-General.* Commission on Population and Development, thirty-eighth session, New York, April 4–8.

United Nations Foundation. 2003. *UNF in Action.* Washington, DC: www.unfoundation.org/unf_action/unf_action.htm.

United Nations General Assembly. 1999. *Twenty-First Session of the General Assembly for an Overall Review and Appraisal of the Implementation of the Programme of Action of the International Conference on Population and Development.* A/54/442. New York.

United Nations Millennium Project. 2005. *Investing in Development: A Practical Plan to Achieve the Millennium Development Goals, Overview.* New York: United Nations Development Program.

United Nations Population Division. 1953. *The Determinants and Consequences of Population Trends: A Summary of the Findings of Studies on the Relationships between Population Changes and Economic and Social Conditions.* Population studies no. 17. ST/SOA/SER.A/17. New York.

———. 1978. *The Determinants and Consequences of Population Trends: New Summary of Findings on Interaction of Demographic, Economic, and Social Factors.* Population studies no. 50. ST/SOA/SER.A/50/Add.1. New York: Department of Economic and Social Affairs.

———. 2003. *Urban Agglomerations 2001.* New York: United Nations, Department of Economic and Social Affairs.

———. 2004a. *World Population Prospects: The 2004 Revision.* New York: United Nations, Department of Economic and Social Affairs, and

United Nations Population Division online data retrieval service, http://esa.un.org/unpp.

United Nations Population Division. 2004b. "Seminar on the relevance of population aspects for the achievement of the Millennium Development Goals," *Population Newsletter.* New York: United Nations, Department of Economic and Social Affairs, No. 78:2.

———. 2009. *World Population Prospects: The 2008 Revision.* New York: United Nations, Department of Economic and Social Affairs, and United Nations Population Division On-line Data Retrieval Service, http://esa.un.org/unpp.

United Nations Population Fund (UNFPA). 2000. *UNFPA and Government Decentralization: A Study of Country Experiences.* New York: Office of Oversight and Evaluation, UNFPA.

———. 2001. *State of the World Population, 2001.* New York: Oxford University Press.

United Nations Population Fund (UNFPA). 2002a. *Asia and Pacific: A Region in Transition.* New York: UNFPA.

———. 2002b. *Financial Resource Flows for Population Activities in 2000.* New York: UNFPA and the Netherlands Interdisciplinary Demographic Institute.

———. 2002c. *Global Estimates of Contraceptive Commodities and Condoms for STI/HIV Prevention, 2000–2015.* New York: UNFPA.

———. 2002d. *Reproductive Health Essentials: Securing the Supply.* New York: UNFPA.

———. 2002e. *State of the World Population, 2002.* New York: Oxford University Press.

———. 2003a. *Donor Support for Contraceptives and Condoms for STI/HIV Prevention, 2001.* New York: UNFPA.

———. 2003b. *Financial Resource Flows for Population Activities in 2001.* New York: UNFPA and the Netherlands Interdisciplinary Demographic Institute.

———. 2004a. *Funding.* New York: UNFPA website, unfpa.org/about/funding.htm.

———. 2008. *Financial Resource Flows for Population Activities in 2006.* New York: UNFPA and the Netherlands Interdisciplinary Demographic Institute and resourceflows.org/index.php/articles/288.

United States Agency for International Development (USAID). 1992. *Project Grant Agreement No. 386–0527 between the President of India and the United States of America for Innovations in Family Planning Services.* Washington, DC.

————. 1996. *The Innovation in Family Planning Project: Management Review*. Washington, DC: USAID Bureau of Global Programs.

United States (U.S.) Department of State. 2000. *Administration of Foreign Affairs, Budget for Fiscal Year 2003*. Washington, DC.

————. 2001. *International Assistance Programs*. Washington, DC.

————. 2003a. "Subject: your meeting with the President regarding the Mexico City policy and US funding for AIDS," unclassified briefing memorandum from Arthur E. Dewey to Secretary Powell, Washington, DC, February 11.

————. 2003b. "Adding family planning to PMTCT sites increases the benefits of PMTCT," *Issue Brief*. Washington, DC: USAID Bureau for Global Health.

United States (U.S.) General Accounting Office. 2003. *Foreign Assistance: Strategic Workforce Planning Can Help USAID Address Current and Future Challenges. Report to Congressional Requesters*. GAO-03–946. Washington, DC.

————. 2004. *Global Health: USAIDS Coordinator Addressing Some Key Challenges to Expanding Treatment, But Others Remain.* Report to the chairman, Subcommittee on Foreign Operations, Export Financing, and Related Programs, Committee on Appropriations, House of Representatives. GAO-04–784. Washington, DC.

USAID Bureau for Global Programs. 2002. *USAID's International Population and Family Planning Assistance: Answers to 10 Frequently Asked Questions*. Washington, DC: http://www.info.usaid.gov/pop_health.

van den Berghe, Pierre L. 1994. "Parasitism and corruption: state behavior in the throes of deepening global crisis," roundtable commentaries, *Politics and the Life Sciences* 13(1): 29–30.

Visaria, Leela, Shireen Jejeebhoy, and Tom Merrick. 1999. "From family planning to reproductive health: challenges facing India," *International Family Planning Perspectives* 25(6) (Supplement): S44–49.

Warwick, Donald P. 1982. *Bitter Pills: Population Policies and their Implementation in Eight Developing Countries*. New York: Cambridge University Press.

Watkins, Susan C. 1993. "If all we knew about women was what we read in *Demography*, what would we know?" *Demography* 30(4): 551–77.

————. 2003. "Review of Catherine Campbell, *Letting Them Die: Why HIV/AIDS Intervention Programmes Fail*," *Population and Development Review* 29(4): 736–40.

Wattenberg, Ben. 1987. *The Birth Dearth*. New York: Pharos Books.

Wellcome Trust. 2003. *Health Consequences of Population Change: A Research Funding Programme*. London: www.wellcome.ac.uk/en/1/biosgintpop. html.

Wilson, Edward O. 2002. "The bottleneck," *Scientific American* 286(2): 82–91.

World Bank. 1984. *World Development Report*. New York: Oxford University Press.

———. 1987. *Financing Health Services in Developing Countries: An Agenda for Perform*. Washington, DC.: The World Bank.

———. 1993. *World Development Report: Investing in Health*. New York: Oxford University Press.

———. 1998. *Project Appraisal Document on a Proposed Credit in the Amount of SDR 185.5 Million (US$250 Million Equivalent) to the Government of the People's Republic of Bangladesh for a Health and Population Program Project*. Report number 17684-BD. Washington, DC.

———. 1999. *Investing in Health: Developing Effectiveness in the Health, Nutrition and Population Sector*. Washington, DC.

———. 2000. *Population and the World Bank: Adapting to Change* (rev. ed.). The Human Development Network: Health, Nutrition, and Population Series. Washington, DC.

———. 2001. *Engendering Development through Gender Equality in Rights, Resources, and Voice*, A World Bank Policy Research Report. Washington, DC.

———. 2002. *Integrating Gender into the World Bank's Work: A Strategy for Action*. Washington, DC.

———. 2007. *Population Issues in the 21st Century: The Role of the World Bank*. Washington, DC.

Zheng, Xiang and Shiela Hillier. 1995. "The reforms of the Chinese health care system: the Jiangxi study," *Social Science and Medicine* 41(8): 1057–64.

INDEX

Breinigsville, PA USA
23 November 2009
228038BV00003B/2/P